TALES OF BREXITS PAST AND PRESENT

'*Culkin and Simmons new book offers an insightful, timely and fresh perspective on Brexit.* Tales of Brexits Past and Present *provides a novel historical perspective of prior Brexit-type situations interwoven with evaluations of future impact. Since the EU referendum in June 2016, attention has been invariably focused on the rationale behind Britain's decision to leave; however, as we approach the start of the transition period, the real question for the UK's economy is what will Brexit mean in terms of entrepreneurial innovation and growth? The authors present a series of questions and pointers towards potential solutions in order to understand the many challenges and opportunities that Brexit offers for entrepreneurs, innovators and policy makers. This book offers a meaningful and valuable contribution to the debate that I would highly recommend.*'

Dr Paul Jones, Editor in Chief,
International Journal of Entrepreneurial Behaviour and Research and Professor of Entrepreneurship & Innovation,
Swansea University, Wales

'*There is a sense that Brexit is territory uncharted, that what we are experiencing is entirely unprecedented. This book explains that, really, there have been similarly disruptive experiences in Britain, and in England in particular. The book is part history lesson, part stakeholder manual and in part a stepping stone to help wider public debate. It advocates socially responsible policy to enable people to aspire, a focus on supply and markets, and in a departure from most economic and political narratives, it uses the experiences of the past as underpinners for a rational approach to how opportunity might be engendered in the future. In doing that, in the current context of panic-laden Brexit noise, it delivers informed commentary and sensible suggestions.*'

Dr Laura Galloway, Professor of Business & Enterprise,
Edinburgh Business School, Scotland

*'It is said that History repeats itself, first as tragedy, second as farce.
But what if Brexit is already the fourth time the same drama unfolds?
In their socio-economic tour through English history, Culkin and
Simmons provide three illuminating case studies of how the English
have tried to break away from the continent before. A highly
enjoyable and informative read that will provide new arguments for
both "Remainers" and "Brexiteers", as well as much needed insight
for European scholars trying to make sense of British sensibilities.'*

Dr Norbert Morawetz, Associate Professor in Entrepreneurship,
Henley Business School, England

*'"There is nothing more difficult to carry out, nor more doubtful of
success, nor more dangerous to handle than to initiate a new order
of things". Machiavelli (1513)*

*The one certainty, at this stage of developments is uncertainty, no
one really knows how Brexit will all pan out. We can speculate,
that's all. As ever the matters in Ireland, in particular the border in
Ireland is proving an obstacle and possibly a brake on a smooth
exit for the UK. Will there be a hard border? And so, what if there
is or even where will it be? In a recent survey undertaken by the
Ulster University Business School most business entrepreneurs in
Northern Ireland who responded felt they could deal with the
uncertainty that BREXIT would throw up at them. NI's business
owners have demonstrated themselves to be entrepreneurial in the
past, they are the sort of people who know a thing or two about
how to deal with uncertainty and change. Culkin and Simmons
present us with a radical new perspective on the issues, providing us
with a different lens through which to view the possibilities and
challenges facing modern-day UK. Historically Britain has been
here before and survived. The authors contribute to the ongoing
debate thrown up by BREXIT as to its benefits and threats. It is
likely to be one that will go on for some time yet, engaging opinion
in Ireland and across the European Union, never mind the UK.
This text is a timely addition to that debate.'*

Dr Pauric McGowan, Professor of Entrepreneurship & Business
Development, Ulster University Business School,
Northern Ireland

TALES OF BREXITS PAST AND PRESENT

Understanding the Choices, Threats and Opportunities in Our Separation From the EU

BY

NIGEL CULKIN
RICHARD SIMMONS

United Kingdom — North America — Japan — India — Malaysia — China

Emerald Publishing Limited
Howard House, Wagon Lane, Bingley BD16 1WA, UK

First edition 2019

British Library Cataloguing in Publication Data
A catalogue record for this book is available from the British Library

ISBN: 978-1-78769-438-5 (Print)
ISBN: 978-1-78769-435-4 (Online)
ISBN: 978-1-78769-437-8 (Epub)

ISOQAR certified
Management System,
awarded to Emerald
for adherence to
Environmental
standard
ISO 14001:2004.

Certificate Number 1985
ISO 14001

INVESTOR IN PEOPLE

CONTENTS

LIST OF ABBREVIATIONS

AFME	Association of Financial Markets In Europe
BIS	Bank of International Settlements
DARPA	Defence Advanced Research Projects Agency (in United States)
DFID	UK Department For International Development
ECJ	European Court of Justice
EU	European Union
FANG	Facebook, Amazon, Netflix and Google
GPS	Global Positioning System
ILO	International Labour Organisation
IMF	International Monetary Fund
MSME	Micro, Small and Medium-sized Enterprise
OECD	Organisation for Economic Cooperation and Development
OEM	Original Equipment Manufacturer
UKIP	United Kingdom Independence Party
UNCTAD	United Nations Trade and Development Organisation
WTO	World Trade Organisation

FOREWORD

Writing any book concerning contemporary issues runs the risk that events will overtake the narrative; this is especially true with a book going to press just as the Brexit saga reaches one moment of natural climax, namely the agreement and ratification of the UK treaty to withdraw from the European Union. Every day brings a new twist and turn to the story. Will there be a deal? Will Parliament ratify a deal? Which government minister will resign today? Against this febrile backdrop an obvious question, then, is why write such a book now and not after we know the actual Brexit deal?

The answer is as simple as it is challenging.

As we see it, the wounds of the 2016 Brexit Referendum have not healed — they have seemingly intensified. It is easy to imagine similar thoughts and emotions in the early 1530s at the start of the Reformation. It was when things started to hurt citizens on the ground (such as closure of the monastic welfare system in the mid-1530s) that serious trouble in the form of insurrections (e.g. the 1536 Pilgrimage of Grace) started to brew.

Brexit is potentially a more substantial change than the Reformation that is likely to impact both the economic and social dimensions of British life, rather than just one of them. It is not always apparent that the current round of negotiations is a starting rather than an ending point in the Brexit narrative 585-page draft 'Withdrawal Agreement' together with a short seven-page outline looking to a future that commits both sides to "combining deep regulatory and customs cooperations, building on the single customs territory provided for in the withdrawal agreement". These talks have led to publication of a "draft". The detailed discussion about future arrangements will continue after the UK leaves the EU and either be 'eased' by a transition agreement or take place against a sharp change, if there is no transition. This statement remains true despite a collective UK Cabinet decision to support the draft withdrawal agreement made on 15 November 2018. The furious reaction to the proposed deal on 16th November with ministerial resignations and talks of votes of "no confidence" reinforce the already uncertain atmosphere.

It seems like we now face an inflection point in the debate, as reality sets in and the grand statements are translated in to material actions that will impact on individual lives. Reality has a habit of either forcing change or forcing conflict notwithstanding the reams written about what sort of trade deal is best, and what sort of Brexit Britain wants. In practice, these discussions will, just as in the Reformation, only become real for most people if and when their daily lives are impacted. For example, if Brexit means the UK is effectively excluded from pan-European manufacturing supply chains we expect this to engender a vibrant debate as to what employment will replace the substantial number of relatively well-paid jobs dependent upon existing pan European supply chains. At the moment, the elements involved in this debate are being aired through 'megaphone diplomacy' where one side of the Brexit divide shouts at the other and vice versa. Listening and reasoned debate is often an early casualty of political and economic invective.

At some point, usually when change actually happens, reality dawns and one of three things can occur. If the change is benign, people will likely grumble a bit and adapt. On the other hand, if the change is perceived to be destructive, two further options present themselves. The first, what we term the golden option, is that a reasoned debate takes place about what to do to next; and the second (sometimes the more common) is that the divides harden, often with very unpleasant social and economic consequences.

Our book is about this second *"reality"* stage of Brexit, when peoples day to day lives start to be impacted as reality starts to bite. In this context, we pose the question, *'How can we make Brexit work as an engine for UK economic success and social coherence over the next quarter of a century and beyond?'*

We make no apologies for identifying that entrepreneurs and innovators need to be at the heart of this future story; it will only be by constant adaptation to build and maintain a competitive edge in today's that economic "social" success will be realised.

Our book is intended to contribute to the 'debate yet to happen'. Just as Ebenezer Scrooge was forced to witness his Christmas Past, Present and Future, we have Brexit Past, Brexit Present and Post Brexit Future. Unintentionally our narrative in some sense 'mimics' Dickens as ours are intertwined with each other; and yet our future seeks to offer a way of breaking with our present through understanding some of the better moments in our past and applying these insights into today's complex and ever-changing world.

This book is for the Brexit Leaver, Remainer and Agnostic alike. There are no right or wrong answers in it. Our conclusions are in one sense a set of informed observations towards potential solutions. Perhaps one necessity for success could end up being all of us 'Taking Back Control' not only from Brussels but also from the 'Westminster Political Village' and its associated ecosystem of lobbyists, think tanks and consultancies.

If the entrepreneur is central to our future success, we collectively are central to equipping them with the practical framework to succeed. This book is about practical realism rather than high-minded theoretical dogma.

We would like to thank our publisher, our families and all of those around us for their support as this book has moved from clouds of ideas into words on paper. Especial thanks need to be given to John Cox for his thoughtful comments on an early draft of part of the manuscript, to David Finch for his very clear exposition of 'Leave Campaign' underlying concerns, to Michael Simmons for his help with the proofing and to all our colleagues and peers who have given their time to thoughtful debate on these issues.

For us, and we hope for you, this book should be a positive starting point and a springboard to action as to 'what comes next' in the 'Brave New World' of Brexit.

Prof N Culkin

Hertfordshire, UK

R Simmons

Riyadh, Kingdom Saudi Arabia

December 2018

INTRODUCTION

Every act of rebellion expresses a nostalgia for innocence and an appeal to the essence of being.

Camus (1956)

Brexit for some, is a rebellion against globalism and the European and domestic political establishment, and for others a desire for a return to a world of certainties, or may be an expression of hope for improvement with a leap into an unknown future. All these sentiments convey a feeling that something in society is implicitly broken and needs fixing; a feeling that has grown significantly since the 2008 Financial Crisis.

Today's society is fluid as to how social groups both form and dissolve. Social and broadcast media, advertising and many other influences now engender the rapid formation and dissolution of social groups. In the Brexit context, both groups — Leave and Remain — feel their group and therefore their nation will 'win' if their policies are followed. Leavers were told it is possible to leave the European Union without a cost and gain significant longer-term rewards, whilst Remainers were told that to 'Leave' will come with substantial costs and few, if any rewards.

This book is about teasing out strategies and actions that deliver hope for economic improvement, realise sustainable social balance and where possible avoid social and/or disruption costs. The implicit assumption in this approach is that 'Take Control' should not mean 'Create Chaos'. In doing this, we draw upon three underlying threads.

First is the need to understand why people who voted 'Leave' did so; the juxtaposition of which is what do they want to change to make their lives better? Second, we seek to unpack experiences from the past and see what we can learn from the successes, failures, strategies and choices made in previous historical Brexits and third, we pose the question as to what must change in the UK today if Leave aspirations are to be realised? Our observations or reflections are not restricted to Brexit, but rather look at how the UK can build a competitive edge in todays rapidly changing and unstable world.

INSIGHTS FROM THE PAST CAN HELP US TODAY

This is not the first time England has split from Europe. There have been previous Brexits; for example, the end of Roman Britain, the Henrician Reformation and the Elizabethan Settlement. If we look at the ruptures following the break with Rome in the 1530s, we see sharp divisions between Catholics and Protestants, some of which persist in some form right up to today. Will today's divisions be as persistent? As the Italian philosopher George Santayana (1863-1952) said, *those who cannot remember the past are condemned to repeat it.* What can we learn from these previous Brexits? How can we apply these lessons to today?

Brexit I: The End of Roman Britain — Economic and Political Brexit

Arguably, the Roman Empire was the first 'European Union' with a Single Market and borderless trade stretching from Hadrian's Wall in Britannia to the Eastern Empire and the Near and Middle East. Britannia's AD 410 break from the Roman Empire is, despite considerable recent archaeology, previous antiquarian studies and much writing over the ages, still 'opaque' in the precise narrative of events, a bit hazy on the timing (approx. AD 408 to AD 430) and unclear in its exact impacts over time.

Following on from previous disturbances in the late 4th Century and a tendency for the elite to move from living in towns to living on country estates, this first Brexit was triggered by the Emperor's removal of the Imperial Army from Britannia in AD 408, due to a pressing need to suppress the Gauls. It had happened before, but this time round it coincided with a cessation of tax payments to Rome by Britannia. One can imagine the sentiment 'why pay for something if I have no benefit? Better I organise it myself'. An early fifth-century form of 'Taxpayers Alliance'?

Ceasing to pay taxes had indirect (and no doubt) unexpected consequences. Tax payments needed to be made in Roman Coin, and without them shipments of coinage largely ceased to Britannia after about AD 411. Without coinage, complex supply chains broke down and over time urban conurbations saw economic and political decline.

Despite archaeological finds such as Sutton Hoo and the writings of Bede, for the common urban dweller, Britannia slipped from the rich urbanised Province of Rome to a rural peasant-based Dark Age. Whilst every town was different, in general, urban settlements fell into disrepair (with some later revitalised during the Anglo-Saxon years), the monetary economy largely collapsed and markets and supply chains that enabled trade, and impacted the ordinary person seemingly disappeared (although evidence of limited volumes of high value imports at a slightly later time exists). This Brexit was bad news for towns and industries, but good news for agricultural economies based around gentry-held rural estates.

Brexit II: Henry VIII's Legal Brexit

We move on to our second Brexit. In the 1530s, Henry VIII's Chief Minister Thomas Cromwell executed a 'Legal' Brexit that separated the English State from the clasps of the Roman Catholic Church, notwithstanding that this Brexit was one immediate result of Henry's need to divorce his current wife. This rupture in relations with Europe was also associated in England with a desire to promote the 'nation state' and in particular the ever-present need to fill the National Treasury. Despite the 1393 Statute of Praemunire that allowed the King to block church courts in the event of a clash between Church and State prior to the break with the Roman Catholic Church, accepted legal practice restricted the ecclesiastical court to matters specifically reserved for church courts.

Sometimes as in the EU today, contentious issues were resolved by carefully crafted 'fudges'. Henry VIII was unfortunate that some of the usual flexibility to solve delicate issues (such as his divorce) were not available through the politics of 'fudge' when he needed them most. Negotiating options had been significantly reduced by international events such as the 1527 Sacking of Rome by Hapsburg troops loyal to Holy Roman Emperor

Charles V. Charles was the nephew of Catherine of Aragon, the wife Henry VIII was keen to divorce, meaning the Pope was temporarily under enhanced influence of one of the rulers who was against the divorce.

Henry VIII decided to force matters after Anne Boleyn became pregnant in late 1532. Thomas Cromwell was instructed to drive a series of bills through Parliament to enable the divorce, change the Royal Succession to reflect the new state of affairs and break with the Roman Church and its Ecclesiastical courts, whilst sequestrating church assets to bolster the King's Treasury. As the legislation progressed towards the end of 1533, Cromwell started to organise an anti-papal campaign to stir passions to engender support for the legislation.

Legislatively successful, it is striking how these reforms unsettled both gentry and peasants and grew into the 1536 Pilgrimage of Grace insurrection. This revolt across Northern England caused Henry considerable concern, sufficient for him to take a lead role in quelling it. Overall, one is left with an impression that despite legal success, the changes of the 1530s had not bedded down in the country. There was alienation from the political elite in London, unrest due to challenging economic circumstances for peasants, dissatisfaction with taxes, a fear of losing the past and concern that local welfare for the poor was being dismantled.

Brexit III: Elizabeth's Mercantilist Brexit

After the death of Henry VIII in 1547, his 10-year-old son Edward VI succeeded the throne, and England was governed by a Regency Council until the young king's coming of age. This Council became deeply unpopular due to its religious, enclosure and currency debasement policies, which led to revolt. The rebellions of 1548 and 1549 (the Western and the Kett's revolts) were especially serious.[1] Ferment and insurrection across Britain continued into Mary I's reign with Wyatt's rebellion of 1554 against the new Queen Mary (Henry VIII's eldest daughter) marrying Philip II, King of Spain. Political unrest was combined with economic difficulty due to falls in real wages and significant inflation associated with the Great Debasement of the coinage (1544–1551). Added to this, there was instability in religion as Edward VI's government followed a strongly Protestant policy to be succeeded by Mary I who banished the Protestants and reverted England to Roman Catholicism.

Following this turbulence, Elizabeth I, not surprisingly, faced considerable challenges upon her accession to the English Crown in 1558. England had been through over 20 years of deep change following her exit from the European Catholic System in the 1530s, to be then reintegrated into the same system by Mary I. There had been revolts from both gentry and peasants, falling real wages, a huge debasement of the coinage and so on and so forth.

Against this background of continual turmoil, Elizabeth was to execute yet another Brexit in early 1559 as she had Parliament pass the 'Act of Uniformity' and the 'Act of Supremacy' that together represent the 'Elizabethan Reformation'. Notwithstanding these changes, in an early display of pragmatism, the Queen was able to be sufficiently "opaque" as regards her long-term intentions so as to avoid excommunication by the hard-line Pope Paul IV; an act that would have undoubtedly inflamed domestic Catholic opinion. In tandem, she avoided war with her European neighbours and successfully stabilised her succession.

Elizabeth's Brexit is typified by pragmatism and together with a reliance on trusted relationships to enforce a separation from Europe that was more distinct and certainly far longer lasting than that of her father Henry VIII. At the same time, she was able to maintain England's economic access to continental – especially the all-important – cloth export markets. Despite continued challenges to real wage levels for agricultural labourers, her reign delivered economic improvement including the nascent growth of some important industries and, advancements in supply chains across England and Wales to support the increasing urban importance of London. The trade deficit was eliminated, the national debt repaid (albeit repayment came from plundering the Spanish Main) and a process of diplomatic and commercial expansion into exotic lands of the East set in progress. Elizabeth's Brexit was more than a reordering of relations with Europe, rather it was an opening to a more internationalist, entrepreneurial, buccaneering and mercantilist age.

THE NEED FOR ENTREPRENEURIAL EXCEPTIONALISM

If part of Elizabeth I's success came from some of the colourful adventuring and entrepreneurial characters around her, the need for risk-taking entrepreneurs to innovate new products and markets remains just as relevant today.

Nostalgia and hope for improved economic circumstances are key aspirations of the Leave voter; but these aspirations need to be realised in a world where many of yesterday's certainties seem to soon become today's unknowns.[2]

The UK in 2019 faces a rapidly evolving world. Change is everywhere and in almost everything; technical change, economic change, political change and social change. Many of today's key technologies were figments of public imagination 20 years ago. Who in 1989 when the Berlin Wall fell could have imagined that the world in 2018 could be facing a global trade war or that Donald Trump would be the US President? Who could have conceived in 1990 that so much human interaction could now occur on social media?

In 1989, China had yet to emerge as one of the 'workshops of the world', yet today is the globe's second economic and an increasingly assertive global power. Even in 1999 less than 20 years ago, there had been no Western financial crisis in living memory, there had been no second Iraq War, no 9/11, the Good Friday peace deal was just being sealed and Russia was still enmeshed in the chaos of the Yeltsin years. Germany grappled with reunification; the Euro was yet to happen and the Lisbon Treaty had not even been thought of. We lived in a mono-power world with a single global power – the United States of America.

With the passing of each of the above events, old certainties died. If geopolitics have changed, who could have imagined how technological change brought about through smartphones, social media (from Facebook to WeChat) and e-commerce would impact on our world? The digitalisation of so many products and services have transformed consumer habits and buying patterns. High streets are increasingly threatened by moves to online purchasing as complex supply chains ripple across the world moving jobs, incomes and investments around countries and continents. We live in a world of uncertainty and change. There is every reason to suspect that this will be the new norm.

Economic success and economic well-being demands we keep up with and adapt to each and every trend. In this context, the most pressing question is, if and how we can turn Brexit into an opportunity for the UK to lead and succeed in this state of global flux? Success comes from the actions taken by individuals. Creating new products, markets and services that address changed circumstances is the life blood of opportunity-seeking entrepreneurs.

Perhaps the key ingredient for the UK's future prospects will be in building, supporting, affirming and unlocking UK entrepreneurial exceptionalism.

SUCCESS HEALS DIVISION

As we navigate our way through previous Brexits to see what insights they offer, and explore how the UK can lead the way in such a rapidly changing world, for many there may be a sense of déjà vu. One question that may present itself is how can we avoid the current 'Leave vs Remain' and 'Old vs Young' divides becoming as deep and bitter as the Catholic vs Protestant splits that developed from the sixteenth century?

Perhaps the best chance of healing these divides can come from generating success and making such rewards shared between those who create it and contribute to it.[3] Finding the right formula to develop and build the UK's entrepreneurial capability to innovate, create world beating new products post Brexit, will be key to enabling this success. The good news is there are always entrepreneurs waiting in the wings, who can provide solutions just when they are needed. The perennial question is, will we be smart enough to recognise and listen to that entrepreneur and support them?

In 1564, England faced economic calamity as Margaret of Parma, Catholic Regent of the Netherlands closed the Antwerp wool market to English wool (the Antwerp handled the bulk of English exports at that time) on the pretence of plague in London. Relief was at hand as canny entrepreneur George Needham had already built relations with an alternative market location in Emden and had good relations at Court.[4] The English sold their wool in Emden and Antwerp reopened. English entrepreneurial exceptionalism had outwitted Hapsburg centralism. Could the current tussle over UK participation in the European Single Market be an echo of Margaret's earlier policy?

As we embark on our journey through previous Brexits, the first half of this book is structured as a tour through a gallery of former Brexits, where each hall holds its own collection and a final hall summarises our situation today. Following in the footsteps of nineteenth-century composer Modest Mussorgsky, we have animated this journey with a number of 'Promenades' as we walk from one hall to the next.

Each Promenade is designed to hold certain aspects of the 'essence' of our journey. Collectively, the Promenades form a detailed introduction to the later chapters, which in turn seek to 'star gaze' and chart a path towards a future economic success and associated social healings onto our blank canvas. So, in the second half of the book, we enter an artist's studio — where we come to understand the pictures, their brush strokes and textures and other attributes to help us pose the question in our final chapter: which Brexit will it be this time?

1

MOTIVATION, MYTH AND REALITY

Whatever your views on the Brexit debate [...] the monopoly of the EU membership model has now been shattered. The story behind this remarkable swerve now forms a part of our nation's tale. It slots into a thread on sovereignty stretching back through the breaking of the line at Trafalgar or the fireships at Calais; or in less incendiary terms, via our founding role in EFTA, the volumes of Adam Smith and the Statute of Praemunire. Our country['s] [...] history is also that of an ancient nation state; one with a profound sense of the limitations of its institutions that was already considered shocking by its Capetian and Valois counterparts.

(Rotherham, 2018)

On 11 April 2018, a UK Museum of Sovereignty[5] was announced to celebrate British Exceptionalism. In view of the geographic distribution of the '2016 UK Referendum' with majorities to leave in both England and Wales, should we perhaps say 'English and Welsh Exceptionalism'?[6] This impression of 'identity voting' was underpinned by the 2016 Annual Social attitudes survey that interviewed Brexit Leavers and found that a sense of 'national identity' coupled with a firm set of social attitudes characterised the typical 'Leave Voter'.[7] Complementary analysis of the polling results found age and home ownership were especially important in determining a disposition to vote leave[8] with older home owners (and social housing tenants) more likely to 'vote leave'.

For some, when they think of an individual Brexiteer, it may conjure up one of two mental images. First, someone from England who is perhaps older, maybe a pensioner, and who has done well financially over the past 40 years. They own a property that has been appreciating in value and are secure in their mind that this nest egg will maintain its value. (S)he also feels the world has drifted away from some 'core values' of English civility, towards a bureaucratic state driven by European red tape. They are also deeply uncomfortable with the idea of unlimited immigration, sensing that 'terrorist' human rights are prioritised at the expense of the indigenous population. Secure in their mortgage-free home, with a defined benefit occupational pension, a triple locked state pension and free health care, it is very hard for them to see how any Brexit Shock could hurt them. Voters from social classes A, B and C1 amounted to 59% of the Leave vote suggesting almost two-thirds of our Leave voters fit our first mental picture.[9]

A second impression might be that some Leave Voters could be members of the 'Left Behind' who are often typified as white working class, maybe at the lower end of school academic attainment, lacking further education, and perhaps younger rather than retired. A member of the 'Left Behind' is someone who faces challenges in the labour market and, following the 2008 Global Crash has found it difficult to step on the housing ladder. This group often blames immigration for depriving them of their 'natural rights' to housing and employment. One core part of this group, representing some 12% of the overall population (and of which 95% voted 'Leave'),[10] is also likely to be fiercely nationalistic, often passionate followers of the England Football team, a reader of a 'red top' tabloid such as *The Sun* or, if aspiring, possibly the *Daily Mail*.[11] As a whole, the 'Left Behind' group is estimated at 21% of the overall Leave Vote.[12]

We are also told that the United Kingdom Independence Party (UKIP) and by extension 'Leave' supporters are more likely to be older, working class, male and white. It has been argued that some pensioners might see UKIP as a political party offering a refuge from a society where social change is seen by some as undermining the key characteristics of traditional 'Englishness', a group rooted in a nostalgic idea of a 'Great' Britain with an Empire compounding feelings amongst poorly qualified members of the working class of being 'Left Behind'.[13]

Eric Kaufmann penned a 2016 blog, 'It's NOT the economy, stupid: Brexit as a story of personal values', in which he argues that voting Leave in the Referendum was all about expressing 'national identity', citing a preference for the death penalty and a fear of immigration as pointers towards having a predisposition to Vote Leave.[14] As part of the Economic Social Research Council's, 'UK in a Changing Europe' programme, a study on prereferendum voter attitude data painted a picture of a nation regarding the European Union (EU) as bent on eroding sovereignty, enabling terrorism, destabilising peace in Europe and undermining local society.[15] A total of 47% of prospective voters viewed the EU as encouraging terrorism, whilst 28% did not. The same number (28%) saw the EU as positive for sovereignty and 51% as negative. Could it be that Leave supporters feel they are protecting their country against foreign forces, giving them a clear, collective, historically rooted and determinate identity?

The 'Englishness' and to a lesser extent 'Welshness' (England and Wales both voted to Leave) contrast with Scotland and Northern Ireland's majority vote to Remain (Electoral Commission, 2016). In this context, we suggest that for many in England, a vote to leave the EU was synonymous with a passion to 'Save England'. Perhaps this 'nationalistic sentiment' helps explain how two surveys can contradict each other on the importance of immigration as a driver to vote 'Leave'. In a British Social Attitudes Survey, Clery et al. (2016)[16] found a clear relationship between a fear of immigration and a disposition to 'Vote Leave' whilst in a specific study of Referendum voter behaviour, immigration is nowhere near so distinct in its association with a vote to Leave.[17]

Could a desire for a distinct 'English National' identity have in some ways emerged in response to both the devolution of power to Scotland and Wales and, the receipt of EU laws from Brussels? In this narrative, the reassertion of an English National Identity for some becomes the dominant theme, notwithstanding previous primary identities that may have been associated primary and primarily in same sentence with economic capability or class status. Seemingly this 'English National Identity' aligns to the feeling of English Exceptionalism we mentioned earlier.[18] There is anecdotal evidence that a Leave vote was felt by many as a patriotic imperative on a par with standing firm at Dunkirk, Waterloo and Trafalgar. In such circumstances, could a leave voter be seen as rooted in 'English Exceptionalism' as we describe in **Box 1**?

The desire to affirm a separate 'English' identity seems to have increasingly replaced party loyalty as a motivational characteristic. There is evidence that Leavers may have been searching for a party that would represent their views. The UKIP tribe in 2015 may well have been Labour voters in

Box 1. English Exceptionalism Over the Ages

The concept of English Exceptionalism draws upon thinking that developed in late sixteenth century English post-Reformation Society. Starting in 1610 with the publication of William Camden's *Britannica*, which focused almost entirely on England and Wales, there is an expression of the English nobility as the cultural heirs to the Roman Empire.

> *[Britain] is certainly the masterpiece of nature performed when she was in her best and gayest humour [...] I need not enlarge upon its inhabitants nor extol the vigour and firmness of their constitution, the inoffensiveness of their humour, their civility to all men, and their courage and bravery, so often both at home and abroad, and not unknown to the remotest corner of the earth.*[19]

Camden focused on links to Roman Britain, one deepened and extended by Antiquarian William Stuckley:

> *They are cursuses of the ancient Britons, long before the Romans came hither. I mean the first aborigines Brittons in heroic ages, when the Druids first began; before the Gaulish nations came over, somewhat above Ceaser's time; those Brittons that made the mighty works of Abury, Stonehenge, &c. [etc.]* (W Stuckley, 1 Sep 1736[20])

Stuckley mirrors Camden's journeys through the counties of England unearthed as he finds and describes relics from Roman and earlier times; his narrative extends Camden as he suggests that the English noble man is the natural heir of Roman Civilisation, a transformation made possible through the subjugation of the children of English Chieftains' (or more correctly the Chieftains of the tribes of Roman occupied Ancient Britain) to Roman Rule.

Well connected and a respected authority on English Antiquity, it is not difficult to see how the ideas of Stuckley (and others around him) became an undercurrent of English Tory and Whigg thought.

Neither is it difficult to find echoes of this 'Heroic Englishman' narrative in today's Brexit pleas to recapture sovereignty.

2005, migrating to the Conservatives in 2010, before arriving at the doors of UKIP in 2015. Such voters include a significant cohort of small business people and self-employed, and aspiring lower middle-class voters in junior supervisory positions. In all cases, there is some suggestion that the media or the 'oxygen' of publicity has had a significant impact.[21,i]

So, our typical Leave Supporter, especially in England, is older, in stable accommodation, with a smaller subset younger and maybe from the one of the lower socio-economic groups. At the heart of their narrative is a sense that 'English Exceptionalism' – what made England great – is under threat from immigrants and foreign (alien) powers. In this narrative, immigrants act as a new and distinct tribe that facture communities by refusing to integrate, take jobs natives could otherwise have undertaken and drive down wage rates. Additionally immigrants seem for many Leavers to occupy what affordable housing exists, 'sponge' off welfare services and expatriate welfare support by for example, having child benefit paid for children in their home country or tying up the country's health service.

How could a great nation that has within folk memory ruled a Global Empire, that won two world wars, be so reduced? To some, it must be the fault of unelected greedy remote non-UK bureaucrats who know nothing of austerity and use hard earned tax revenues from the English to subsidise their luxurious life styles and fund white elephant projects that are scattered around Europe. Examples of such foreign waste seem to flow into popular media and are substantiated and highlighted by the European Court of Auditors in its investigations that have unearthed apparent abuses such as the building of unwanted and unused airports in Estonia, Greece, Italy, Spain and Poland and using €666 million of EU grants in the process. No wonder that the EU deems such activities as *poor value for money*.[22]

IMMIGRATION

We have already mentioned that conflicting opinions exist as to how important immigration was as an issue in the Referendum. Equally there is a paradox that areas where the immigrant population is highest, such as London

---

[i]The data employed to study the determinants of voting in the EU referendum were generated by a part of the University of Essex Continuous Monitoring Survey.

were generally citadels of Remain, whilst areas with lower levels of immigrants were more worried about it. In a recent comparative study on assimilating immigrants in the UK and Netherlands, immigrants are seen to be more *different* when they fail to speak English as their first language at home, where they fail to have a community of English friends and where their points of socialisation differ from English social norms, for example, if they object to meeting in the pub.[23] Such opportunities to connect have not been helped in places where immigrant groups dominate specific urban areas. Geographic proximity reinforces human tendencies to focus on bonding with like people. For example, around 90% of people identified friendships as being within their own ethnicity.[24] Alike people tend to stick together thereby accentuating feelings of distinctness. Despite all the noise about immigrants threatening jobs, a recent study found little evidence of this for either of their sample occupations, a bricklayer or an IT worker. However, the importance of paying local tax was seen as important across the socio-economic spectrum with a slight bias towards lower socio-economic groups – suggesting some support that the more disadvantaged are more likely to brand immigrants as 'welfare scroungers'.[25]

The overall picture painted is rather surprising. Civic integration ranks over religion, which in turn ranks over economic considerations. A French immigrant is seen as preferable to a Chinese one who is preferable to a Polish one, but bottom of the pile sit African immigrants, followed by those from the Indian Subcontinent. Anti-Islam bias in a survey found 63% of respondents believe Arabs have not integrated into society, rising to 75% amongst the retired. Leave voters also felt migrant Arabs were not beneficial to the UK/Europe (61%) with less than 10% seeing them as a positive influence.[26] In contrast, 47% of Remain voters thought this group was beneficial to UK society. This impression is further reinforced when one compares the results of the European Social Survey in 2002 and 2014. The findings demonstrated a significant hardening of attitudes against non-EU immigration rather than immigration from poorer EU countries[27] although overall negative attitudes towards immigrants seem to have receded since 2017.[28]

Whilst it is unclear how directly correlated the immigration narrative is to the Leave vote, there has been a discernible rise in race related hate crime since the Referendum. Such an increase can be conflated with some finger pointing (e.g. by the 'left behind' tribe) as they believe specific ethnic and racial groups are the reason why those born English cannot find good stable jobs and cannot afford secure housing.

Contrasting hate crime in London in the three months before the Referendum and the three months after, the Metropolitan Police[29] found a 30% increase in reported hate crimes with racist crimes showing the highest rise (34%). Concerns relating to this hate crime rise were later echoed by the United Nation's Special Rapporteur on Racism.[30] **Box 2** discusses how this rise in hate crime and the associated narrative reverberate from a previous dark age.

Box 2. Worrying Echoes from a Darker Age

English Exceptionalism is typified by feelings of greatness, a narrative that *in extremis* may assert that Great Britain is great because it is led by the English. Arguably in this paradigm the English are "Great" because they are the true inheritors of the Roman Empire. They are the children of the Chieftains of the Great Tribes that gave the world wonders such as Stonehenge who were subjugated to Roman customs that they then adopted and modified to grow a great 'Anglosphere' Civilisation.[31] Notwithstanding, we are reminded that indigenous pre-Roman Britons contained a substantial group of people who did not share the classic white Anglo-Saxon genetic characteristics so often associated with being indigenous 'English'.[32]

This sense of 'national exceptionalism' has disturbing parallels in history. For example, the early Nazi obsession with castles and medieval ceremonies underpinned the *Volksgemeinschaft* or 'people's community' of the Third Reich. In addition to much needed employment in a depressed country, the German castle and monument renovation programme of the early 1930s gave 'icons of place' a popular focus of expression of a 'heroic Teutonic' tradition.[33] These historic icons became inseparable with a symbolic bonding into a presumed heroic age of perceived 'German Exceptionalism'.

Another parallel comes from some of the voting groups that supported the Nazi party. Analysis of pro-Nazi voting groups found that support was concentrated amongst the working poor (including self-employed and small shop keepers) and domestic workers and family members helping someone in the household together with middle class members with investment incomes and fixed salaries/pensions who had been especially impacted by the 1923 Weimar hyperinflation.[34] Explicitly, more than one study found that the unemployed and poor workers in Catholic areas where there was some form of social support were not in the main prime Nazi voters.

In summary, the Nazi regime came to power partly by legitimising itself in the context of historical greatness and partly through the support of those on fixed incomes or pensions, by the aspiring poor and those at home. How does this contrast with the UKIP and Leave support coming from the 'at home' and the aspiring lower middle class or left behind?

DO REMAIN SUPPORTERS HAVE A COLLECTIVE IDENTITY?

Remain supporters provide a striking contrast to Leave Voters. First, "Remainers" tend to be younger, better educated and working rather than retired. Surprisingly, a study of Labour Remain voter motivations, found that they held common views to Leave voters on issues such as immigration.[35] Arguably, "Remainers" are more persuaded by economic arguments, with data suggesting 95% of Remain voters were persuaded to vote Remain by the fear of economic damage.[36] The geographic distribution and demographics tell a story of younger people in more economically successful and cosmopolitan centres such as London and Manchester voting Remain. By contrast, the Remain vote is much broader in Scotland and more rural in Northern Ireland.

TRIBE AND VOTER COALITION IN THE BREXIT WORLD

The 'Leave' and 'Remain' narratives are very different. Leave aspirations for many seem to be deeply rooted in a sense of 'English Exceptionalism', the protection of the English nation and the metaphorical repelling of foreign invaders. Remain on the other hand, whilst sharing many of the concerns Leaver's have on issues such as immigration are arguably driven by economic concerns.

A recent study[37] found that in the post-modern world, groups or tribes as we might call them, form dynamically in relation to people's self-defined roles, social perception and relation to others. This is a significant change from previous societal arrangements where families and genetic links formed the tribe and the tribe dictated the role of each member. For example, research[38] has found English DNA gene pools have remained relatively stable since the sixth century AD. In effect the ancient Saxon Kingdoms seem to be 'tribally' based, according to the Latin word *tribus* that is used to describe a group of families and their organisation.

Contrasting this post-Saxon theme to later Roman Britain, we find a tendency for Citizens to assume a more state facing identity as conveyed by the use of the word "citizen" which in itself is originally derived (via Norman French) from the Latin word *civitas*. We gain an insight into the meaning of *civitas* through Cicero (51 BC) who describes this as expressing their common community interest through the institutions of the State. It has been argued elsewhere that the pre-Roman identity of Britain was a *civitas* one, where groups of people identified with a central regional authority focused on *oppida* or regional capitals.[39]

In one model (*tribus*), we have common genetic bond (English Exceptionalism) and in the other model (*civitas*), we have a common social bond focused on a common perception of governance issues. From Maffesoli (1988), we gain a sense that post-modern *tribus* or tribes are formed via self-identification rather than genetic links; notwithstanding distinct DNA gene pool differences in different English regions.

Arguably Leave voters could be grouped into a Maffesoli post-modern tribe, whilst Remain voters (living in conurbations, younger and more mobile so paradoxically being more DNA mixed) have a tendency to group via *civitas* or state expression of their collective will. The latter have been on the 'winning side' – economically in terms of jobs, status and career paths over some considerable time, most likely since the late 1970s.

No wonder the two groups are so divided and find communicating difficult, if not almost impossible. According to a 2017 study on attitudes, the divisions between, Leavers and Remainers are hardening.[40]

TODAY'S PRE-BREXIT WORLD

The Britain of 2018 is very different from the Britain of 1950, which in turn was very different from the Britain of 1975 and arguably from the Britain of 2000. In 1950, households were still facing food rationing (which continued until 1954), young people were conscripted into National Service (this ended in 1960), television had one channel that was only available in selected regions (the first 'national' TV event is generally considered[41] to be the 1953 Coronation) and the UK was just starting to divest itself of Empire. By 1975, the UK had seen the 'swinging sixties', Beatlemania, the 1973 oil crisis, the British Leyland debacle and its association with union activist such as 'Red Robo', a three-day week and fall of a government during a Miner's Strike; was on the threshold of another balance of payments crisis that this time would see the IMF being called in.

Roll forward a further 25 years to 2000 and the UK had been through a massive economic restructuring as traditional industries faded away in the 1980s, the cold war was over, London had developed into a global financial hub, union power had become a shadow of its former self and the years of 'Cool Britannia' were setting in. As Britain crossed into the new millennium memories of 1950's, food rationing had faded as consumerism took hold. An economic and cultural journey that spanned 50 years saw living standards rising. In the first half of the post war period, wealth rose as real wages rose, and in the second half of this period after the mid 1970's such improvements in wealth tended to come from steep house price increases. Wealth generation for the many moved from earned wealth accumulation to

---

Box 3. An Englishman's Castle or a Pot of Gold?

UK Residential housing prices have risen as a multiple of average wages for many years. Much of today's narrative has been focused on these prices being due to restrictive Planning Laws as demonstrated by the substantial differences in land valuations between agricultural and building land. These differences provide evidence of a distorted land market, and associated restrictions to new housing supply. Less attention has been paid to market distortions on the 'demand side' due to post-1970 changes in financial regulation.

Post-1945 financial liberalisation and deregulation started with the publication of 'Competition and Credit Control' in 1971[42] and accelerated with the reforms of the 1980s. Taken together, these reforms had a significant impact on housing finance availability and by implication house prices. Deregulation enabled commercial bank lending into the residential mortgage market starting from the changes in financial regulation in the early 1970's. Within a few years, additional providers had entered the market as both Barclays and Midland (now HSBC) banks entered the market, with Lloyds

TSB joining the market in the 1980s.[43] The sums lent by these banks have been and continue to be substantial. When significant additional funds enter a market (as a result of new providers and increases in lending multiples of income), and there is no matching increase in supply, prices rise.

The scale of the change was substantial. From a position of nearly nil commercial bank lending to the residential mortgage market in 1970 mortgage assets have grown to become major business for banks. The commercial bank lending to the residential mortgage market was estimated in 2014 at around £800 billion or over 60% of their retail assets.[44] Analysing the impact on house prices over the long term Muellbauer et al.,[45] state

'Theory suggests that financial liberalisation of mortgage markets in the 1980s should have led to notable shifts in house price behaviour. The evidence supports the predictions of theory, suggesting shifts took place in wealth effects, as in the consumption function, and that real interest rates and income expectations became more important.'

This strong rise in house prices, is associated with insufficient new build, vast net lending flows and relaxations in the loan income ratios. The consequences are that today, houses are for many unaffordable for younger people on average incomes, especially for those in, and around, London. As prices have risen, home ownership levels have started to fall as affordability challenges for younger people with no inherited wealth from 'the bank of mum and dad' have made home ownership unaffordable for them. Overall home ownership for the 16 to 34-year-old age group declined from 54% in 1996, to 34% in 2016.[46] Whilst house prices have risen (so excluding younger generations from the prospect of housing related capital gains), real wages have stagnated, making wage-based capital accumulation more challenging.

These changes in home ownership trends indicate that house prices have moved out of line with incomes. When house prices are out of line with incomes, there can be financial instability.[47] It can be assumed that the market will, at some point, force adjustment by reducing asset (e.g. house) prices until they align with earned incomes across all generations as these incomes represent the cash flows that ultimately support the prices houses are bought and sold at. Such an adjustment happened in 2008 in the USA, Spain and Ireland. It did not happen in the UK largely because of Government and Bank of England monetary policy intervention targeted at encouraging "Lender Forbearance" and above all reductions in interest rates. Ultra-low interest rates, state pressure for lender forbearance, activist monetary policy to support residential mortgage lending and an active Help to Buy subsidy scheme averted a UK house price crash.

wealth based upon rising asset values, especially rising house prices (see **Box 3**).

The 2007/2008 financial crash represented a sharp shock. For some, it was the sight of depositor queues outside Northern Rock offices, for others it was the fear of losing their job; and, for many young people, it was the difficulty of finding any job, let alone one with prospects and rising real wages.

In 2018 the certainties of earlier ages are for some, especially the young a distant memory. Young people sometimes termed 'millennials' (those born in the 20 years from 1980) face relatively poorer earnings than their predecessors and consequent difficulties joining the housing ladder. This is the first generation in living memory who are likely to be poorer than their parents.[48] Younger people can face zero hours contracts (that lock an employee into a company but do not guarantee a weekly wage), which for some not seeking the benefits of flexible hours working, have become a key entry point to the labour market. Welfare for those in work has been squeezed while non-working pensioners have been protected from austerity by a pension triple lock. These changes represent a break from historical norms. Previously a young person could normally look forward to a job or succession of jobs

---

Box 4. Austerity to Cool Britannia and Back to Austerity

How things have changed. In 1950, families were subject to food rationing as Britain continued to struggle to recover and rebuild from the war years. Austerity was combined with rebuilding traditional industries, employees in the main expected career routes with the same employer and the challenges were to rebuild. Things eased in the 1960s with a 'Swinging Decade' of the Beatles, cultural liberalisation and expectations of a 'white hot' technological revolution. By the mid-1970s, optimism had faded as the first energy crisis and union unrest dented confidence. Unemployment and inflation rose, leading to the sharp structural adjustment of the 1980s as Mrs Thatcher's government let whole industries such as mining and steel go through large scale restructurings. Yet, for many others, living standards rose as North Sea Oil helped free the UK from it's notorious balance of payments constraint; consumer lending rose and housing wealth started to grow as house prices rose.

By the late 1990s, after a painful recession, Tony Blair's Labour government was viewed by some as young, equable and appealing; the term

'Cool Britannia' was, for a time, seen as the main driving force behind a feeling of euphoria and optimism in Britain. In an interview for the *Independent* newspaper, the Culture Minister Smith acknowledged that Cool Britannia was the Spice Girls, *The Full Monty* and London's Soho on a Saturday night. There was a sense that there could be a form of post-industrial capitalism that combined hard-nosed profits with a fuller recognition of the human creativity on which the profits hinged.

The wheel of fortune turned again in 2007/2008 as the Global Financial Crisis took hold. Banks toppled, uncertainty came, the public deficit ballooned and by 2011, the narrative was once again about public austerity.

that would enable them to buy their own house and leave them wealthier than their parents. We discuss these trends in **Box 4**.

Post 2008, the UK has found itself in a more uncertain world, with power seeming to shift from the United States to a rising China; real wages stagnating, public sector austerity, and the shock of seeing banks, regarded by many as the pillars of modern commercial life needing to be rescued by taxpayers, notwithstanding the relatively huge rewards some of the people working in them had / continue to receive. Many young people have come to face the twin challenges of finding affordable long-term housing and stable well rewarded employment. At the same time, these previously accepted certainties have been challenged, mass adoption of social media has opened the door to more fluid social groupings. It is unsurprising then that Brexit for many should represent a siren call for a return to stability (by taking back control) and a belief that success can only be regained by shaking up and replacing old compromised structures.

PROMENADE I: CRITERIA FOR MEASURING SUCCESS

The June 2016 EU Referendum Leave result synthesised two very different aspirations. If we assume that most 'Remainers' continue to anticipate Brexit challenges, we need to look at 'Leaver' aspirations to establish how we should measure whether Brexit is a success or not. We return to some dominant themes from this chapter by assuming that most people are less than excited by the minutuae of regulatory directives, European Court Advocate General reasonings or any of the many other technical parts of the operations of modern states and supranational bodies. We believe that most Leave Voters voted Leave as an expression of hope that a break with the European Union will allow the reordering of UK society to build a more certain, more prosperous, more stable world. It is (we believe) the 'big picture' items (that are confirmed by the detail of day-to-day life) that drive views and opinions.

For the Leaver, we have seen a dominant desire to reassert English Exceptionalism. A key feature of this includes a desire to recover a sense of 'greatness' that has nostalgic roots in the folk memories of the British Empire, encapsulated in Churchill's famous 4 June 1940 speech to the House of Commons:

> *we shall prove ourselves once again able to defend our island home, to ride out the storm of war, and to outlive the menace of tyranny, if necessary for years, if necessary alone. [...] We shall go on to the end [...] we shall defend our island, whatever the cost may be. We shall fight on the beaches [...] we shall never surrender [...] our Empire beyond the seas, armed and guarded by the British Fleet, would carry on the struggle, until, in God's good time, the new world, with all its power and might, steps forth to the rescue and the liberation of the old.*
>
> (Churchill, 1940)

The same speech has special resonance to some of today's headlines such as the 'Enemies of the People'[49] in its passage on the 'enemy within'.

> *We have found it necessary to take measures of increasing stringency, not only against enemy aliens and suspicious characters of other nationalities, but also against British subjects who may become a danger or a nuisance should the war be transported to the United Kingdom. [...] Parliament has given us*

the powers to put down Fifth Column activities with a strong
hand, [...] until we are satisfied, and more than satisfied, that this
malignancy in our midst has been effectively stamped out.

(Churchill, 1940)

Our second theme is economic, where Brexit is for some perhaps synonymous with a narrative of hope. We see this as especially the case for the
left behind, often white working-class males who face challenges in the
labour and housing markets and may feel a sense of exclusion from their
own native land. Additionally, English Exceptionalism is in a sense nostalgic,
reflected in the marked skewing of the 'Leave Vote' towards older generations. Equally the "Leave Vote" economic narrative is skewed towards
regions which have over time become associated with many who have been
'left behind'. From these narratives, we can set two key criteria by which a
Leave Voter can assess if 'Brexit Works'.

The first success criterion is nationalistic and has two components that
mirror each other. Internally within the UK, English Exceptionalists will
want to see an end of the 'tail wagging the dog', where ethnic minorities and
devolved nations are seen to 'game the system' against the English and then
make the English pay for the benefits they receive. Externally there is a
demand that Europeans and especially France and German respect the UK
as 'senior partner' in any arrangement, as other nations only have their liberty as a result of the British blood and resolve that has been shed to defend
them, especially during the Second World War.

The second criteria for Brexit success for a Leave voter, especially a 'left
behind' Leave Voter, will be measured by if they feel better off financially; a
hope in part engendered by Leave Campaign references that post — Brexit
they will stop paying taxes to Brussels. Perhaps the most striking example of
this aspiration is the suggestion that after Brexit day, as the UK has regained
control of its own finances, the National Health Service and Adult Social
Care will receive large amounts of additional funding without any matching
tax increases as a tangible 'Brexit Dividend' for all.

2

BREXIT TODAY: THE CURRENT STATE OF PLAY

In this chapter, we focus on two specific themes. The first is the process of leaving the European Union (EU), a subject that is filling untold newspaper column inches. The second looks at the UK's underlying economic situation as it faces Brexit. Our starting point is the June 2016 Referendum, Article 50 of the 2007 Lisbon Treaty,[50] which has become the gateway to Britain's Brexit journey.

ARTICLE 50

After the UK voted to leave the EU in an advisory Referendum held on June 2016, notification of that decision was given[51] to the European Union via Article 50 of the Lisbon Treaty on 29 March 2017.[52] This set in motion a two-year negotiation process for the UK to formalise its exit from the European Union. The mechanics of the negotiation are explored further in **Box 5.**

Prior to submitting the Article 50 notice to Brussels, British Prime Minister May set a number of 'red lines' for how the Brexit process would be negotiated in a January 2017 speech. These red lines can be summarised as (1) ensuring that the European Court of Justice (ECJ) has no jurisdiction in the UK; (2) no barriers will be allowed within the boundaries of the United Kingdom (which has had special relevance for the discussions in respect of Northern Ireland); (3) there will be no 'freedom of movement' for people; and (4) that the UK will leave the EU single market and customs

Box 5. Article 50 – The Road to Freedom?

The only previous voluntary departure from the EU was Greenland, which joined the EU in 1973 on account of its being a part of Denmark. Having attained Home Rule in 1979, Greenland voted by 53% to leave the EU in a Referendum in 1982 that was held as a consequence of a dispute over fishing rights. Exit negotiations (for the island of 56,000 people) took three years after which the final treaty was confirmed by a second Referendum in 1985 in which 52% voted to leave. The final outcome saw Greenland leave, technically in charge of its fish but with the EU retaining a broadly similar fish quota, whilst continuing to be part of the Kingdom of Denmark and joining the 25 Overseas Territories (e.g. French Polynesia) that are not part of the EU, but do have a special partnership with the block.[53]

The 2007 Lisbon Treaty was the first to offer a way for a Member State to leave the Union. The UK's decision to exit is the first time the mechanism has been used. This exit is very different from Greenland, as the UK is a full Member State in its own right and it is not looking to become an Overseas Territory affiliated through another Member State after its departure. Equally it is the first state to use the Article 50 exit process, which itself is fairly loose. The relevant wording states:

> '*In the light of the guidelines provided by the European Council, the Union shall negotiate and conclude an agreement with that State, setting out the arrangements for its withdrawal, taking account of the framework for its future relationship with the Union*'. (Lisbon, 2007)

There is no clause in the Treaty of Lisbon explaining what happens if a withdrawal notice is revoked and there are differing opinions as to whether it could be unilaterally revoked by referring to Article 68 of the Vienna Convention of Treaties.[54] Some argue it is possible to revoke unilaterally whilst others argue the reverse.[55] The question of whether the Article 50 can be revoked will be decided by the European Court of Justice following a referral by the Scottish Courts in September 2018.[56] In any event the provisions in the Treaty allow the two-year Article 50 negotiation period to be extended if there is a unilateral vote for this in the European Council.

union.[57] The intention to leave the jurisdiction of the ECJ led to formal notice for the UK to depart from a number of other bodies such as Euratom. The consequences of these decisions are complex and will continue to unfold over the coming years.

With Brexit, it is striking how complex and interrelated each strand is. Making a decision to leave the jurisdiction of the ECJ implicitly makes the decision to exit all the bodies that come under the Court's jurisdiction. For example, the ECJ has ultimate jurisdiction over all the EU Regulators, so removing the Court's role de facto means leaving the regulators under its judicial supervision. Each regulator has its own specialist staff, knowledge and procedures, so as new replacement bodies are created, growing the capability to replicate the existing European Regulators is likely to be complex, time consuming and expensive. Implementation of new regulators may also be technically challenging as these bodies contain large amounts of accumulated knowledge in their staff and crucially, relationships with the other similar regulators globally. These regulators operate within a context of global rule setting organisations, such as the WTO, IMF and the BIS (and its component Basel Committee on Banking Supervision) and within a series of international treaties that in some circumstances accord mutual recognition. A number of regulations enacted by the EU have their origin in other multilateral bodies. For example, the Capital Requirements Directives that control Bank Capital have their origins in the Basel Committee on Banking Supervision. These regulations will continue after Brexit as they relate to international rather than European conventions.

Some relationships are governed by specific treaties. One such treaty is the EU/USA 2011 Air Safety Treaty that accredits the European Aviation Safety Agency and its US counterpart (the Federal Aviation Authority) with each other giving mutual recognition to each other's Air Worthiness Certificates, Pilot Licences, etc. These official documents are the fundamental basis of civil aviation worldwide. Planes and crew without valid and mutually recognised certificates cannot fly globally. In April 2018, the EU Commission formally warned the Aviation Industry that as of Brexit Day existing UK certifications will cease to be valid.[58]

On the expiry of the Article 50 negotiation time period, the UK will no longer be an EU Member State with no access to the Bilateral Treaties that the EU has signed with non-EU countries. In **Box 6**, we examine how UK treaty relationships with non-EU states will change on Brexit Day (11 p.m. on 29 March 2019).

Box 6. A Brexit Britain Without Less Global Access?

Much of the UK's non-EU trade is currently enabled by EU third country Bilateral Treaties that in addition to forming the tariff basis of the EU's trade, govern a number of key functions such as mutual recognition of regulators, air safety, peaceful use of nuclear materials, data safe harbour and mutual recognition of court judgements for enforcement. Whilst the EU has indicated that it would have no objection to these treaties being rolled over during a transition period, such a rolling over requires consent from all the Treaty Parties.

Norway seems happy to give access to a post Brexit UK to its agreements with the EU and others such as Japan and Canada have reportedly indicated a willingness to grandfather their agreements. In contrast, South Korea and Chile are rumoured to be looking for UK trade concessions in order to undertake a 'modified' grandfathering of the current EU agreement.[60] Transatlantic tensions over trade policy also beg the question as to what the US President Trump administration's approach will be, given the USA currently has a trade deficit with the UK?

Without access to these agreements, the new Brexit Day Global Britain risks leaving the EU and reducing its access to the rest of the world as it is excluded from any treaties that have not been "rolled over".

Even with a transition agreement, the UK as a 'third country' cannot access any trade treaties signed by the EU in its own name. A legislative research paper[59] identified 1,149 EU negotiated treaties of which 746 are bilateral Third Country Treaties between the EU and Third Countries that the UK will lose access to on Brexit day, unless, they are agreed for rollover by all the signatories to these treaties.

BREXIT EXECUTION STREAMS

Having notified the European Union of the intention to leave through Article 50, two separate, but intertwined workstreams, were created by the UK to implement the changes that enable the UK to make Brexit a reality.

The Exit Negotiations

The first work stream relates to the exit negotiations themselves. Stresses in the UK negotiating team have become evident, culminating with Dominic

Raab being appointed Brexit secretary after David Davis resigned from the government on 7th July 2018. Mr Davis quit saying Theresa May had 'given away too much too easily'. At the insistence of the EU negotiators and in line with the wording of Article 50, the exit negotiations have first focused on drafting and agreeing a 'Withdrawal Treaty'. This treaty deals with key legacy matters between the UK and the EU such as residual financial liabilities, the status of nationals who find themselves either side of the Brexit divide after Brexit (for example UK nationals resident in the EU and EU nationals resident in the UK) and how to maintain the conditions of the Northern Ireland Good Friday Peace Agreement.

The UK had hoped to synchronise discussions on its future relationship with the EU at the same time as it negotiated the exit agreement. However, it was forced by EU negotiators to agree the withdrawal treaty detail in principle before it could move on to discussing a memorandum of understanding as to what a future trade treaty might look like. Although a transition agreement (subject to completing the withdrawal agreement) has been outlined that will maintain UK arrangements with EU (but not guarantee access to the Third Country Treaties) with the EU until December 2020, this does not specify what arrangement will apply after 2020 or any subsequent UK customs "backstop" arrangement in respect of the Irish border. This awaits the negotiation of an EU/UK trade treaty. At the time of writing neither the Withdrawal Treaty nor an Agreement on a future trade treaty have been finalised. The September 2018 European Summit in Strasbourg ended with a rejection of current UK proposals for both the Irish Border (key to the withdrawal treaty) and UK proposed free circulation zone for goods only, thus suggesting the negotiations are proving difficult.

The Legislative Programme

In parallel, a significant legislative programme to implement the legal frameworks required for Brexit was outlined in the 2017 Queen's Speech and is now being implemented into UK legislation.[61] This work programme may be summarised as (1) the EU Withdrawal Bill that repeals the 1972 European Communities Act and makes provision to transpose European Law into UK law; (2) the Customs Bill to replace the EU Customs Union; (3) the Trade Bill to enable new trade deals; (4) the

Immigration Bill to control the movement of people; (5) the Fisheries Bill to control fishing quotas; (6) the Agricultural Bill to replace the Common Agricultural Policy; (7) the Nuclear Safeguards Bill to replace UK Membership of Euratom; and (8) the Sanctions Bill to enable the UK to impose sanctions after it leaves the European Union.

Underpinning these bills (especially the EU Withdrawal Bill) are a plethora of detailed rules and regulations that relate to existing EU Regulatory Agencies; all of these will need to be adapted to whatever Regulatory Agency will be used in the future. It was reported in June 2018 that the UK may now seek to keep membership of these Regulatory Agencies. It remains unclear, how this request will align to Mrs May's January 2017 redline that the ECJ that regulates these EU Agencies agencies shall have no post-Brexit jurisdiction in the UK.[62] Until there is certainty as to which regulators will be used, it is challenging to imagine how existing and future regulations will be both set and administered. A transition to the end of 2020 merely 'kicks' this can down the road for a few months. Undoubtedly further legislative instruments (especially statutory instruments sometimes called 'secondary legislation') will be required, (most especially in the event of a 'No Deal' Brexit where there is no transition agreement).

To deal with the complexity of the process, the UK Government has requested wide powers to submit 'secondary legislation' with minimal parliamentary scrutiny to allow them to adapt rules and regulations to shoe horn European law onto the British Statute Book. These powers will be germane to replacing EU Regulators (including if there is a 'No Deal Brexit') that the UK has previously requested (for example the European Air Safety Agency) to stay in. We note that in passing the EU Withdrawal Bill in 2018 Parliament insisted on more Parliamentary scrutiny than originally envisaged, which may lead to a 'log jam' of legislation needing confirmation in a very short period of time especially if there is a 'No Deal Brexit'. The prospect of a 'No Deal' Brexit continues to be felt by many a significant possibility due to either a negotiation collapse or UK or EU Member State ratification failure.

Box 7 briefly contrasts today's Legislative approach approach with that of Thomas Cromwell in the 1530s.

Box 7. Following in the Footsteps of Thomas Cromwell?

Thomas Cromwell was the legislative mastermind behind the 'legal' Brexit of the 1530s. How does his mastery compare with today's legislative programme? The immediate and striking contrast is how Thomas Cromwell legislated on an incremental step by step basis and being the main author of the legislation had an overwhelming understanding of the detail. Cromwell crafted each bill incrementally to fill a hole that had been created by a previous bill, thereby giving himself a process to adjust for difficulties as he met them.

Whilst establishing a legal revolution in a very short period of time, Cromwell's approach was intended to ensure that the upheaval was, if possible, restricted. The legislation removed the power of Rome over church courts; removed the power of Rome to receive funds; ensured the Royal Succession became a 'national' matter; seized the property of the church through the dissolution of the monasteries; and, ensured clerical appointments came within the King's control. It did not reorder England and Wales's commercial, foreign relations or immigration, which were left largely untouched in the 1530's. By way of contrast all of these items that untouched by Thomas Cromwell will be items that Brexit will change, in addition to seeking to remove the jurisdiction of the European Court of Justice.

Cromwell's changes were in themselves very significant and had deep implications for contemporary society. The upheavals resulted in social unrest that can most easily be seen in the 1536 rebellion of the Pilgrimage of Grace and subsequent instability.

Yet Cromwell's changes feel modest in comparison to the changes being executed within the current Brexit. In addition to removing EU influence over British courts, Brexit 2019 will change almost all of the UK's foreign trade relations, its internal product and service regulatory standards, its connections to global supply chains and many of its main diplomatic relationships all at the same time.

Making an omelette always requires the cracking of a few eggs, but a successful omelette requires cracking them with the certainty that the frying pan is waiting to accept the mixture. Despite Thomas Cromwell's many and rapid changes, he was always conscious of the need to drop them into a stable process, even if the rebellions starting in 1536 suggested that Cromwell sometimes misjudged how Royal Court politics interplayed with local gentry.[63]

One emerging issue today is the sheer complexity of what will change. How confident can we be that the Brexit implementers will be more successful in implementing changes that are far more extensive and sudden than those of the 1530's than Thomas Cromwell, who was renowned for his command of every detail? This raises the question as to whether the finished Brexit omelette will have any resemblance to the one advertised in the original 'Brexit Recipe'.

ECONOMIC BACKGROUND

Brexit aspirations and the 'Leave Vote' have a complementary economic dimension expressed as an aspiration (especially by the 'Left Behind') for 'better days'. Such aspirations need to be understood in the context of recent UK economic performance.

Post-2008 Crash Economic Impact

The 2008 Global Financial Crisis represented a major economic shock to both the global and the UK economies. The process of recovery has been slow across the developed world, with the United States leading, the UK following and the Eurozone (despite varying growth rates between its members) overall dragging its feet behind. Despite the recovery in the UK, there had still been a significant overall loss of GDP estimated at 6.9% by 2014 when compared to pre-crash forecasts and trends.[64] This loss contrasts with estimates of a 2.4% loss in the USA, 4.7% in Germany, 0.9% in France and 23.8% in Greece.

In the UK, GDP loss would have been greater by a further 1.2% had it not been for an increase in labour force participation (that is more people joining the workforce).[65] The loss can be accounted for by poor overall productivity (reduced by 7.6%), most especially to lower total factor productivity (output achieved per unit of input) and a shortfall (against previous forecast) in the amount of capital (e.g. machines and associated technology) per employee. There is evidence that for smaller firms, productivity has fallen at the same time as investment fell, resulting in a lower capital intensity ratio thereby reducing output[66] per person.[67] This poor productivity performance is one of the key reasons for the overall falls in real wages in the period after 2008.[68]

Employment, Growth and Real Wage Pressures

International dimensions make any overall business effectiveness assessment complex, as wage patterns have also been impacted by companies moving low value-adding labour intensive manufacturing operations to low wage economies. Jobs that would have previously been filled by the 'Left Behind' have in many cases been exported overseas or, in some cases filled by lower cost immigrant workers. Higher skilled activities have where possible been retained in higher income countries.[69] One example of this phenomenon is the Apple iPhone, which is designed in the United States but mainly manufactured in lower cost regions such as China. Overall wage level changes for employees reflect the composition of jobs, between sectors and each sector's average wage rates, productivity growth and the distribution of income (between labour, entrepreneurs, rentiers and capital providers) in each sector plus to a lesser extent immigration[70] combined with the overall level of pay in the economy.

In the UK, these globalisation factors plus the post-crash loss of output have been combined with an increase in labour force participation and immigration to impact real wages. Although the overall rewards to labour have largely remained stable over a period of 40 years, the distribution of wages across earners has changed (with inequalities widening) and more of the labour share has been targeted towards benefits than wages (e.g. pension contributions). The latter two effects have been striking in their impact on low earners. Productivity grew 42.5% faster than the median wage in the period 1972–2010, whilst the overall share of labour in GDP remained broadly constant; the gap between the increase in productivity and the increase in the median wage reflects how companies have diverted pay increases to higher earners and into funding defined benefit pension schemes. Rising wage inequality and increases in non wage labour costs (mainly pension contributions) have had roughly the same impact in this decoupling of median wage growth from productivity growth.[71] In summary, wage earners have suffered lower pay rises to ensure companies maintained the 'final salary' pension schemes of the retired and older (often higher earning) pensioners.

Squeezed real wages for lower earners (our Left Behind tribe) are in a large part the consequence of supporting current and future pensioners in defined

Table 1. Sector Employment Growth Q1 2008–Q1 2018.

Rank	Sector	Change	% Change
1	Real estate activities	109,290	41.5
2	Mining & utilities	135,634	30.0
3	IT	293,053	28.6
4	Hospitality	334,708	24.2
5	Professional services	433,844	22.4
6	Other services	324,843	21.5
7	Health social	695,676	19.5
8	Education	388,864	13.7
9	Admin services	157,222	11.2
10	Agriculture	16,676	5.0
11	Public services	81,611	4.1
12	Retail, wholesale & car repair	74,576	1.8
13	Transport & storage	−36,438	−2.3
14	Financial services	−27,395	−2.7
15	Manufacture	−230,412	−7.3
16	Construction	−204,874	−8.1

Source: ONS (2018a) contains National Statistics data © Crown Copyright.

benefit pension schemes and in improving rewards for higher earners. The sectoral composition of the employment growth is shown in **Table 1**.

It is notable that manufacturing has a higher productivity growth rate than services, although Riley et al.,[72] found that post-2007 firm level productivity is still better than it would have been if resources had been allocated randomly. The high rates of growth of employment in sectors such as real estate and utilities demonstrate the relative employment strength of sectors that are less exposed to global competition.

Slow productivity growth, sectoral employment shifts and generational / income distribution effects have combined with the impact of the 2008 global crash to drive a significant reduction in real wages. In the period 2008–2014, median real wages fell by 10% (males experienced a higher fall (12%) than females (7%)). The biggest sufferers were young people with

18–24-year-olds suffering a 16% cut in real wages. This translated into a 7% *income fall* for working families in contrast to a 4% *income rise* for pensioners.[73] Anecdotal data related to specific towns suggest that the 'Left Behind' are likely to be in low productivity growth sectors. **Box 8** briefly explores living standards on low earners.

Raising real wages will require rising productivity plus a new look at both income inequality and intergenerational balance between working families and pensioners.

Box 8. Working Life on the Bottom Rung of the Ladder

In the period since 1980, Machin[74] found that real wage inequalities have significantly widened, although they remained broadly constant during the period following the 2008 Financial Crisis, with the lower paid suffering only a slight relative disadvantage in their real wages during this period.

Overall, there has been a significant increase in inequality between top and bottom decile male earnings since 1979 which a significant part of this increase being due to reduced hours relating to lower decile male earnings. Attempts have been made to compensate for this increase in inequality at a family level by changes made to the tax and benefits system from 1994 onwards and, the introduction of the minimum wage in 1999.[75] Current planned cuts to the UK welfare budget have led to a projected 2%+ drop in real income before housing costs (4%+ drop after housing costs) for the bottom decile between 2017 and 2020.[76] Whilst subject to much debate the evidence in general suggests that immigration has had a minimal impact on real wage levels,[77] although there are some suggestions of a small impact (under 2%)[78] in the bottom decile of the income distribution.[79]

To complete the overall earnings picture, self-employment and sole traders need to be included. In the UK, 13%–15% of the workforce are self-employed, sole traders or working in personal service companies; 800,000[80] more sole traders were registered in the period from 2007/8 to 2015/16 representing a 25% increase in numbers, while at the same time, there was a fall in the overall turnover of the sector of around 19%.[81] This group which includes some nascent entrepreneurs has materially reduced capital investment – as measured through their use of capital allowances against tax – over this period.[82] Could this group include 'enforced entrepreneurs' who cannot find stable work elsewhere?

Two other work classifications need to be highlighted. First, there are around 1.8 million people who have 'zero hours' contracts that do not guarantee them a fixed number of working hours of which about 901,000 are thought to view such contracts as their main job. These contracts are concentrated in industries such as administrative services and hospitality and tend to be focused on younger rather than older workers.[83] Second, there are agency and fixed term work contracts of which there are around 650,000[84], and these are less secure than full time work contracts.

Finally, there is the 'grey economy' that acts outside established rules and regulations to reduce the price of products by minimising investment and wages to compete with prices from less developed countries. Evidence of such poor practices can be found in the textile sector in Leicester which is focused at providing cheap 'fast fashion' merchandise to internet and other retailers. Selling 'fast fashion' garments at £6 or £7 (UK Sterling) per piece does not leave much room for wages or for capital investment, meaning that these businesses (which tend to have short lives) pay under the minimum wage with scant concern for working or employment conditions. The businesses pop up and disappear on a regular basis, thereby proving a challenging environment to enforce minimum standards. The companies argue that if they changed their method of operation then the jobs would go elsewhere.[85]

For those in the formal economic sector, the minimum wage rise masks significant 'real income' challenges affecting especially males in the bottom decile of the earning distribution. These challenges may not have been helped by migration, but primarily result from insecure jobs being created in lower productivity sectors, combined with changes in the income distribution that favour higher earners and switches from rewarding labour in wages to rewarding in benefits (primarily in pension benefits).

The Productivity Dimension

It is an obvious 'home truth' that economic success depends upon producing goods or services that a customer wants to buy, at a price that allows for a reasonable return for all the various inputs. According to Schumpeter[86] the inputs can be classified as labour, rent, capital and the entrepreneur's skill. Capital can sometimes come from the entrepreneur and sometimes from a professional finance providing sector (whose ultimate aim is for the lowest possible risk with the highest possible return). The distribution of profit[87] to each stakeholder needs to be balanced with how much needs to be used for capital investment. Assuming that good projects are selected for capital investment these will either (1) expand capacity to serve more customers and/or (2) change products and associated underlying technologies to raise productivity.[88] Wise capital investment when combined with effective innovation raise future financial returns for all. We will return to this issue in Chapter 6.

The UK has a poor record of capital investment, with recent capital investment levels failing to meet the level required to replace worn out capital.[89] Between 2011 and 2015, per annum growth in gross value added was 1.9% of which 1% came from higher employment levels, 0.4% came from improvements in labour skills and the balance of 0.5% from improvements in the capital stock (of which 0.1% related to IT investments). Total Factor Productivity Growth in the UK fell by 0.1% per annum.[90]

Raising productivity depends on many factors including (1) ensuring appropriate capital equipment and associated production technology, (2) having products and services that can attain market prices that provide appropriate profit margins and (3) good organisation and management practices.

According to Andy Haldane, Chief Economist at the Bank of England,[91] sector-based analysis indicates that even within sectors, some firms are leaders and some are laggards. A recent study comparing these firms found that management competency and exposure to external competition are key factors in driving productivity.[92] The importance of competition, especially foreign competition in driving productivity is emphasised by a 2018 study that indicates higher productivity companies tend to be exporters.[93] A more technical discussion relating to the relationship between productivity and the sector the firm can be found in the end notes.[94]

It is likely that an effective productivity raising strategy needs to be developed and focused on a sector by sector basis as 'one size does not fit all'. In all events, raising capital investment rates and associated investments that embody product innovations and latest technology are together one important enabler.

Innovation In Today's Rapidly Changing Products/Markets

Businesses need to constantly innovate both products and associated underlying technologies to be competitive. With today's world of rapid product innovation, new products and new companies can spring up wherever an aspiring entrepreneur happens to be located and is able to obtain the resources they need to fulfil a market need. We give one example of how rapidly new products can emerge in **Box 9**.

Box 9. A Payments Revolution from a UK Aid Project

With a 2017 Purchasing Power GDP per head of US$3,491, Kenya is ranked the 151st economy in the world. This ranking can be compared to the UK which with US$44,118 per head is ranked 28th in the world.[95] Kenya has incubated the ground breaking mobile payment system M-Pesa with software designed and built in the UK (part-funded by a £1 million grant from UK development ministry DFID) and supported commercially by UK business Vodafone. M-Pesa was used by 18 million Kenyans in 2017.[96] The ability to recruit local agents to process the cash interface in the system was a critical launch factor in the roll out of M Pesa. The UK provided the software, the UK aid budget the seed funding and Kenya provided the market.

Entrepreneurs need an idea, the money to convert it to reality and a ready market to adopt the product. Mazzucato[97] has highlighted that for aspirational high growth potential entrepreneurs who need to compete on a global scale, there is often a need for external state support to mitigate the risk the new venture faces; risk that commercial markets often refuse to bear on their own. M-Pesa is an example of such an approach.

Supply Chains

In the face of rapid innovation, one way industries have protected themselves is to split the innovation and manufacturing processes resulting in competitive advantage being built by integrating technology across a company's supply chain. Supply chains are economically important to UK manufacturing competitiveness. The OECD uses the import content of exports as one measure of supply chain interconnection. In 2014, this ratio stood at 21.9% for the UK compared to 15.3% in the USA and 25.4% in Germany.[98] This shows that the UK, like Germany is far more dependent upon international supply chains than the USA. An alternative analysis estimates that 48% of the UK's export activity is related to participation in global supply chains.[99]

Global supply chains have evolved on a 'tiered approach', whereby there are a number of contracting tiers, of which each is responsible for different aspects of the product, its manufacture and its development. At the top of the structure is the 'Brand Company', more formally known as the 'Original Equipment Manufacturer' which then has a number of contracting tiers coming into it. We discuss the possible Brexit impact on one successful 'Supply Chain' industry in **Box 10**.

Box 10. Brexit and the Automotive Sector

The automotive industry (including its supply chain) employs over 800,000 people in the UK with a £75+ billion turnover. It is a significant UK industry (SMMT, 2018) in which companies such as BMW or Jaguar Rover are defined as the 'OEM' of the sector. Selling to them are 'Tier 1' suppliers such as GKN Drivetrain[ii] or Robert Bosch. Tier 1 suppliers provide whole assemblies that are then brought together at the final manufacturing location. Below them are a host of micro-, small- and medium-sized enterprise (MSME) component suppliers and raw material suppliers in Tiers' 3 and 4. The whole supply chain is managed cohesively both on an operational level (driving just-in-time delivery and associated inventory reductions) and increasingly at an R&D and innovation level.

Tier 1 OEM manufacturers to a large degree specify their product development and timeline requirements. Especially in Germany, the automotive sector then uses existing supply chain relationships, to develop trust and informal collaboration in increasingly complex networking between supply chain members, with the goal of raising innovation levels.[100] In contrast, a study found[101] the UK's East Midlands automotive supply chain capabilities have limited innovation capacity due to '*Management often* [being] *too busy to innovate*' in many MSME Tier 2 and Tier 3 suppliers.

Automotive supply chains stretch across Europe's borders with components and assemblies crossing multiple borders before final assembly. Free trade deals insist on a specific percentage of local content (usually 60%+) sourced locally to allow finished items to attract zero tariffs. Notwithstanding, the successful drive to increase local UK content in UK manufactured automotive products, this was 44% in 2017.[102] With the

---

[ii]Now owned by Melrose Industries.

EU being the most important market for UK automotive exports, any tariff will be unhelpful to sales. Non-tariff barriers are also very important in this industry. For example, any additional documentary and other checks at ports will require increased inventory holdings and associated costs. Honda estimates a 15-minute port delay will cost the company £850,000 per annum in addition to the need to pay a customs declaration fee for each movement across a border.[103] Increased costs, tariff penalties and more complexity as management deal with additional port flow supply chain uncertainties are unlikely to be helpful to this industry's competitiveness.

Perhaps most importantly, Brexit will focus management energies on maintaining the existing business whilst elsewhere managers are investing and adapting for a world of electric, and in some cases, self-driving vehicles. These emerging technologies will require wholesale product and supply chain re-engineering over the next 20 years as product updates require matching changes in the supply chains that support the Tier 1 OEM manufacturers. Missing the next automotive technology wave could have significant long-term negative economic implications for the UK.

Managing logistics and inventory across the whole supply chain has become crucial to ensure 'just-in-time' manufacturing and retailing. Consumers have benefited from these developments as lower inventories have reduced working capital costs, thereby limiting price increases and improving product availability. Making supply chains work seamlessly on minimal inventory requires common regulatory frameworks, (so multiple product variants are avoided), single regulatory inspections (avoiding time consuming multiple inspections as products move to different countries), minimal customs and border formalities and avoiding tariffs and upfront taxes. For products entering the EU from the UK after Brexit, VAT will need to be paid in advance, customs declarations will need to be made and paid for[iii] and product technical conformity will have to be proved. This procedures will affect and negatively impact both manufacturing and trading supply chains.

For example, currently most plastic crockery from China is imported to the EU via the UK. After Brexit, assuming that there is no treaty agreeing

---

[iii]Additional post – Brexit declaration costs are estimated at £6.5 billion per annum in the UK and same in the EU making a total of £13bn per annum.[104]

common standards and regulators (e.g. a single market), 1 in 10 of these shipments will need to be given a health inspection when they enter the EU to ensure they do not have biological contamination, as Chinese plastic cutlery has a reputation for contamination risk.[105] Unsurprisingly, if cost rises and delays are anticipated or occur, one can expect both pan European and Global Supply Chains to adapt to the new cost realties as Brexit unfolds. Such adaptation is likely to see the gradual realignment of existing UK based supply chain activity away from the UK into the EU single market. It can be assumed the UK proposition of July 2018 (commonly known as the Chequers proposals) that envisaged the UK continuing to fully participate in the EU single market for goods after Brexit were in part, made to reduce the risks that companies would re-engineer supply chain activity away from the UK.

Making a Global Living

Today, the UK's Current Trade Balance Deficit is running at just over 3.5% of GDP.[106] Significant falls in sterling in both 2008 and 2016 have not successfully closed this gap.[107]

Funding this Trade Deficit relies on *the kindness of strangers* according to the current Governor of the Bank of England, Mark Carney.[108] This funding currently comes from foreigners making capital deposits as either (1) investments in UK businesses and real estate (purchasing existing UK assets such as the foreign investors buying UK companies, which have sometimes been described as selling the family silver) or (2) as portfolio or short-term balance investment, (mortgaging current and future family silver as these monies will eventually need to be repaid). This second category, being easier to liquidate and move to other money centres carries significant risks of a sterling currency crisis in the event of a loss in confidence in the UK. Should these capital flows stop, let alone reverse, the UK currency is likely to face challenging times with potential for significant falls in the value of sterling.

Long term, paying one's way in the world matters. There are suggestions that there are certain limits as to the size of trade deficits relative to GDP above which there can be sharp currency adjustments. Former US Treasury Secretary Lawrence Summers writes *'close attention should be paid to any current account deficit in excess of 5 per cent of GDP, particularly if it is financed in a way that could lead to rapid reversals.'*[109] Such sharp falls in

the value of a currency are often associated with negative impacts on economic activity. Such adjustments, as was seen with the 1998 Asian Financial
Crisis, can be very painful. We shall return to this issue.

Recapping, there are two ways long-term deficits can be funded. First, by
foreign investments in the country that has the deficit; second, by loans or
money flows into that country. The second method has a special relevance
for countries such as the UK, that act as Global Financial Hubs. The money
flows associated with such a financial services hub can more than compensate for a trade deficit. Large flows of short-term investment cash (portfolio
capital flows) are of especial importance for both the United States (where
the US Dollar has a special role as the world's main trading currency and US
dollar assets are seen as a 'safe haven' in times of a crisis), and for the UK
because of London's importance as a major financial centre. Other financial
hubs such as pre-2007 Iceland also previously benefited from these capital
flow effects only to find the benefits turn into a nightmare as confidence was
lost and the money flows reversed. Some UK financial features can be seen
as being somewhat similar to those in Iceland in 2006. These include the
high UK levels of personal indebtedness as percentage of GDP (which can be
an early warning that an adjustment may be coming)[110] and inflated house
prices vs income that can be a warning a housing market adjustment is due.
Housing market adjustments can also be associated with larger scale economic shocks as we saw in 2008.[111]

The inter-relation between the financial and real economy (especially in a
balance of payments context) is complex. There has been some attempt at
modelling this interaction[112] although this is an area that is still ripe for further study. Some have argued that huge capital flows in and out of a global
centre mean that for countries with these centres, the trade balance can be
ignored. If this is the case then one could suppose that even if Brexit significantly disrupts whole exporting industries, this will not matter because capital flows will fund whatever level of trade deficit the UK incurs. IMF Chief
Economist Maurice Obstfeld is clear that this logic is erroneous. Substantial
trade deficits matter.[113]

One strand in this argument has been labelled the *Lawson Doctrine* which to
paraphrase states that the current account balance results from private and public economic decisions, but private decisions are always rational; so, whatever
trade balance results from private activities, it will always be the correct one.
The doctrine states that instability and adjustment can only come if the

government spends too much and runs a deficit.[114] We return to this issue in a later chapter.

The 'Lawson Doctrine' theory is not supported by events in the real world. A study of 42 countries from the 1970s to the 2000s found that it was the trade deficit and not the public-sector deficit that was found to trigger 'Sudden Stop' crises.[115]

When the trade balance becomes too large relative to the value of exports, adjustment happens and as Eichengreen and Gupta[116] found it can lead to 'Balance of Payments Sudden Stop Events', such as the 1998 Asian Financial Crisis or the 2008 Iceland crisis. The impact of some such events is shown in **Table 2**.

In the event of any loss of confidence in the UK economy, the UK's complex relationship with global markets due to London's role as one of the world's main financial hubs will have significant impacts. We focus on the Financial Services Industry in **Box 11**.

Both Brexit and any risk that capital outflows lead to a 'Sudden Stop' event could risk London's long-term global role. Global financial centre relocations have happened before. The history of financial centre relocations suggests that, as a whole, financial services like to concentrate in one location as when they disperse this can be the start of a longer-term strategic shift. This was the case of Antwerp in the 1560s and Amsterdam in the late

Table 2. Sample Sudden Stop Events.

Event	Timing	Narrative
AD 410 Brexit	Starts in AD 410	The change in GDP in undocumented although archaeological evidence suggests urban collapse whilst agricultural GDP (the most important GDP component at that time) being maintained[117]
Great Depression	1929–1933 Worldwide impact	GDP decline 30%–40% in real prices. (Markuss & Kane, 2007)
Asian Financial Crisis	1998	GDP decline 3%–16%. (Barro, 2001)
Iceland	2008	GDP c10% over 2 years. (Krueger, 2016)

Source: Authors.

Box 11. Financial Services

The Financial Services industry matters to the UK. The sector contributes 11% of GDP and employs around 1 million people directly, rising to 2.2 million people if one includes linked services.[118] Brexit will mean change for this industry. Currently, global financial firms trade across EU countries from a single organisation in London using 'passporting', a system allowing financial firms licenced in one member state to operate in all the other EU members into EU markets. It is expected that the 'passporting' regime will end for UK-based firms with Brexit. From comments on the current state of the negotiations, there seems little immediate prospect of 'mutual recognition' that gives a stable regulatory environment through a treaty that would confirm UK regulators and their regulatory frameworks are fully acceptable to the EU. Instead, both market participants and regulators are facing a world where they will rely on less secure 'equivalence' arrangements (where regulations are judged as being the same, but where this judgement can be removed without notice) or 'delegation' (where companies in one state contract companies in a non-EU Member State to perform activities for them) procedures. In the face of such a change, many financial services companies have started to open new offices or boost existing staff complements in continuing Member States.

The extent to which activities and staff will move is not yet clear and will to depend upon the views market participants have as to future regulatory arrangements and the long-term stability of these arrangements. Should financial services find itself needing to trade under a regime of regulatory 'equivalence' then recent events in Switzerland may lead some firms to fear the EU may change the rules in the future. Khan[119] found Switzerland is facing 'regulatory uncertainty' as the EU is threatening to end its 'regulatory equivalence arrangements' for share dealing. There are suggestions that this change could be the prelude to the EU looking to force the Swiss to accept full EU Regulation of its financial services sector. Delegation procedures are also reported to be under threat of significant change.[120]

With relocation comes the issue of critical mass. If relocated operations require separate capital bases resulting in fragmenting of regulatory capital bases this could have knock-on effects as to the sustainability of the the UK banking cluster. Expert financial association AFME[121] recently found that restructuring costs in respect of Brexit could be €15 billion requiring €20 billion more equity and a further €20 billion of Tier 2 risk capital. Relocating activities also raises the risk of serious knock on negative multiplier effects into London-based professional/business services, risking a reduction in activity in these sectors.

Additionally, restructuring could affect the location of funds under management by UK-based asset managers. A recent study[122] identified £.6.9 trillion of assets under UK management of which £2.7 trillion are owned by overseas clients. This makes the UK Asset Management industry the second largest in the world. Of the £6.9 trillion, under management £1.7 trillion is in UK managed funds domiciled either in the UK or overseas. It is unknown how much of this is in sterling assets that are susceptible to being sold in the event of a loss of confidence in the UK. Abstracting published data investment holdings,[123] one can estimate maybe up to £2.3 trillion of the £6.9 trillion is held in UK equities and UK debt, assets that are very likely to be Sterling denominated. UNCTAD[124] found that 2017 showed the first evidence of an outflow in Foreign Direct Investment from the UK with a fairly modest outflow of some US$80 billion compared to inflows in recent years. If this outflow grows and feeds into portfolio flows there could be a significant negative impact on sterling, and this could be the harbinger of a 'Sudden Stop' balance of payments event. All capital flows (both gross and net) matter and strong changes in capital flows can have marked economic effects.[125]

seventeenth and eighteenth centuries; disruption that leads to some functions moving can act as the first step in the financial sector relocating.[126]

Public Sector Austerity & Private Sector Short Termism

The UK's productivity leaders are its export sectors,[127] which in many cases have integrated supply chains into the EU. As a whole, the UK has a poor track record of capital investment for the future. The OECD[128] found that the UK's publically quoted companies are focused on short, rather than medium term goals due to investor pressures. Private companies, insulated from investor pressures have much higher fixed asset levels at 128 times sales when compared public companies at 25 time sales, suggesting that private companies invest more and have a longer-term horizon. There is a view that adapting publicly quoted companies to operate on longer-term horizons would result in public firms having a capital stock that could be several times higher than at present. Such a change would result in a knock-on rise to capital investment rates.[129]

Raising investment in technology and innovation, assuming it is properly and entrepreneurially managed will raise growth, productivity, export penetration and real wages. World beating products from world beating companies win world beating returns for themselves and those who work for them.

Instead of focusing on raising investment levels, the post-2010 narrative in the UK has focused on the need to reduce the size of the public sector (austerity) and later on, freeing the UK from the "stranglehold" of Brussels regulations via Brexit. In its simplest terms, the suggestion is that austerity stops the public sector crowding out the private sector and Brexit frees entrepreneurs to invest without fear of bureaucratic regulations. Hard experience and cold logic suggest that investment and innovation raise economic performance. Cutting waste can free resources but blanket austerity is of little value in a modern open economy, unless it is associated with a rise in investment in innovation and capital investment. It is unclear how austerity policies have or could have these impacts. The public sector cannot 'crowd out' private investment in a world where private banks can create new money to fund good loan opportunities[130] but they can allocate credit to non-productive requests. We will return to this theme in a later chapter.

PROMENADE II: WHICH GROWTH MODEL IS NEEDED?

Our "Left Behind" Leavers are looking for an improvement in living standards. Arguably at the end of 2018, they are less convinced than they were in 2010 that austerity and shrinking the size of the state will deliver this. Perhaps, Brexit can unlock the genie from the bottle. If so, how?

Tax Cuts and the Laffer Curve

Some argue that if you reduce personal tax rates economic growth rises. The idea was conceived on a restaurant napkin by Arthur Laffer, Dick Cheney, Donald Rumsfeld and journalist Jude Wanniski during a lunch in 1974. The napkin itself is on display in a Washington museum.[131] Intuitively true that economic growth rates and investment will rise if personal tax rates cut from 99%, this argument is not supported by evidence if personal tax rates are at more modest levels.[132] The deregulation argument is epitomised by proponents of 'Economic Shock Therapy'[133] that sees deregulation, capital flows and free trade as the keys to force business to change and adapt to global markets.[134] In this nexus, such policies also need to be combined with a deliberate policy to reduce the size of the state sector and reduce the size of any public-sector deficit to stop the state distorting markets and 'crowding out' resources from the entrepreneur.[135]

The evidence for this policy mix working is, in itself mixed. In extremis where the state share of GDP is 98% clearly there is crowding out, but in other cases, the argument is highly dubious. Indeed, experience from the 1990s, when these policies were applied to former Soviet States such as Russia there was substantial economic dislocation, which led to a body of academic research to explore if a more gradualist approach could more effective. Gavin[136] found that shock therapy may be theoretically optimal in neo-classical economic terms, but the policy's unemployment consequences may require a more gradualist approach. Aghion and Blanchard[137] developed a model to sequence reforms to reduce the rate at which unemployment increases. Whereas Dehejia[138] suggested that shock therapy needs to be accompanied by income redistribution between different societal groups, and that this may lead to political preference for a more gradualist approach.

Notwithstanding all the research and studies, this deregulating and tax cutting approach linked with free trade is seen as one of the key opportunities of Brexit by some such as Professor Patrick Minford and his colleagues at the organisation, Economists for Free Trade.[139]

The Global Innovation Economy

Global change is accelerating. Today's new product is rapidly becoming tomorrow's museum piece. Whole established industries are on the threshold of huge disruption as technologies become greener (e.g. electric vehicles) and products become smarter (e.g. home automation via the internet of things). In this context, libertarian deregulating tax cutting free traders risk missing the main point, namely that to be globally successful in the current century requires constant capital investment and innovation in new and updated products and technologies. Innovation and globalisation trends will not stop because the UK is leaving the EU; but by leaving the UK and losing the protection of the EU's protected markets, the UK must become a stronger force of innovation and change in global markets. Post Brexit, the UK will no longer be able to participate with the same level of vigour in complex Pan – European Supply chains (as non-tariff trade barrier impacts shift economic gravity away from the UK) and will not be protected by the dynamics of the EU's Internal Market.

This will have significant implications for the UK's business landscape. To be competitive, rates of capital investment will need to rise and skills will need to improve and become flexible enough to allow UK business to take on the role of 'early adopters'. Public infrastructure, especially public data infrastructure, will need investment, to become leading edge; and, to address short termism it is likely that the public sector will need to partner the private sector, to ensure capital flows to projects and innovations that may have great long-term potential but threaten lowering short-term yields.

Shifting from Consumption to Investment

Raising capital investment levels increases the prospect of needing to shift resources from those living off their wealth towards those who generate the wealth. In practical terms, the older generation will need to relinquish some of their wealth to the younger generation. Perhaps this can occur voluntarily, through tax rises and potential means tested contributions for health and social care for the over 60s. Alternatively, change is likely to come about through market adjustments, as asset prices and most especially house prices, adjust to reflect the incomes and payment capabilities of the younger generation. Whichever way the adjustment happens it is unlikely to be pain free.

Rebalancing to Help the Entrepreneur

Success will depend upon the UK's entrepreneurial community in companies of all sizes. Big companies, small companies, private and public companies all have potential entrepreneurs in them who need nurturing and supporting. There are many different ways of doing this. Part of the story lies in ensuring that financial markets support entrepreneurs provide both angel and venture capital and, access to affordable loan finance. Another part of the story is in how non-quantifiable Knightian Uncertainty[140] can be reduced, so that entrepreneurs and financiers face well enough defined landscapes in order to take the commercial risks innovating new products, technologies and markets require.

Recent evidence[141] demonstrates that whilst statistical measurable risk can be dealt with in the R&D and Venture Capital process by raising the threshold rate of return; pure uncertainty (Knightian uncertainty), as encountered when opening the door to new technologies, is usually met by a reduction in project adoption as the degree of uncertainty cannot be easily assessed. This is a key area where the State, (an *"Entrepreneurial State"* in the words of Mazzucato), can play a key role in helping make the risk commercially bearable.

Facing this challenge, different countries have adopted different strategies. For example, DARPA in the US (who were involved in building GPS) operates by 'seeding' innovative projects.[142] By way of a contrast, the Frauenhofer Institutes in Germany provide an applied research backbone for the German Mittlestand[143] to reduce risks and help commercial adoption of new technologies. There are many examples where the state has successfully enabled ground breaking innovation for example today Google Earth is taken for granted, yet it started in 2003 with a tiny company Keyhole Inc funded by CIA venture capital, only to be acquired by Google in 2004.[144]

3

BREXIT MK I AD 410

Britannia had been a colony of the Roman Empire for over 400 years, when in a relatively short period, we see a significant change commonly described as the end of Roman Britain. As with any simplistic generalisation, the patterns that underline such an event are invariably more complex. However, a snapshot of Britannia – essentially England as it is now – in AD 400 compared with that of AD 440 portrays a different landscape, with previously active towns moving into decay and civic life fragmenting into rural islands around villas of the nobility. Hard Brexit fifth century style had happened.

Notwithstanding a popular narrative that sees the fall of Roman Britain as synonymous with invasions from barbarian Angles and Saxons, change was more internally than 'barbarian' driven. The 'barbarian' narrative seems to have been largely engendered by historians remote from events in both time and distance; writings such as the Gallic Chronicle of 452. Archaeology paints a rather different picture.

THIRD CENTURY TRIAL BREXIT?

Much of the Western Roman Empire – most notably Gaul and Germany – had been deeply affected by the troubles of usurping Emperors in the third century. Britannia on the contrary, being remote from the continent had continued to flourish. However, this prosperity masked underlying structural change. Londinium had declined as stresses and disruption had taken place in its main continental markets. Esmonde Cleary[145] found that previous luxury pottery industries faded away to be replaced with new ones (e.g. in the

New Forest); these tended to have a narrower geographic distribution, whilst still producing a small amount of top quality items or 'purple ware'. Whereas many continental supply chains had been disrupted by the changes of the third century there is evidence suggesting some trade still occurred with Germany. Changing trade patterns meant that structural change was inevitable.[146]

Drawing conclusions from pottery remains, there seems to have been sufficient economic dynamism in the late third century Britannia economy to effect a structural change, that led to a reorientation towards domestic rather than continental markets. The first 75 years of the fourth century saw continued and growing prosperity. New well decorated villas[iv] were built and public buildings in towns were maintained and refurbished in many towns across the country. The economy seems to have been in good shape, which was in stark contrast to the fate of towns in Gaul.

Why then in early fourth century was Britannia in such better economic shape than say Gaul or Germany? Both these colonies were nearer the centre of power in the Imperial Seat at Trier than Britannia. Most likely, the island nature of Britannia insulated the colony from many of the continental difficulties, so its basic industry − agriculture − is likely to have been somewhat less disrupted than on the continent. The difference is striking; contemporary buildings in Gaul (France) tend to be reusing stone from previous structures whereas, construction in Britannia uses new stone. The fourth century supply chain shock was still felt in localities with deep continental supply chain connections − as witnessed by the relative decline of Londinium − but fundamental disruption seems to have been avoided in Britannia.

There was a second key factor. The role of the army. The Roman Army not only protected towns, it also acted as an economic engine to drive them. The Army bought produce and effects for its own operation, thereby stimulating both the agricultural hinterland and local artisan industries. **Box 12** describes some of the economic impacts of the Roman Army and Roman State.

The whole edifice was dependent upon both the army and the state, which as well as being the political authority was the economic engine supporting the market economy. The State was the most important customer, it provided the physical security for the towns that housed the markets where

---

[iv]Some of the most elaborate villa mosaics date from this period.

Box 12. A Fourth Century Entrepreneurial State?

Mazzucato[147] describes the role of the state as an economic and innovation engine through its willingness to take risk that is too high to be borne by the private sector. There is evidence that the Roman State acted in an entrepreneurial manner. It was the key economic engine in the Empire mainly through (1) the role of the Roman Army and (2) ensuring grain purchases to feed the population of Rome.

The State acted as a customer, as a promoter, a guarantor of markets and as the security authority that enabled long complex supply chains to function across the ancient world. Its role as a customer can be separated into two parts. First, the Army, which was often stationed at frontiers thereby acting as the economic engine for the communities that grew around security posts.[148] Second as the overseer of grain purchases for the city of Rome and associated transport of this grain.[149] These roles took place in a monetarised market economy, but an economy in which the State was by far the most important purchaser, one who acted entrepreneurially by creating functioning markets where there were none. This entrepreneurial role was further enabled through both public buildings used for trade and commerce, taxation that had to be paid in Roman Coin (creating a monetary economy), and through establishing legal certainty on contracts and the terms of trade. The character of the Roman Forum can be seen in the following quote:

> *Before he comes out,*
> *I will direct you to all classes of women and men.*
> *You would find it easy to find a willing mouth.*
> *Decent or vile, esteemed or without worth.*
> *For perjurers, try the Comitium.*
> *Liars and braggarts hang around the Shrine of Cloacina.*
> *Rich, married ne'er do-wells by the Basilica.*
> *Packs of prostitutes there too – but rather clapped-out ones.*
> *In the Fish-Market, members of the dining clubs.*
> *In the lower Forum respectable, well-to-do citizens out for a stroll.*
> *In the Middle Forum, flashier types along the canal.*
> *By the Lacus Curtius you will find bold fellows with a tongue in their head and a bad intent in their mind.*
> *Great slanderers of others and very vulnerable to it themselves*
> *By the old shops, the money-lenders – they will make or take a loan.*

> *Behind the Temple of Castor there are men to whom you*
> *wouldn't entrust yourself.*
> *In the Vicus Tuscus are men*
> *who sell themselves.*
>
> Plautus (ca. 250–184 BC) from Lendering (2002)
>
> The long supply chains protected by the Roman Army to bring grain to Rome encouraged other trade (e.g. in olive oil, pottery and luxury goods) and thereby enabled a state sponsored economy. The State's importance can best be seen in retrospect. As the State withdrew in the fifth century, supply chains were no longer reliable, the supply of coin facilitated by these supply chains dried up and the major customer disappeared. Temin[150] describes how once these failed the 'market economy' fails, even though individual markets remained. The connections that supported the 'market economy' and the principal customer that drove the 'market economy' had disappeared.

the trading was done and it provided the money that made the trading possible. There was a semblance of an Empire wide banking system as well as considerable 'Angel Investment' from wealthy nobles, but again this depended upon the stability of the Empire.[151] There were also according to Ward–Perkins a complex series of economic dependencies expressed in the supply chains that traversed the Empire.[152]

Despite the role of the State, the economic model was decentralised, notwithstanding the state guaranteeing the market through coinage, security and its purchases. Is this an early form of state capitalism?

Common Roman coinage had an especially important role in facilitating the market's smooth operation. Coinage flowed into Britannia to buy supplies that were then integrated into a supply chain that stretched across the Empire. Coinage flowed from the colony back to Rome as taxes were paid to the Imperial Centre and money flowed back to the colony to pay for imports. As an incidental aside, according to Esmonde Cleary[153], the estimated effective tax rate on much of the population was somewhere between 25% and 33%, paradoxically close to today!

There is evidence that in Britannia things started to change in the towns towards the end of the fourth century. Whilst towns were still occupied, the use of public buildings started to change. In general, these were maintained and adapted to a world in which, with State Religion having become

Christianity, some former uses of these buildings were no longer appropriate. Wooden buildings started to crop up in forums and some of these buildings seem to have been used by artisan trades.[154] The economy was in a state of change with signs that a possible recession set in some time after AD 375.[155] Perhaps, this was linked to strains in the Roman World. We don't know for certain. Despite some cities flourishing (e.g. Trier) more generally this period saw significant economic challenges in continental Europe.[156] Britannia had become an exception in the Western Empire, as it experienced economic growth during the fourth century whilst other provinces such as Gaul were retrenching.

FIFTH CENTURY HARD BREXIT?

In AD 407, Emperor Constantine III, facing the possibility of losing Gaul after the AD 406 barbarian invasion across the Rhine had breached the Empire's Northern Frontier, took the standing army from Britannia to restore order in Gaul, not least to preserve communications with Britannia. The campaign could not be described as a great success; in AD 409 the people of Britannia began to organise their own defence against barbarian invasion. A year later, the Emperor Honorius informed the cities of Britain to defend themselves, and following the Roman Army's defeat at Arles in AD 411, there was little prospect of the Roman Army's return.

Somewhere in this three year period taxes stopped being paid to Rome and coin in turn ceased being shipped to the colony. Tax payments needed to be made in Roman Coin, and without them all shipments of new coinage ceased to Britannia after around AD 411; although according to researchers from the British Museum a notable exception was made with the discovery of a Roman coin shipped to Richborough in about AD 421.[157] **Box 13** gives a picture of the extent of coinage in the years leading up to AD 410, which can be contrasted with the disappearance of new coinage after AD 410. These coinage records describe a sharp break in the established monetary economy.

Notwithstanding suggestions in the Gallic Chronicle (AD 452) that AD 411 saw a mass invasion of the Saxon hordes, there is little archaeological evidence to support this. Rather, the immediate impact of the departure of the Roman Army and the cessation of shipments of Roman Coinage seems

---

Box 13. Sources of Coin Data for the Late Fourth and
Early Fifth Centuries

Britannia was endowed with a comprehensive numismatic record. The quality and quantity of coin data available for study for the late fourth and early fifth centuries AD is remarkable, comprising not only hoard data, but excavation assemblages and 'site' finds. Records exist for 232 hoards with a *terminus post quem* of AD 388.[158] Although this is in part a reflection of Britain's established record of reporting hoards, there are proportionally a higher number of hoards from this period than any other province in the Roman Empire.[159] A large number of these hoards such as the Hoxne, Haynes and Coleraine hoards include other objects, such as precious metal jewellery, plates, ingots and spoons, illustrating the complex relationship between bullion and currency in this period.[160]

Hoard Composition	Number of Hoards
Gold	16
Gold and silver	31
Silver	90
Silver and bronze	34
Bronze	56
Gold, silver and bronze	5
Total	232

Notably, notwithstanding such a rich record, finds of Roman coins after AD 410 become very rare, indeed nearly non-existent as only coins minted early in the reign of Constantine III have been found[161] demonstrating the likely sharpness of the monetary shock.

---

to have been economic rather than military. The economic shock appears to have been beyond the capability of the urban economy to deal with, whilst the impact that may have benefited local agricultural economies focused around landed estates.

Previously, Britannia had successfully adapted to an economic shock during difficulties of the third century, through changing its centre of economic gravity. This entailed a raised focus on trade within the colony as opposed to depending upon the supply chain flowing north and east through Gaul, which had come under pressure due to military and security challenges. Such a change reflects a shift in 'spatial gravity' that with today's techniques can be modelled using a series of equations to optimally position economic activity in relation to centres of income (e.g. markets) and distance from these.[162]

Tinbergen[163] (using a contemporary example) alludes to the importance of this gravity in the context of international as well as national economies. This economic gravity effect was significant after AD 410 as the locus of economic activity moved from the towns into the countryside, responding to the local pull and power of the nobility living there. The change in the fifth century, with its breakdown of demand from the main customer (the Roman State) and the sharp reversal in the monetary economy was too big a shock for most urban centres to absorb. So, the centre of economic gravity drifted away from these locations out to the country estates, which being less dependent on the monetary economy continued to function and may even have prospered, despite no longer having access to certain products they had previously sourced in towns.

These changes in the post AD 410 English economic landscape were uneven geographically, being rapid in the East and quite slow in the West, reflecting the uneven changes in the overall security situation. Whilst the economic effects started to impact fairly rapidly, it took 30 years or more for the third component, security, to fail to the extent that control in some specific localities slipped away to invading tribes. We know that in AD 446, there was an appeal to the last Roman Commander in Gaul, Aetius, for help to stop the barbarians driving the local population into the sea. Bede dates the Saxon invasion to AD 449 although it would appear nothing was as clear cut as that. There were a series of invasions and battles during the second half of the fifth century, culminating in the great Romano British victory of Ambrosius Aureliaius at Mount Badon. Mythology casts Ambrosius and the legendary King Arthur as one of the same.

The Saxons did not mix well with the local population. Ward–Perkins[164] echoes Gibbon[165] in describing the invasions as conquests rather than assimilations, suggesting that one important element of the change related to occupation. We can see one such, lack of assimilation in the Saxon village of West Stow, located on sandy soil near the rich fertile pastures of the Lark Valley, near Bury St Edmunds in Suffolk. The location of West Stow is distinctly separate from the old Roman Settlement and on poorer land. This settlement dates from about AD 420, suggesting the old Roman System was still operating and local landed estates were strong enough to protect themselves at that time.

Indeed, the Roman System seems to have endured far longer in the West than the East. For example, there is evidence of a monetary economy continuing in Wroxeter until the sixth or seventh centuries, long time after the supposed end of Roman Britain in AD 410. There is also evidence that some industries such as specialist pottery in specific areas, such as Porchester continued to function in reduced form for until 430/440.[166]

A FIFTH CENTURY MONETARY AND SPATIAL SHOCK?

We have seen that the end of Roman Britain appears to have less to do with marauding Saxons and more with a breakdown of civic fabric and an associated decline in towns. In short, the withdrawal of the Roman Army and the ending of tax payments and associated coinage led to an economic event from which most towns were unable to recover. The centre of gravity moved to where the wealth and power was, the villas and estates of the gentry. An economic shock that rewrote the spatial geography; one occasioned by both the loss of the state as a customer, the breakdown of wider supply chains and the absence of new coin (so impacting the monetary economy). The consequence was that the economy reverted to its agricultural base.

PROMENADE III: LESSONS FROM THE END OF BRITAIN?

Sometimes Change Can Happen Rapidly

The speed with which a market economy can be damaged is striking. In just a few years following the departure of the Roman Army from Britannia, the supply chains break, coinage is no longer received and taxes are no longer paid. The centre of economic gravity moved away from the towns into the country.

The post AD 410 experience is not unique. Monetary and financial shocks today also have rapid and severe impacts. We know this from the experiences of the Great Depression (1929–1933), the Asian Financial Crisis (1997) and the Great Recession (2008).

Today, London is one of the world's foremost financial centres. We know from the experiences of Iceland in 2008 that – if for any reason – there is a significant disruption in a financial centre's global role, effects are felt in the real economy, almost immediately. This is what happened in AD 410. Should disconnection from the EU in today's Brexit lead to a change in London's financial role, the associated monetary adjustment could give a sharp economic shock. We will deal with this in more detail in a later chapter.

Supply Chains Matter

We can see from AD 410 that supply chains matter. If they mattered in AD 410 then they are likely to matter today. Indeed, given the complexity of how things are manufactured today with sub-assemblies and components moving across borders multiple times, any red tape or bureaucratic impediments to free flows could lead to rapid structural change. Again, we will deal with this in a later chapter.

The State Matters

Paradoxically in the free market economy of the Roman Empire one of the lessons is that the state matters. It is an important economic actor and plays four key roles in a market economy (1) as market enabler through contract certainty given by the rule of law, (2) as the monetary authority providing a secure and known means of exchange, (3) by guaranteeing certainty on the functioning of supply chains and (4) by acting as the purchaser that can take risks the market itself is unable to bear. In AD 410, all these broke down at once. As we develop our narrative, we will examine how the forthcoming Brexit may impact on each of these issues as changes start to happen.

4

BREXIT MK II THE ROAD FROM ROME IN THE 1530's

In 1491 Henry VII had a second son, Henry. At birth and during his first few years, there was no expectation that Henry would become King. He had an older brother, Arthur, who as Prince of Wales was destined for this role. It is understood that Henry was initially being groomed to become Archbishop of Canterbury and his early spiritual education was focused accordingly.[167] However, the situation changed suddenly in 1502 when Arthur died some 20 weeks after marrying the Spanish Princess, Catherine of Aragon. In 1509, Henry first inherited his elder brother's claim to the throne, then soon after, having initially rejecting her, married his late brother's wife Catherine. The stage was now set for Henry's eventful reign.

England in 1510, having recovered from the earlier 'Wars of the Roses', which ended with the accession of Henry VII in 1485 had become engaged in a complex competition between nation states that was also intertwined with a somewhat secular Renaissance Papacy. The world of the 'Renaissance Prince' was one in which alliances were forged and then broken. This was the backdrop to the European Power Politics of the day. England, France, the Papacy and the Holy Roman Emperor were in a state of constant tension as France and the Emperor struggled against each other for primacy across Europe. Under Henry VII, England had tended to avoid overseas adventures, but following the accession of Henry VIII to the throne it was now engaged in Europe both militarily (through for example the successful 1515 campaign against France) and politically (with the English brokered Universal Peace struck in London in 1518).

This was a world of intrigue and diplomatic innovation.[168] With all this pomp and nationalism, there was continual budget stress as displays of pageantry were required to project an image of strength.

Turning our focus to religious matters, the Roman Catholic Church was in control of matters spiritual, notwithstanding the Pope's desire to find secular independence through firm control of the Italian Papal States; and, his constant need for money to fund a desire for monuments and artwork. Famously, Pope Julius II (who commissioned Michelangelo to paint the Sistine Chapel ceiling) was equally well known for leading his troops into battle. His predecessor but one was Borgia Pope Alexander IV renowned for the exploits of two of his four children, Lucrezia and Cesare Borgia. The Papacy which was inevitably part spiritual and part temporal, was influenced in many of its decisions by the immediate political environment, whilst also facing popular scrutiny as to its assumed moral probity.

Against this background, the Papacy was attuned to using diplomatic fudges to flatter Rulers and build supportive secular relationships: as demonstrated by how Henry VIII was granted the title 'Defender of the Faith'. The Pope granted Henry the title for life in recognition of a religious book he published that challenged the arguments advanced by Martin Luther. Diplomatic wrangles followed to make the title hereditary, ending with a classic diplomatic fudge saying the title was 'yours for ever'. It took the Reformation and Parliamentary Legislation to formally make it hereditary.[169] Any Renaissance Pope could have felt at home in Brussels today!ᵛ

In England at a national level, there had in the early years of the sixteenth century been tensions between Church and State, although these stresses were constantly changing in temperature.[181] **Box 14** compares and contrasts the periods in the 30 years leading up to the break with Rome in the 1530s and today's European situation.

ᵛThe reader is encouraged to explore the structures of today's European Union (EU) in Appendix 1 and judge how close today's EU institutional framework is to the narrative that we will unfold on the sixteenth century Roman Church.

Box 14. Current Echoes from a Long Gone Age?

Competing Powerful States

Looking at Europe in 1519, there were already three Great Powers and a fourth working to secure its independence from the others. The Great Powers were the Holy Roman Empire (Germany, Netherlands and the Spanish Empire under Charles V), France under Francis I and England under Henry VIII. The fourth power (struggling to maintain its independence) was the Papal States in Italy with the Pope striving to maintain his independence. Papal policy was often nuanced (as we have seen with the saga of Henry's title of Defender of the Faith) to accommodate the competing interests of the major states.

If we look at Europe in 2018, nearly 500 years on, arguably and controversially there are three Great Powers in Western Europe – Germany, France and the UK – plus a number of other significant powers such as Italy and Spain in attendance. Unlike in the sixteenth century, today there are also three mega-powers all with some form of interest in Europe; the United States, Russia and China. The EU is neither a country nor a federation but something in-between.

Could one, as an observation, liken today's EU to the sixteenth century Papacy, strong through its body of shared law (*acquis communitaire*) but weak in the face of any coalition by its principle Member States? How confident can we be that the EU will not bend to more powerful member states? There have been a number of examples where it looks like it has.

For example Article 282 (3) of the Lisbon Treaty[170] expressly states that the European Central Bank (ECB) is independent of the Member States and the European Institutions. Yet arguably in the Greek Euro Crisis, it was the refusal of the Central Bank to fulfil its Treaty Responsibility to act according to Article 127 (4) as guardian of financial stability through providing banking system liquidity that forced the Greek Government to submit to the political will of the European Institutions. This action was challenged in the European Court of Justice but thrown out for a lack of evidence as to the damage the ECB's decision was causing, notwithstanding a Greek bank run was seemingly caused by the Central Bank's decision.[171] Would the ECB refuse help if German or French banks need emergency funding? Post-2008 actions suggest this would not be the case, not least as the evidence demonstrates the ECB did act as a Lender of Resort for commercial banks in these countries.[172]

Disconnected Elites

A second similarity can be drawn by looking at disconnected elites. Day-to-day contact between the Roman Church in the sixteenth century was by means of the local clergy. Many parishes had been appropriated by both monasteries and were nominally run by 'gentlemen' non-resident clergy to give them an income,[173] meaning the great majority of local ministers were substituting for absent priests as 'hired help', paid minimal salaries, whilst the funds intended for local clergy were paid to absentee clergy. Eliminating 'phantom priests' from these posts was a major demand in the 'Twelve Articles' resulting from the Peasants War in Germany (also widely circulated in England) in 1525.

As with the current social media revolution, the early sixteenth century saw the advent of 'new media' as the printing press opened the doors to wider and more diverse communications that enabled criticism of the elites. This innovation enabled the circulation of a number of anti-clerical abuse tracts such as the *Julius Exclusus by* Erasmus.[174] In this tract, Pope Julius II arrives at the gates of heaven to be denied entry by St Peter. Peter on being challenged by the dead pope declares '*Signs of impiety in plenty [...] body scarred with sins all over [...]*'. This anti-elite theme is developed by Tyndale when he writes '*our holy prelates and spiritually religious, who ought to defend God's word, speak evil of it instead, and shame it all they can*' (Tyndale, 1528).

Although there were some like brewer Raynold Darrye who wanted that '*all priests were hanged and had lost their heads*', court records are more suggestive of a deeply conservative parish laity who really wanted continuity in worship and tradition. For example, the Abbot of Missenden was to reap the reward of his parishioners when he called himself the '*Sovereign*' of his local parish church. They broke down the doors, damaged the building and assaulted the abbot and his staff. Needless to say, in general, disputes were very local and related to individuals within individual parishes.[175]

Moving to today, alienation from Brussels has been growing in many Member States. For example, Gaston[176] found that only 11% of EU citizens felt very attached to the EU, whilst 56% of those interviewed identified with their own country. Frustration for some also comes from how EU regulations are implemented locally. For example in London and Edinburgh, all taxicabs must have disabled access, whilst in other cities, this is not the case. The decision for 100% mandatory access is local one, but sometimes conflated and confused, with the less stringent overall European Requirement for disabled people to have access to public transport.[177] Equally, high-profile issues such as fishing rights, just as sixteenth century anticlericalism, can be misunderstood. UK fishermen complain about inadequate fishing quotas from the UK, but a significant part of the UK quota (over 50% of the English quota and 88% of the Welsh) has been sold by the same fishermen to foreign trawler owners.[178]

Falling Real Wages

A third element is the squeezing of real wages in lower earning groups. In 1500, agricultural wages equated to an index value of 121 (1860 = 100) and then steadily fell 22% of the peak to an index value of 94 in the 1520s.[179] Contrast this to real wage experience in the UK from 2008 to 2016 when median real wages fell by 4%, with the richest 10% seeing an increase in real wages of 2% and the bottom 10% seeing a fall of 6%.[180]

HENRY'S DIVORCE

Henry VIII smitten with Anne Boleyn also wanted a male heir. By 1529, he was keen to obtain an annulment from his existing wife, Catherine of Aragon. For the ecclesiastical lawyers, it was unfortunate that the King's desire to change wife required ecclesiastical approval under one of the matters specifically reserved for the church courts. The Pope, having seen Rome sacked by Catherine's nephew two years previously was extremely reluctant to solve King Henry's marital matter and thereby upset her uncle. Henry VIII's desire to force matters, gained especial urgency after Anne Boleyn became pregnant in late 1532.[182]

The scene had by this point been set for Henry to use rising lawyer Thomas Cromwell to execute a 'Legal' Brexit, separating the English State from Roman ecclesiastical law. The initial objective was to free Henry from the shackles of 'Church Law' and obtain an annulment for him from Catherine. It was Cromwell who was to appreciate the implications and complexities that this simple statement implied.

Through a series of Parliamentary Statues, he transformed England's relationship with Rome and arguably its method of governance. The philosophy behind this is encapsulated in the following extract from the 1532 Ecclesiastical Appeals Act (24 Hen 8 c 12):

Where by divers sundry old authentic histories and chronicles it is manifestly declared and expressed that this realm of England is an empire, and so hath been accepted in the world, governed by one supreme head and king having the dignity and royal estate of the imperial crown of the same, unto whom a body politic, compact of all sorts and degrees of people divided in terms and by names of spirituality and temporalty, be bounden and owe to bear next to God a natural and humble obedience.

Ecclesiastical Appeals Act (1532)

According to Cromwell, England was to become a Sovereign State free from any outside interference as a result of this legislation. One can imagine that any Brexiteer would celebrate a more 'secular' form of Thomas Cromwell's 1532 wording as the preamble to any 'Brexit Treaty' between the UK and the EU.

It has been argued[183] that this legislative campaign (led by Thomas Cromwell) saw the beginning of a professional national bureaucracy although this position is challenged by others.[184] Whichever conclusion holds it is striking how Thomas Cromwell, the son of small business owner (a smith and fuller) could – despite a somewhat chequered and entrepreneurial youth – reach the apex of power in the early 1530s during which he masterminded Henry VIII's Brexit.[185]

SIXTEENTH CENTURY LEGAL BACKGROUND

Law in the early sixteenth century partly came from ecclesiastical law for family, religious and moral matters and from the English 'common' law heritage, derived from Saxon times.[186] Although there is some dispute as to how effectively Canon Law or more formally 'Learned Law' was enforced in the period leading up to the Reformation, two trends can be discerned: (1) whilst Papal Authority was unchallenged, interpretation of Ecclesiastical Law was local and flexible varying from country to country and (2) English resentment at receiving law from Rome had an influence in developing English Common Law in an opposing direction.[187]

No discussion of this period can go by without mentioning the 'Great Statute of Praemunire' of 1393 (which actually followed two previous ones in 1353 and 1365). This statute has achieved a certain notoriety not least because Victorian constitutionalists such as Stubbs (1875) and Ramsey

(1913) portrayed the Act as being as important as the Reformation in shutting down Rome's legal authority in England.[188] In fact, the Statute was far more limited in its application and despite landmark decisions such as the 1515 Ryecroft case, in pre-Reformation England there was generally a reasonable working relationship between church and secular courts.[189]

Praemunire's notoriety perhaps came from its later use as a threat by Henry VIII against the whole clergy in 1530/1531. Arguably this demonstrated as much about the limitations of Praemunire as it did in failing to solve Henry's marital problem; instead the threat was resolved by the payment of a substantial fine from the Clergy to the King. It was to be Thomas Cromwell's 'Ecclesiastical Appeals Act' of 1532 that finally enabled Henry's divorce by stopping Appeals to Rome that was to allow the King to obtain the annulment he wanted.

Today, areas of UK Law are required to align with EU Law under the European Communities Act 1972, with the consequent assertion that the EU has become the 'source' of UK Law in these areas.[190] The process of alignment is implemented through legislating local British Law. This often takes place through utilising Secondary Legislation otherwise known as Statutory Instruments (reviewed by Parliamentary Select Committees), rather than Primary Legislative Acts debated and enacted through Parliament as a whole. Specifically, existing Statutory and Common Law is modified and combined as appropriate through the 'local transcription' of EU Directives into each Member State's local jurisprudence and adopted body of Law. Consistency between states is monitored by the European Commission and enforced by the European Court of Justice. We explore whether the EU has a Praemunire type legal device (subsidiarity) in Appendix 2 and again leave it to the reader to judge how Subsidiarity and Praemunire compare.

This framework of local implementation and interpretation combined with a central review for overall consistency across states feels somewhat similar to the situation of Canon Law in the pre-Reformation sixteenth century.

THE BREXIT BREAK OF THE 1530's

The 1530s Brexit break was executed by Thomas Cromwell piloting a series of bills through Parliament that (1) enabled Henry's divorce, (2) changed the Royal

Succession to reflect the new state of affairs, (3) broke with Rome and (4) seque-strated church assets to bolster the King's coffers. Henry VIII's Treasury always seemed to be under strain, and Cromwell stands out as the only 'Chief Minister' in the first 50 years of the sixteenth century not needing to debase the coinage to find additional funds for the King. 1530's Brexit did bring a short-term dividend to public finances, although by the mid-1540s, these finances were in trouble again.

As with all change there were unexpected consequences. It is striking how Thomas Cromwell's changes unsettled both Gentry and Peasants. Cromwell reacted by trying to bully the population through showpiece executions for treason, such as that of Elizabeth Barton in 1534. Despite this high profile campaign, the unrest could not be quelled As the resistance to the break with Rome continued prosecutions for treason rose and a new Treason Act was enacted in November 1534. Some 308 people were exe-cuted for Treason in the years leading up to 1540, exceeding the number that Mary I (otherwise known as "Bloody Mary") was to execute during her reign.[191]

Still, unrest persisted; eventually growing into the 1536 Pilgrimage of Grace insurrection that took place in the north of England. This revolt caused Henry sufficient concern that he felt the need to take a personal role in supressing it. Eventually order was restored by the King who (after sack-ing and executing Thomas Cromwell in 1540), in 1541 made a 'Progress' (or journey) to visit York, and force submission to him personally by the local Gentry in areas where the rebellion had occurred.[192]

It has been argued that this insurrection reflected the concerns held by both gentry and peasants regarding the loss of local religious traditions, buildings and artefacts and the loss of the poor relief system the monasteries provided.[193] Upon quelling the uprising – something that may have taken both the fall of Cromwell and the Royal Visit to Yorkshire in 1541 – the Crown suppressed the rest of the monasteries (for political more than eco-nomic reasons) and used the economic bonus from selling monastic lands to balance an already stressed National Treasury.

One rebel demand was that Parliament should meet in York – suggesting local alienation from the London-based Parliament. Some, such as historian Michael Bush[194] see the revolt as being religious, whereas others[195] stress the economic element. By contrast Geoffrey Elton[196] sees the revolt as being gentry-led and related to Royal Court politics. Tudor history just like Brexit is able to generate much controversy.

Overall, one is left with an impression that despite legal success, even by the 1540's the changes of the 1530s had not bedded down in the country. There was alienation from the political elite in London, unrest due to challenging economic circumstances for peasants, dissatisfaction with taxes, a fear of losing long held customs and dissatisfaction that local welfare for the poor (which had previously been delivered by the now dissolved monasteries) had been dismantled. Evaluating how successful the changes were at a local level is challenging, with many historical accounts from this period coloured by the viewpoint of the author. In **Box 15**, we explore potential author bias and the idea of 'fake news'.

Box 15. Fake News in the Sixteenth and Seventeenth Centuries

Shaping and controlling public opinion has always been important. Before the printing press, this was largely an exercise in 'Word of Mouth'. The printing press developed during the second half of the fifteenth century, came into its own in the first half of the next century. This was the internet of its time, with some well researched publications and some not so well researched ones. We catch a glimpse of how many sixteenth century writings were '*fabulists whose scurrilous lies and malicious omissions spawned wholly inaccurate narratives*' (Popper, 2011). Many of the more bizarre writings were influenced by Annio de Viterbo (c. 1432–1502) who in his 1498 'Antiquities' suggests that he had found documents and artifacts that explained how Noah (of biblical flood fame) had ruled the Etruscans as his own ancient kingdom from Annio's town Viterbo and that Noah was the original Pontifax Maximus![197] Although these and many other claims were fake, just like today's 'fake news' circulates around the internet, they spread around sixteenth century European World. For example, they influenced John Bale (an English Reformer who was hauled in front of the Archbishop of York in 1534 for preaching a sermon against invoking saints) and John Speed. In Speed's 1611 History of Great Britain he references Annio and includes suggestions that St Peter preached in England before he preached in Rome. He also suggests that the first Christian King in the world had been King Lucius in England, that Henry VIII had banished the 'usurping Roman Beast' and therefore God is on England's side. This era's fake news seemingly aligns to English Exceptionalism.

Ad hoc pamphlets, often containing unhelpful narratives for those in power were to varying degrees a 'live issue' throughout the sixteenth century. As the Reformation Legislation progressed towards the end of 1533 and into 1534, Cromwell tried to turn this trend to his advantage and seize the initiative by organising an anti-papal media campaign utilising the printing press. Propaganda was used to stir passions to engender support for the Reformation legislation.[198]

Recapping and expanding upon Thomas Cromwell's use of executions to reinforce his message; there were showpiece executions for treason to encourage conformity such as that of Elizabeth Barton in 1534. Despite this there was continued unrest and prosecutions for treason rose in response to resistance to the break with Rome, eventually leading to a new Treason Act being enacted in November 1534. Broman[181] (2014) found 308 people were executed for Treason in the years leading up to 1540,[199] exceeding the number that Mary I executed during her reign. Overall, it was found there were an average of over 2,000 executions (mostly hangings) in each year of Henry VIII's reign, a total of over 72,000, contrasting to a fraction of this number during Queen Elizabeth I's reign.[200]

PROMENADE IV: LESSONS FROM THE 1530's FOR TODAY?

SIMILAR OR DIFFERENT?

There is much that is similar between the 1530's Brexit and the current one. Both seek to remove the legal constraints of a foreign super national power, both are executing this strategy through a series of new statutes and changes to legal frameworks, both prompt deep and seemingly irreconcilable (in the short term) fractures in society, both operate in a world of new media (the printing press in the sixteenth century and social media today), both exist in a world where media targeting and fake or spurious news is being used to manipulate attitudes, both are following attempts to reinforce the role of the National State and both are occurring against a background of disruptions to the established welfare state, grumbling about taxation and deficits and challenging economic circumstances for some sections of the population.

Although there are many similarities, there are obvious differences. Who could we label today's Thomas Cromwell? Can one argue that Brexit zealots in all Parties through calls to respect 'the will of the people' apply the same pressure as a moody and autocratic King Henry VIII could? Although there was a 'will of the people' in the 1530's this was far from organised and certainly subjugated to the 'will of the king'. There was no Brexit Referendum in the 1530s.

The two Brexits are not the same, but they are we would argue sufficiently similar for there to be some useful lessons drawn to help guide us on our current journey. Both Brexits focus on laws and legal pathways; both Brexits focus upon the distribution and execution of power between the nation state and other competing bodies. Both Brexits are executed in a country with deep divisions across the Brexit divide. In the sixteenth century, this divide was so sharp that the whole process was reversed by Mary I, (a later monarch who is associated with her own bloodbath as we can read in *Foxes Book of Martyrs*). Both Brexits started at a time when the government felt short of money and was facing a deficit. Both Brexits took place at a time when some sections of the population have been facing real income challenges.

Despite the differences between the ages, we argue that the similarities are sufficient to allow us to ask if there are any simple lessons to be drawn from the experience of the 1530s that could be relevant today?

LEGAL SUCCESS DOES NOT MEAN A BREXIT SUCCESS

The experience of the 1530's suggests that short-term success from a legal break may not deliver solutions to long-term problems. The 1530's Brexit was a success for the King, as he was able to divorce his wife with the added bonus of filling his Treasury and fixing the deficit in the National Treasury at the same time. But as events were to unfold, both his new wife and the deficit fix were short-lived benefits. The second wife failed to give the king a male heir and was executed in 1536, replaced by a further four wives before Henry himself died. The King's financial deficit started to re-emerge by the mid-1540s and by the end of the decade the 'Great Debasement' of the coinage had started.

UNINTENDED ECONOMIC AND SOCIAL CONSEQUENCES?

Despite delivering a successful legal Brexit, Thomas Cromwell – the King's Chief Minister and Brexit architect – was executed on Tower Hill on 28 July 1540; the same day Henry married Catherine Howard. Cromwell's demise was partly brought about by the significant unrest associated with the Pilgrimage of Grace Rebellion. Short-term legislative success had given way to near term unrest and long-term societal ruptures as Radical Protestant (later Puritan) and Catholic (later expanding to include Laudian churchmen) became two different 'tribes' facing off each other over the centuries that followed. Notwithstanding the Elizabethan Settlement, one might argue this division was only finally resolved in England with the Glorious Revolution (with hangovers such as Catholic emancipation lasting into the nineteenth century) and continuing to this day in Northern Ireland. Such ruptures are defined by bitterness, failure to listen across the divides and *in extremis* Civil War.

Shorter term, the changes of the 1530s and associated unrest culminated in a sharp economic shock during the reign (1547–1553) of Edward VI with the 'Great Debasement' of the coinage and a sharp fall in real wages. Agricultural Real Wages fell from an index value of 94 in the 1520s to 89 in the 1530s, recovering to 95 in the 1540s and then plummeted to 78 by the 1550s in the face of the Great Debasement and instabilities of reigns of Edward and Mary.[201] Recovery came via the mercantilism of the Elizabethan era, but even then, was slow and faltering. Such a view is contested by some[202] who argue that in freeing England from the continental system the way was opened to society adopting the Protestant Work Ethic and the wonders of the Industrial Revolution. It is however difficult to imagine today's voters being prepared to wait even five years for a positive Brexit impact let alone 200!

5

BREXIT MK III ELIZABETH I: THE PRAGMATIC PROBLEM SOLVER

I mean to direct all my actions by good advice and counsel.
Elizabeth I (first speech as queen; Hatfield House, 1558)

Following the turmoil of Henry VIII's Brexit and the reigns of both Edward VI and Mary I; Elizabeth I faced considerable challenges upon her accession to the English Throne in 1558. England had been through over 20 years of deep change, having exited from the European Catholic System in the 1530s and then re-entered it some 15 years later under Mary I. For example, there had been revolts from both gentry and peasants, falling real wages and a huge debasement of the coinage.

BUILDING STABILITY

As the daughter of Anne Boleyn, Elizabeth's own legitimacy had been challenged by her predecessor Mary I. In addition to settling doubts over her right to the crown, Elizabeth inherited a domestic kingdom under stress. Elizabeth was immediately pitched into international power politics and the fractious religious divide between Catholics and Protestants. Protestants on the continent and in England saw the prospect of Elizabeth taking the 'Augsburg Confession' as offering a natural alliance that would bind England into the emerging family of 'Protestant' nations. By juxtaposition, many Catholics at home and abroad saw the new Queen as illegitimate and not the rightful heir, so favoured succession by Mary Stuart (who was married to the French teenage king Francis II), Queen of Scotland in her own right. As with Brexit today, the country was deeply divided. There had already been revolts against Phillip II of Spain in Mary I's reign, and before this against Edward VI as we see in **Box 16**.

Box 16. Tudor Brexit and Remain Rebellions

Sir, is your only quarrel to defend us from overrunning by strangers?
      Unknown doubter to Sir William Wyatt in 1554[203]

The Tudor Age saw rebellions both before the 1530's Brexit and after it; so rebellions in a Tudor context should be seen a continuing rather than exceptional theme. Indeed, the Tudor dynasty itself had come to power in 1485 as the result of a baronial civil war. Having said this, the rebellions after the 1530's inevitably became enmeshed with a combination of the changes that had and continued to occur, baronial and court politics and to a lesser degree, economic change.

Mary I's reign saw a number of risings. The most notable of these was Wyatt's Rebellion of 1554, when Thomas Wyatt marched to London in the belief that London would rise up against both the marriage of Philip II to the Queen and the fear of England was becoming re-Catholicised. As events transpired, London did not rise against its monarch.[204]

Elizabeth's reign also saw uprisings, most notably the 1569 Northern Rebellion[205] which again was prompted by a combination of baronial politics and dissatisfaction with the religious changes brought about by the Elizabethan Settlement. It's difficult to assess the risks of these rebellions to the Crown, although undoubtedly, all Tudor rulers would have needed to keep a watchful eye that the changes they were making would not destabilise the baronial power brokers and risk stirring up rebellion.[206]

As an historical footnote, Kett's Rebellion of 1549 during the reign of Edward VI seems to have been different (and perhaps a foretaste of some of the more extreme movements that came to the fore during the English Civil War). It was typified by a desire to remove property owning rights from the baronial class, and was triggered by a combination of the chaotic economic circumstances of the later 1540s and landowner moves to enclose land. In some ways, the language and idealism of the Kett rebels can be said to have some resonance with the Momentum movement for change and the language of the Labour Party's Corbyn leadership.[207] The rebellion lasted three weeks before it was supressed. Even today major changes can cause unrest if these are thought to disadvantage people. A recent parallel would be the 1990 Poll Tax riots in London.

Against this backdrop, the first and most urgent need was for the new Queen to re-establish stability. The French were lobbying the Pope to have her declared illegitimate and so have the succession pass to Mary Stuart (Mary Queen of Scots). There was already a state of war between England and France, so if Mary acceded to the English Throne, the French would end the war and combine the Kingdoms Scotland and England into their own. At the same time, the Spanish and the Protestant Princes of Augsburg were wooing Elizabeth to bring her into their own spheres of influence.

First Elizabeth had to take a position on the religious split, the most divisive issue of her time. Elizabeth took England back into the Protestant camp as she executed yet another Brexit in early 1559 via the 'Act of Uniformity' and the 'Act of Supremacy'. In an early display of both her pragmatism and diplomatic skills, she was able to avoid Papal Excommunication (an act that would have inflamed domestic Catholic opinion and risked early civil unrest in what was already a challenging international context) and avoided war as she stabilised her succession.[208] The young Queen handled the hard-line Pope Paul IV (who died in July 1559) by listening to and utilising people (such as Sir William Carne, Elizabeth's Ambassador to the Pope) who already had positive relationships and credibility with him, to build a constructive engagement. This skill of working with and through others to deliver results was to serve her well throughout her reign.

REBUILDING THE ECONOMY

In addition to facing political instability, Elizabeth inherited an economy that had been traumatised by the political and religious changes of the past 25 years; one that was still recovering from the inflation of the 'Great

Debasement', the loss of Calais and a balance of payments deficit with imports running about 17% ahead of exports.[209] The Tudor economy had seen a period of export led growth (mainly via cloth exports) during the first half of the sixteenth century, and most especially during the 1530s and 1540s. Arguably this was the result of England's continued devaluation of its currency, setting English cloth prices at a very competitive level on the continent. This changed in the early 1550s when with a desire to reverse the monetary chaos of the late 1540s and early 1550s, changes in the effective exchange rate led to a rise in the relative price of cloth, a consequently challenging sales environment and an economic downturn.[191]

The recession broadly coincided with both Elizabeth I's accession to the throne and, the start of 40 years of economic troubles on the near continent due to religious wars that only came to an end with the Edict of Nantes in 1598. Elizabeth's reign had started at an economically and politically challenging moment.

Elizabeth's 'England First' Policy

In one sense Elizabethan commercial policy can be described as 'England First' as rules and regulations were established to protect English merchant interests. By the late 1550s, over 90% of cloth exports[vi] were made through the Port of London, and this trade in turn was monopolised by the London Company of the Merchant Adventurers. One school of thought sees such monopolies, and their associated regulations, as impeding growth by favouring specific merchant interests and reducing the level of competition.[192] By juxtaposition, another set of analyses has seen these measures as essential to protect the national interest against the chaos on the near continent, with a strategic aim of developing 'economic autarky'.[193] It is also possible to see both narratives as complementary.

Could there be some today who see Brexit as a way of removing the EU's mercantile monopoly protections (so opening the way to a new era of competitive innovation) and others that see Brexit as establishing 'Fortress Britannia'?

[vi] As measured by customs records (Stone, 1949).

In the second half of the sixteenth century, there can also be no doubt that chaos on the near continent was impacting the all-important English textile export trade. Most especially, the closure of Antwerp in 1564 and soon after its reopening its closure again in the face of the Dutch revolt. Inevitably in all this turmoil, there were tensions between the winners and losers and demands to break open the monopoly of the London Merchant Adventurers. These came to a head with the 1604 Free Trade Bill that was more about trying to allow excluded groups into trading networks than about classic free trade.[194] We look at these Elizabethan 'free trade pressures' in **Box 17**.

Box 17. Different Types Trade

Debates over 'Free Trade' are not new, and indeed there was a lively debate on 'Free Trade' in the House of Commons in 1604 that focused on the subject of opening trade to ports outside London for the cloth trade.

The London Company Merchant Adventurers (whose control of the English textile trade was formalised through its 1564 Charter of Incorporation[195]) had centralised almost all of the cloth trade into London.[196] Sir Raymond Bulkley intervening in the debate[197] stated that the issue under consideration was the Merchant Adventurers' monopoly.[198] Free trade in this case was defined as letting other groups (both the Staplers Company and the so called 'Out Ports' group) into an on-going monopoly.

This debate contrasts with the later nineteenth century 'Corn Laws' debate. In 1605, the question was about allowing new entrants to an existing monopoly, whereas during the 1840's the debate was about removing all barriers and tariffs to allow a free for all.

Lobbying group Economists for Free Trade[199] argue the 1849 repeal of the Corn Laws yielded significant benefit, and that unilateral free trade Brexit under WTO rules should therefore lead to a 4% rise in GDP and an 8% fall in consumer prices.[200] These forecasts are disputed by others who point to the potential damage such a move could imply with, for example, an estimated increase in 'Red Tape' regulatory barrier costs of £27 billion annually if the UK has no EU trade agreement and is forced to use WTO rules.[201] A total of 70% of this additional cost is focused on five sectors: financial services; automotive; agriculture, food and drink; consumer goods; and chemicals and plastics.

Although Tudor data is sparse and unreliable, we shall attempt to contrast the impact of Elizabethan 'Mercantilist' free trade with the post-Corn Law repeal classic 'free trade'. Using data from Keynes's Treatise on Money, economic historian John Nef[202] found an England of widening profit margins in the final 25 years of the sixteenth century that was undergoing a mini industrial revolution as industries such as iron, bricks and pottery both grew and were established in new localities. This picture is reinforced by Stone[203] who argues that the formation of an English 'Internal Market' during the Elizabethan Age was driven largely by increasing urbanisation in London, as the power of the Mercantilist companies drove trade through London (a trend that grew during the later Stuart era). A further pressure for change came from the rebalancing of English supply chains following the rebasing of the currency, which led to agricultural changes away from grazing, and redeployment of some resources into the industries that were developing to feed London.[204]

By way of contrast, in the mid-nineteenth century, Britain set the international trading rules through its Empire and military might. O'Brian and Pigman see Britain as the global rule setter during the second half of the nineteenth century.[205]

The 1860 Cobden Chevalier Treaty between France and the UK reduced tariffs and duties and introduced 'Most Favoured Nation Status' (MFN) where all MFN treaty status nations gain the same rights even if only one country negotiates a change. Following the 1860s there was a spate of 56 bilateral trade treaties (mostly not with the UK) signed between 13 Europe nations. These agreements were mainly to increase trade with near neighbours (indicating that distance matters when building trade links), to improve or protect an existing export industry and were generally made with larger states first, thereby giving smaller states a possibility to 'free ride' 'MFN' clauses.[206] Bairoch[207] alludes to the post-1860 Cobden Chevalier Treaty between France and the UK creating a unique European Low tariff area that gave the UK a significant advantage due to its more advanced industrial base.

For others such as Glazier (1980) '*Under free trade the gap in development levels between Britain and the Continent became more pronounced, income differentials widened between 1860 and 1880, and investment and innovation on the Continent declined. With the reintroduction of protective tariffs between 1890 and 1913 on the Continent, however... per capita incomes in the less developed (continental) countries rose, while growth in Britain lagged*'.

Global Adventuring

Elizabethan commercial policy represented a second theme as the sixteenth century progressed, and the previously stable supply chains and markets of the near continent dissipated into a world of religious wars. England began to look beyond Europe for both imports and new customers. This search was led by both pioneering individuals and the chartering of new companies such as the Muscovy Company in 1553. **Box 18** describes some of the events surrounding the forging of these new overseas trade links as England looked to become 'Global England'.

Box 18. The Attractions and Perils of Far Off Lands

The later sixteenth century had its share of colourful entrepreneurs looking to open new markets and new opportunities. The story behind these new markets is the story of individuals and their relationships both at home in England and abroad. John Cabot who supposedly discovered Newfoundland in 1497, [208] was originally a Venetian who had chosen to settle in Bristol; but when Henry VIII offered him less than satisfactory opportunities Cabot turned to Spain for whom he discovered the River Plate in Argentina. His son, an anglophile, returned to England in 1553 with the goal of finding a 'North East Passage' sea route to China. Being rather old (76) by then he could not sail himself, so he organised the financing for a company to do the exploring. This new company was initially called *'The Mystery and Company of Merchant Adventurers for the Discovery of Regions, Dominions, Islands and places unknown'*.

Its first expedition was led by another intrepid explorer who had been mentored by Sebastian Cabot, Richard Chancellor who ended up in Russia. Here, Chancellor established a good relationship with Tsar Ivan IV (Ivan the Terrible). This success led to the 1555 establishment of the Russia Company and Chancellor being sent back to the Tsar to continue to grow the relationship. In 1556, he returned to England and bought with him a Russian Ambassador to the English Court. Unfortunately, Chancellor was shipwrecked, and although the Ambassador's life was saved, both Chancellor and the cargo valued at £20,000 were lost. Notwithstanding this inconvenience, the relationship continued to grow and prosper as following Chancellor's death, Anthony Jenkinson became the entrepreneur in charge.[209]

Jenkinson began to have 'itchy feet' to extend the reach of the Russia Company. After obtaining the support of the Tsar to travel to Persia,[210] Jenkinson embarked on his journey; arriving at Shabran, he was housed in the Governor's tent waiting for the possibility of transit to Shamakhi, the regional capital. Middle Eastern hospitality took over at this point as he was given transport and an escort to the Governor Generals palace where he was lodged in the mountain pavilion to avoid the summer heat. The undertone to this hospitality was that the Governor General, as a close relation and confident of the Shah, undertook preliminary questioning of Jenkinson to see if he was suitable to meet the ruler. Such initial screening of people by trusted confidents has continued in the Middle East right up until today.[211]

Jenkinson passed his pre-screening test and moved near to the Shah's residence where he was kept waiting whilst the Shah completed some other business. This transpired to be the striking of a peace treaty with the Ottoman Sultan.[212] The treaty pandered to the aspirations of the Ottoman merchants who wanted to prevent the English having access to the Persian silk trade. Opening the silk trade for England was the commercial objective of Jenkinson's visit. Matters were further complicated by an alliance between the Turks and Persians against the Portuguese. Jenkinson was in both contexts suggested by some to be in Iran undercover to support Portuguese interests. Unsurprisingly, Jenkinson's reception by the Shah himself was difficult partly due to the issues relating to the Turkish peace treaty, but also due to Jenkinson's difficultly in answering questions regarding religion. The result was that this visit was not successful, although Jenkinson did leave with some royal gifts and was not handed to the Turks for interrogation and execution. Whilst in the short term the visit was judged a failure, longer term it was seen as a foundation for future success in opening trade between Persia and England.[213]

This narrative could be transposed into some parts of the twenty-first century Middle East, where personal trust must be built before commercial fruits can flow. Elizabeth I understood that diplomacy and trade needed great personal relationships as much as, and maybe more than formal treaties.

Jenkinson, and before him Chancellor reflected this understanding, as both were acting in a dual role that encompassed both private trade and public diplomacy. Both had their expeditions endorsed by the Sovereign of the time and both carried diplomatic messages from the Sovereign. Equally both had to be flexible and adaptable in the face of unexpected events and local skullduggery. Many of Jenkinson's experiences could be

> replicated today in regions such as the Middle East where trust and per-sonal relationship can have far more importance than more formal con-tract regulated relations.
>
> Could, one ask, if this experience provides any lessons for those who seek to build a 'Global Britain' at the same time as significantly reducing the local UK diplomatic presence and relying on websites to provide commer-cial leads?

Jenkinson was also an important character in dealings with the Ottoman Empire. His 1553/1554 discussions with Sultan Süleyman opened trade rela-tions between the Ottoman Empire and England.[214] This trade involved a variety of goods, including metals for the Ottoman's to melt down and form into guns.[215] Notwithstanding the efforts to increase sales, Stone[216] found the distance and transport costs meant that any overall impact on England's then trade balance was small, in comparison to the cloth sales to Europe.

Privateering

A third entrepreneurial strand was formalised in 1585 by the granting of Royal Licences to merchants and shippers to recover goods seized by other powers. This was the start of Privateering. The Court of the High Admiral was responsible for issuing these licences and entitled to 10% of the pro-ceeds. In a very short time groups were able to obtain the licences without proving loss,[217] and in some cases, they did not even bother with a licence! Over the period 1589–1591, it is estimated there were in excess of 235 privateer vessels in action. Some expeditions were part financed by the Crown in which case orders were given on potential targets, indicating an alignment to state. Overall, privateering started to fall away once inter-national trade took off.[218]

Elizabethan Outsourcing

Elizabeth was content to outsource many activities that today we might regard as firmly within the 'state's' competence, namely diplomatic represen-tation, trade negotiations and tax and customs collection.

Tax farming was used as both a reward for members of the elite[219] and as a way of improving revenue reliability and avoiding a then chaotic public administration system.[220] The London customs farm was lucrative and corrupt if we are to believe Richard Carmarden's 1570 compilation of customs fees and trade data for Queen Elizabeth I in a document entitled *Caveat for the Quene*.[221] In it, Carmarden asserts that perhaps 50% of the duties due to the Crown in the 1560's were not paid due to corruption. Eventually Caramarden was appointed as the Queen's surveyor of Customs, and duty collection was taken in house by the Crown during the 1590's, only to be later outsourced again; but this time under the oversight of Carmarden and later his son on his death in 1604.[222]

Outsourcing seems to have been more successful in the case of trade diplomacy as we have seen in the work of Anthony Jenkinson and Richard Chancellor and described in **Box 18**. Outsourced trade diplomacy was again used to deliver the temporary relocation of the English Cloth Market to Emden when Antwerp was temporarily closed in 1564. In this case it was the entrepreneur George Needham whose personal relationships with the rulers of East Friesland and the Merchant Adventurers that enabled the relocation of the cloth market to Emden at short notice.[223] Privateering represented yet another form of outsourcing, this time combining private profit and enhancing the national naval defences.

One aspect of Elizabeth's genius was to use these outsourced relationships in a flexible manner to achieve what she wanted, at minimum cost but with maximum effect. An additional benefit to the strategy was it also ensured that significant economic interests were naturally bound into Crown policy, so reinforcing political as well as economic stability.

THE END RESULT

The Queen upon her accession to the English throne had faced a country that was at least as divided as the UK today. In her age, the divides were religious whereas today it is political and over Europe. Elizabeth successfully established stability, enabled some economic growth, and delicately avoided many of the power clashes and disputes of continental Europe, a continent in turmoil for most of her reign. Business did develop in the Elizabethan era, with arguably[224] England taking the lead in mining and industrial technology away from Germany. The Elizabethan economy still depended upon trade, especially the cloth trade (which was focused on the Low Countries) rather than as happened in later centuries forcing trade to come to England. For the entrepreneur outside the great Merchant Companies there were still opportunities, even if developments were on the whole small scale, local and fitted into, rather than transforming, existing structures.

Unlike in her father's time, Elizabeth did not break relationships, rather she manipulated them and used them for her own and her nation's advantage. Elizabeth's Brexit whilst not advertised as Brexit, combined a break with the political rivalries of Continental Europe, an opening of horizons and an entrepreneurial spirit that served well in the challenging times she lived through. Pragmatic, stealthy, entrepreneurial and yet at times buccaneering and almost pirate like, Elizabeth's Brexit moves our story on. Reintegrating England to the Roman Church was notwithstanding later Catholic uprisings never again a serious question.

The economy stabilised and started to develop but not in the abundance that some may have hoped for. In the words of the late Professor Frederick Fisher:

> It was an economy heavily dependent on foreign sources for improved industrial and agricultural methods, and to some extent for capital, but in which foreign labour and business men were met with bitter hostility. In it, ambitious young men often preferred careers in the professions and government service to those in business, and fortunes made in business were too readily converted into land. [...] Men increasingly pinned their hopes on industrialisation and economic nationalism [...] but industrialisation was slow to come and the blessings of economic nationalism proved to be mixed. (Fisher, 1957, p. 18)

It makes one wonder how much in the economic sphere has really changed in 400 years?

PROMENADE V: BREXIT THEN AND NOW – THE CHALLENGE LIST

Draw your knowledge of the past [...] and read the ancient tales of
learned lore. Look neither at the page of Homer, nor of elegy, nor
tragic muse, nor epic strain. Seek not the vaunted verse of the cycle;
but look in me and you will find in me all that the world
contains.[225]

Adapted from Photios I (cited in Fowler, 2013, p. 384)

Our journey so far can be summarised as follows. First, we have established
that for Brexit to be judged a success by the Pro-Leave community, two outcomes will need to be delivered. The first requires that this group feels recognition, affirmation and 'fair play' for English Exceptionalism; a rebalancing
in the social narrative that allows room for nostalgia of Empire, a recognition that England dominates the United Kingdom (and subsidises the nation-
alists in Scotland and Ireland) and a recognition that the English have for
many centuries had a crucial civilising influence on our constantly warring
continental neighbours. In summary, a restoration of English national pride
and as Leavers would put it *an end to the tail wagging the dog.*

Secondly, Brexit success needs to see notable economic improvement and
especially the releasing of more resources to (1) fund each of the devolved
nations National Health Services, (2) provide quality affordable houses for
both long term rent and purchase and (3) provide stable jobs with career
prospects especially for white working-class males who have tended to be
left behind in recent decades.

Many in the Remain camp would most likely warm towards the need
for recognition and concession to England's exceptionalism but rewrite
the second criterion to say that Brexit must not damage existing successful UK
industries such as financial services, automotive, aerospace and pharmaceuticals.

It is also likely that many in both Leave and Remain camps recognise that
there is a need for a process of national reconciliation that removes the bitterness, anger and distrust the Referendum stirred up.

POINTERS FROM PREVIOUS BREXITS

Our journey so far has shown us how bitter divides can cause trouble for
many decades and in some cases centuries. The shockwaves from the 1530s
arguably resonated through Elizabethan times into the English Civil War

and beyond. The earlier such divides are healed the less chance there is of perpetuation across generations. Perhaps the best healer is economic success that touches the whole of society and translates into a new feeling of national confidence and pride.

We know from the end of Roman Britain that unintended consequences and change can happen, and they can happen remarkably quickly if fundamental economic structures are broken. The end of Roman Britain emphasises the importance of maintaining a monetary economy (which with the exception of a possible fall in Sterling, Brexit should not threaten) and stable supply chains (which Brexit does threaten). Equally we have learnt from the 1530's that whilst a 'legal only' strategy might fix specific legal issues (such as King Henry VIII's divorce), it cannot effect broad social and economic change unless all the structures of society are fully engaged. If you read any newspaper today, it is challenging to see how Brexit is engaging with non-Brexit advocating stakeholders. The 1530's teach us that although Thomas Cromwell may have been master of Royal Court politics, he was far less successful in convincing groups outside this circle.

Will today's politicians in Westminster prove to be any more successful?

The scale of this Brexit's proposed changes is awe inspiring when compared to previous ones. If we contrast the number of relationships, regulations, regulators and minutia that will change in this Brexit with the changes of 1530s, then the comparison suggests today could be a mega – quake (Richter scale $9+$) compared to the strong shaking (say Richter scale 5) in the 1530's. With such a huge change, there must be a significant risk of unintended consequences.

We also have to ask who today is the UK equivalent of Henry VIII's Thomas Cromwell?

Cromwell with an exceptional eye for detail, an iron grip on court politics and a very focused step by step approach was committed to delivering each element perfectly. This contrasts to today when we can reasonably pose the question, who in government can map out the details of exactly what they are trying to do and by when? As this book is written more than two years after the decision to Leave, there is still no accepted definition in the ruling Conservative Party, let alone the country as a whole as to what post-Brexit customs arrangement the UK wants with the EU, and even less clarity as to what may actually happen.

We know from the Elizabethan era that stability is built on trust and that trust is based upon personal relationships. One aspect of Elizabeth I's genius was to work with a wide variety of people to achieve her strategic goals, and let the people who were in control of the detail worry about and sort out the detail for themselves. Although the circle of Charted Corporations such as the London Company of Merchant Adventurers or the Muscovy Company was relatively small, and competitors from other locations complained about their hold on business, Elizabeth's pragmatic trust and willingness to outsource sensitive state matters to experts in these Corporations and trusted individuals enabled her to reach places other people could not. If we contrast this to today's business engagement in the Brexit process then perhaps we can sense the relative gap.

TRANSITIONING TO THE NEW ORDER

Our narrative has now reached its 'transition corridor', that will take us from looking over our shoulder and into what we all hope will be a light airy modern space, filled with sunlight, optimism and opportunity. However, our transition corridor ends with three doors, each representing an alternative choice. Each door is one way only, there is little chance to say *mea culpa*, go back and try again. Our decision is further complicated as the marks on all the doors are indistinct and change because lobbyists, media commentators and politicians obfuscate, shift and amend their positions. How can we know which option is best if those helping form opinion keep moving the goalposts?

To move us forward, we shall label the three doors by what is behind them, and not by what they advertise themselves to be.

The first door is labelled 'Delusion'. An attractive door on the outside that suggests once we pass through it, most if not all of our problems will go away. Public finances will suddenly be augmented by a treasure chest full of gold that will pay for unlimited spending increases on health and social care whilst removing the austerity caps on areas like defence, education and justice. Real wages will rise and every person who wishes to work will find a stable career job with long-term prospects, whilst the retired will keep their triple lock pensions. House prices will rise but housing for the under 40s will be more affordable and young people will become owner occupiers again.

The second door is labelled 'Continuity'. This door is not so attractive, but does feel very familiar and comfortable. Go through this door and one feels the promise that nothing much will change. Life will go on and we will 'muddle through'. This door suggests (but does not guarantee or even assure) that companies dependent upon complex supply chains will continue to manufacture and invest in the UK, rather than avoid the additional costs by relocating into their main markets. This door also suggests austerity will continue but with the occasional tweak here and there to keep the show on the road. The NHS will be given more funds, but not enough to solve its systemic problems and the adult social care issue will be avoided with resolution left to a later date. Financial services will continue undisturbed, house prices will hold their current level and affordable housing for young people will arrive by a huge expansion of the public housing programme. Reading the list begs the question 'Wishful thinking?' and yet this is probably the door that the current Brexit negotiating team and many others in the UK expect the UK to pass through.

The third door has two names, the first is attractive and says 'Opportunity' and the second is a definite turnoff for most people[226] as it says 'Challenge'. Behind the third door are the tough decisions needed to raise the level of investment and innovation in the UK economy, to move from short-term to long-term thinking. Long term house prices need to align to the earnings potential of those that seek to purchase them. Tough decisions are required to rebalance spending away from wealth consumers into wealth creators. To make these changes requires a significant squeeze on pensioner assets through falls in the price of houses relative to the incomes of those that seek to purchase them (either through price falls or strong increases in real wages). Equally, pensioner incomes from both universal pensioner welfare and, the funding contributions to pension schemes are likely to come under pressure if income is focused on wealth creators rather then wealth consumers (of which pensioners are a substantial component group). Unfortunately, both the 'Delusions' door and the 'Continuity' door could in the fullness of time, lead along ever more difficult passages to their own 'Challenge' door.

What is expected to lie behind each door will vary according to the expectations of the individual opening it. What actually lies behind the door will be determined by the realities of the world. As reality overcomes illusion, we will all be forced to make sharp adjustments to our assumptions as to where there can be continuity after Brexit. Our adjusted assumptions will likely once again point us back to the 'Challenge' door. Unfortunately the new realities may, dependent upon how long we delay taking action, result in facing even stronger challenges than if they had been tackled at the point Brexit happens.

The choice of which door we as a society take matters, as unlike in video games, there will be no 'reset button'. We go through the door we choose and after this we will be stuck with most of what we have chosen.

DRIVING SUCCESS IN THE FACE OF CHALLENGE

How then do we drive success in the face of these challenges? Success requires that the UK be (as it is today) a leading global economy, and that this success is translated into rising living standards, affordable housing and stable work. Employment opportunities need to be open to and reach everyone, including the Left Behind. There will also need to be a revised intergenerational balance that works for all generations and is adapted to the challenges of the UK's ageing population.

Discerning a pathway to drive this success is the subject of the remainder of this book.

In the forthcoming chapters, we will take a pragmatic approach that starts with the importance of generating and supporting innovating entrepreneurs. These entrepreneurs can be in their own companies, leading small and medium sized companies or they can be in large companies.

We start with entrepreneurs and not trade deals, because it is innovating entrepreneurs who create and build the products that excite and delight their customers, which lead to the profit streams that fund the rest of society. We also start with entrepreneurs because the world we live in, the products people want and the technologies that are embedded in these products, imply that customer demands on companies are changing at an ever increasing rate. Behind every new product or service created to meet these changing needs lies an entrepreneur. In the forthcoming discussion, our focus is on how to nurture and support these entrepreneurs to innovate markets, deliver what the customer aspires to and succeed by being the best in their class globally.

The gap from today's starting point is emphasised by the findings from a recent survey of UK small business. Overall, the appetite to invest in new products, innovation and new equipment is weakening and the aspiration to grow turnover is also falling. Fewer small companies want to be involved in innovation (a drop of 4% between 2012/2014 and 2014/2016), fewer want to invest in raising skills (a drop of 6% between 2016 and 2017), and fewer companies want to export because of Brexit uncertainty.[246] The same survey found the number of high growth potential firms is roughly stable. How then can we move more firms from steady state or managing decline into managing for growth?

The remainder of our book is about thoughts and ideas, Brexit or no Brexit as to how to bridge this gap. Success here will open the way to economic success, economic success nurtures confidence, confidence builds self-esteem and success and self-esteem help engender respect. When a representative from a growing, economically successful self-confident UK walks through the diplomatic door, the aura of confidence and success combines with memories of British exceptionalism and everyone in the room will sit up and take notice. Success in itself encourages further success, and everyone likes to be part of the winning team.

Isn't the ultimate Brexit aspiration for the UK to be seen as the 'winning team' everyone wants to be associated with?

Just as it was when Britain ruled the Empire over which the sun never set.

6

THE GLOBAL INNOVATION ECONOMY

When people shake their heads because we are living in a restless age, ask them how they would like to live in stationary one, and do without.

GB Shaw (1928)

Have you ever taken the time to consider how many of the products we use today did not exist ten or fifteen years ago? Many of the products that shape our lives come from companies that did not exist until recently. The now ubiquitous Google, Facebook, Amazon, eBay and others had not been formed in 1990, and earlier innovators such as Microsoft and Apple were simply not around in 1975. Equally, other 'big change' product companies of the last 35 years such as Samsung, Vodafone and Nokia transformed themselves from business to business companies into consumer facing businesses in surprisingly short periods of time. For example in 1980, Racal was a substantial UK defence contractor (prior to merging its defence operations with Thompson to become a constituent part of French Group Thales), that had some interest in the commercial exploitation of defence technology through a patent link with Lord Weinstock's GEC. This "commercial" aspect of their business grew in importance after 1985 with the launch of the mobile phone service that was to become the global Vodafone phone business.

The spectacular growth and market breakthroughs of rising star mega companies originated with the vision and persistence of entrepreneurs. In the Racal case, it was long-term employee Sir Ernest Harrison who took the entrepreneurial step to branch into a new business sector, away from what was already a sizable defence contractor. The "entrepreneurial group" can also be external to an existing company as, by way of contrast, is the case with Google. This now giant corporation started small, by looking to commercialise academic work by Larry Page and Steve Brin whilst at Stamford University. At first, Page and Brin tried unsuccessfully to sell their internet page ranking system to other search engines such as Excite, before Stamford University Professor David Cheriton introduced them to tech start-up investor Andy Bechtolsheim who invested the first US$100,000 in; a company that was about to start its journey to the global megalith it is today.[247]

Transformation and growth are realised as entrepreneurs see an opportunity and then set about persuading other people to help make it happen. To translate an idea into reality, backing for a new idea has to be obtained irrespective of whether the entrepreneur is within an existing company or outside one and seeking venture capital. A key ingredient to success is to have entrepreneurs with the vision, tenacity, ambition and skill to both drive success and the ability to communicate their ideas in a way that motivates others with crucial resources, (such as risk finance), to partner them on their entrepreneurial quest.

Increasingly, short-term profit growth pressures within large listed companies limit the scope for entrepreneurial action.[248] The torch therefore passes to private companies varying from large ones such as Dyson, (a successful innovator for many years) to new or smaller MSMEs. Such companies are especially important in a world of disruptive technology, as rarely do they have existing business models to defend; on the contrary they offer opportunities to change the customer paradigm and technological assumptions in products and markets *à la* Google or *à la* Amazon.

Aspiration and vision are crucial to their success. A 2017 survey of micro-business in the UK found that only 22% wanted to build a 'national or international business' and just 47% expected to grow in the next year.[249] Only 62% are planning to grow in the next three years (a percentage that is year on year falling) and where a lack of ambition can *ceteris paribus* be often associated with a lack of willingness to seek external finance.[250]

Nurturing the ambition to succeed is a key UK growth and innovation issue.

A RAPIDLY CHANGING WORLD

From both a technological and business viewpoint, we live in a rapidly changing world. Products that are ubiquitous today were figments of consumer imagination just 10 years ago. For example, in January 2007 Facebook did not work on mobile phones and was far from being widely used on PC type devices. In December 2007, there were a mere 58 million active users globally. By March 2018, this had risen to 2.2 billion active users active just on Facebook's mobile platform.[251] The first iPhone, the start of the 'Smart Phone' revolution, was launched in June 2007. Then Nokia was still the number one mobile phone company globally with 37.8% of 2007 market. Android phones were unheard of to the consumer; their launch only came about in 2008.[252] In such a dynamic business environment British success has been limited. There have been some winners, including Dyson, recently acquired ARM Holdings (a UK global technical champion in silicon chip design). Equally, multi national established companies such as Unilever and GSK have also been very successful at driving new products into established and emerging markets.

Despite the UK having a number of the top Global Universities and being one of the world's key finance hubs, it has been unable to create a digital 'Platform Company' on the scale of Google, Amazon or Facebook. Could there be something related to the US entrepreneurial climate that explains why these platform companies have grown there and not in the UK? If so how can post-Brexit Britain become a source of global companies that successfully transform global markets with next generation products and technologies?

PLATFORM FIRMS AND BIG BANG DISRUPTION

'Big Bang Disruption' combines with incremental innovation to define the modern business landscape.[253] A 'Big Bang' disruption has the capability to change an entire market, whilst an incremental innovation tends to enhance something that is already there. Well known as market disrupting companies in recent years are each of the western 'FAANG'[254] companies.[vii] [255]

[vii]'FAANG' = Facebook, Apple, Amazon, Netflix and Google.

These businesses (with perhaps the exception of Netflix) together with other companies such as Ebay, Ali-Baba and Baidu have disrupted markets by operating as 'Platforms' for other organisations to trade through. A Platform Company is defined as '*A business creating significant value through the acquisition, matching and connection of two or more customer groups to enable them to transact.*'[256] Such companies are in effect the pure 'digital market place' (where many parties can interact in multiple ways with multiple other parties) as opposed to the 'peer to peer' digital market businesses where parties transact directly with each other rather than via a third party.

Arguably 'Platform Companies' are the internal plumbing of the digital economy, allowing people with a common interest to connect. In a world with no trade or information barriers, these companies will tend to become 'natural monopolies' as ubiquity of information is a fundamental requirement to make them useful. How many people would look for something on Amazon if they thought there was a 1% chance the item would be there? Chinese state policy, according to Lewis,[257] recognises the importance of building Platform Companies by integrating them into the 'One Belt One Road' and 'Internet-Plus' initiatives. This has led to the building of growth companies such as Ali Baba, Tencent and Baidu.

This begs the obvious question: does the UK need any 'Platform Companies' if it is to be a globally leading post-Brexit 'Global Britain'?

The attraction of growing such champions is clear, but the method of growing them is opaque as whilst depending upon open access globally, these companies also 'nip and tuck' to avoid additional costs. They innovate first and worry about the regulations afterwards. Just like Elizabeth I's privateers, these companies don't need conventional trade deals to do business, they carve out their own space until someone stops them.[258] However, they do require a free flow of data across borders. For any Platform Company based in the UK, post-Brexit arrangements with both the EU and the USA will require a specific agreement for unrestricted, free and open data exchanges between the EU and the UK[259] through being granted full post-Brexit access into the EU–US Privacy Shield agreement[viii][260] or some appropriate alternative agreement.

[viii]Implemented by diplomatic notes between the United States and the European Union in 2016.

Providing such a data exchange agreement is in place, and subject to any changes in customs and proof of origin procedures, Platform Companies based in the UK should be able to grow operations without relying on a specific trade deal, thereby opening a possible area for entrepreneurial activity that will not be constrained by trade deal terms.

Despite internet markets rapidly maturing, there is still scope for new Platform Companies. Many sectors remain undisrupted. One area of immediate opportunity for the UK is in the redefinition of boundaries between health and social care. With a single National Health System[261] plus an urgent need to match budgetary constraints to an ageing population the UK could, if it chooses, nurture new delivery patterns of health and social care that could then be adapted and rolled out globally. One example of the UK seeking to address this market can be seen in 2013 UK health start-up Babylon Health, which has led the way globally in online health by combining an artificial intelligence-based question and answer system with online medical doctor consultations that are normally fulfilled within two hours of a request.[262]

TECHNOLOGY CLUSTERS

Having a Platform Company in a specific location does not create a vast business infrastructure on its own. Although these companies can generate a large number of transactions as digital market places, the associated businesses using their platform features can come from any location. The business 'multiplier' effect of having a global Platform Company in a locality comes through the indirect economic benefits associated with it being a focal point for growth culture, venture capital and technical innovation; most especially if it is linked to high quality technology universities. This model is visible in Paolo Alto/Silicon Valley in California. Big tech companies attract ambitious people and become an anchor to build an entrepreneurial culture cluster within a region. We explore the development of this cluster in **Box 19.**

ENTREPRENEURIAL CAPITAL

Entrepreneurs and Risk Capital

At the heart of any business cluster are entrepreneurs who combine their market, technical and business flair with risk capital. This was as true in

---

Box 19. Silicon Valley

When we look at Silicon Valley good geography does not seem to be the key factor in creating a growth hub. How could one of the most important technological region's in the world end up being located in an area that suffered some of the worst destruction outside of San Francisco itself during the 1906 earthquake? Sheriff William White who was visiting the Santa Clara area (Silicon Valley) from Los Angeles in 1906 when the earthquake struck is quoted as saying '*San Jose, which was the prettiest city in California, is the worst-looking wreck I ever saw*' (Russell, 1906: Chapter XIV). The city had been effectively flattened by the San Francisco earthquake.

Recovery from the earthquake saw the Santa Clara County being turned into fruit orchards and agriculture until the World War II, when its close location to Stamford University made it the ideal site for electronic firm Varian to start business. Varian Associates was founded by a group of academics who had been at Stamford in the late 1930s and were responsible for inventing the klystron. The klystron was a key enabler for airborne radar detection in World War II and at the same time the foundation for the microwave technology industry. A close relationship between Varian and Stamford continued into the cold war period with the firm moving into buildings located on land owned by Stamford.[263] A few years after this in 1956, William Shockley (co-recipient of the 1956 Nobel Prize for Physics) opened the Shockley Semi-Conductor Laboratory as a subsidiary of Beckmann Instruments in Mountain View, Santa Clara County. Silicon Valley had its first semi-conductor firm containing a group of scientists who had previously been involved in radar research.

Just one year later, another group of scientists split off from Shockley when they found out the company was not prepared to continue silicon wafer research. This group colloquially known as '*the traitorous 8*' self-funded a start-up to continue the research until they managed to attract investment from the Fairchild Camera and Instrument Corporation giving birth to Fairchild Semiconductor.[264] One of these scientists was Gordon E Moore who went on to found chip megalith Intel.

From these, small beginnings grew today's semi-conductor industry, which was later to be followed by the communications, database handler, mobile phone platform and software industries. This litany of industries is testament to how Silicon Valley has re-invented itself numerous times over the past 70 years as both firms and technologies have waxed and waned. Much of the initial impetus in the 1950s came from military (mainly US navy) contracts, which over time were replaced by Defence Advanced Research Projects Agency (DARPA) and other Federal Government Research programs. Some of the later programmes were undertaken at Stamford University (who also helped to commercialise products if they could) and some by DARPA research initiatives.

As the importance of the technologies in Silicon Valley grew, around the turn of the 1980s, the area started to suck in and create its own venture capital ecosystem. One long standing and key player in the Silicon Valley Venture Capital world is Marc Andreessen, who in the early 1990's was working as a software engineer and co-founded internet browsing company Netscape. Closeness between business, entrepreneur, university and venture capitalist typifies the Silicon Valley ecosystem.[265]

Whilst government basic research has been a key ingredient,[266] commercialisation has been built by a group of individuals who in some cases have worn several hats. They may have been academics, entrepreneurs or business people. Some of them, after cashing in their rewards from their own entrepreneurial companies became Venture Capitalists in their own right. These individuals know the business, the market, the technologies and have the funds, connections and risk appetite to break new ground. If we roll the clock back five centuries we have, with the exception of the university connection, the same dynamics working in the London Company of the Merchant Adventurers as they changed their membership, products and trading locations to make sure they were leading the sixteenth-century cloth market.

England in the final quarter of the eighteenth century as today in Silicon Valley. In the late eighteenth century risk capital had a supportive relationship with entrepreneurs through the catalytic role that it played. For example the Truro based Praed Bank had a key role in the introduction of the Steam Engine into the Cornish Copper Industry. This is described in **Box 20**.

The Funding Paradox

Our story of eighteenth-century Cornish steam engines reaffirms that to achieve success the innovating firm needs an idea or invention that can solve a customer need; a connection to the customers and markets that can

Box 20. A Cornish Copper-bottomed Bank?

The introduction of the Watt–Boulton steam engine represents one of the foundation events in the English Industrial Revolution. The change incorporates both an invention (a new steam engine) and an innovation in the business model created to promote its adoption.

Invention occurs when there is a technical insight that changes the rules of a technical process to create something new.[267] Innovation occurs when an invention or change of a substantive kind is applied into a business model.[268] Watt's invention of a separate external steam condenser transformed potential steam engine efficiencies when compare to the existing Newcomen Engine technology. Having invented the external steam condenser in 1765, Watt was only able to gain modest financial backing until finally with one of his partners Roebuck going bankrupt, Boulton a Birmingham manufacturer become involved. Boulton had varied interests including a factory making parts for Newcomen engines (providing the context) and a loss-making coal mine that was about to fail because it could not pump out the water flooding it fast enough with the existing Newcomen engine technology (so he knew the market).[269] Boulton also created an innovative payment model that allowed customers to buy the engine in instalments which were calculated as a share of the savings the customer was making on their energy bill by using the new more efficient engine.

The new steam engine started to look viable. By 1780, 50% of Watt–Boulton pumping engines had been installed in Cornwall. This raises the question as to why the engine was adopted so rapidly in Cornwall?

The answer to this puzzle lies with the 1771 founded Praed Bank. The owners of this bank were experts in the copper mining industry, copper markets and in finance. The bank itself had few depositors, and all of these were wealthy individuals, looking for good returns. Understanding both the market and the current cost pressures in the business, the bank applied its knowledge and funds to finance both the Watt–Boulton engine's introduction into Cornish Copper mines, and provide support for the manufacturers Boulton and Watt when they were facing cash flow problems in 1781.[270]

Our story has one inventor (Watt), an entrepreneurial industrialist (Boulton) who is the innovator and an entrepreneurial venture capitalist (Praed County Bank) who innovated the financing. The story evokes a late-twentieth-century parallel with the formative years of Google. In 1999/2000, this company had its inventors Brin and Page who had tried various funding routes unsuccessfully, until finding entrepreneur

Bechtolsheim who provided their seed funding and then starting to work
with leading venture capitalists such as Sequoia Capital who gave them
money and a market link with Yahoo.[271]

persuade them to start using the innovation; long-term risk finance to fund
the product, plus the operational competence to deliver the result. It is para-
doxical, that although the UK is home to one of the great global financial
hubs (the City of London), access to affordable and appropriate finance is
challenging for many UK start-ups and high growth companies. The lucky
companies that can find finance are generally in sectors favoured by Venture
Capitalists at that point in time, whilst the unlucky ones – however good
their business plan – can struggle to attract funding in the early years.

Why should such a funding paradox exist? Savers are complaining they
cannot obtain realistic returns on their savings, and entrepreneurs complain
they cannot find funding. Entrepreneurs with successful companies offer better returns than interest on savings accounts, don't the two just need to be
matched? Is this mismatch simply a case of market failure or is there something else going on? **Box 21** explores this issue.

LONG-TERM FINANCIAL RETURNS NEED SUCCESSFUL BUSINESSES

Quality long-term financial returns are underpinned by the growth of successful
and innovative businesses. For savers to be assured of returns on their savings,
the 'national income' needs to be protected by a constant flow of successful
businesses evolving; as old ones become uncompetitive, new ones are already
growing to take their place. We have seen that dynamic 'mould changing'
businesses need financial institutions that are capable of injecting funds to cover
early year losses and that allow them to invest in the assets they need to drive
growth.

Detaching financial markets from entrepreneurs may allow a short-term
rise in financial returns as assets are sold and R&D and innovation are pared

Box 21. Are Modern Banks Capitalist?

CAPITALISM (MASS NOUN)

Definition: a system of allocating capital to entrepreneurs who anticipate risk adjusted profits in excess of the ruling rate of interest thereby demonstrating their proposed product or service will profitably meet a customer need (Author definition).

Our definition aligns to Schumpeter's view that Capitalism is *'the practice of financing enterprise by bank credit, i.e. by money (notes or deposits) manufactured for that purpose'* (Schumpeter Capitalism, Socialism and Democracy 1942, p. 167). Capitalism is about allocating capital to the best productive use. We have a clear example of this (**Box 20**) in the operations of the Praed Bank as it took savings and allocated them to funding the entrepreneurial business activity of buying steam engines to raise productivity and profits in the Cornish Copper Mining Industry. We have a similar example of financial institutions, this time Venture Capital funds at the turn of the millennium allocating funds to develop and grow Google. This is Adam Smith's 'invisible hand at work'.[272]

Smith, insightful as ever repeatedly makes the point as to how money and human motivation are tied together. *As soon as the land of any country has all become private property, the landlords, like all other men, love to reap where they never sowed, and demand a rent even for its natural produce* (Smith, The Wealth of Nations, 1776: Book 1 Ch 6 v08). To generalise Smith's statement, wealth owners like to have a good return from their wealth and a steady income regardless of whether they have sowed the seeds of profitability through capital investment or not. Smith helps to explain why modern financial markets have such a short term, rather than a long-term view.

Savers want safe, risk-free returns for their money so they deposit it in the bank. Outside balances at banks the saver may deploy their funds to seek a capital gain in stocks and shares, property, Exchange Traded Funds or the myriad of other financial products available to them, but on the basis that 'the market' will provide a capital gain. Many of the common types of investments have the benefit that the saver can exit them through the market as they are traded on a regular basis. Direct investments into the visions of entrepreneurs are however different. They are not easily tradable and with no market history existing upon which to assess likely returns.

These attributes have led to financial markets and entrepreneurs becoming to some extent disconnected, as money flows into supposedly 'safer' financial assets packaged from predicable cash flows.[273] The consequence is money deployed from savings is going into second hand assets not to support the entrepreneur. Paradoxically more cash chasing returns from the same assets and associated cash flows leads to financial bubbles and associated crashes.[274]

In the early nineteenth century when the capitalist motor was industrialising Britain, UK banks still funded industrial companies, often along the lines we have seen with the Praed Bank. A number of banks failed and there were voluble protests from savers that their savings were being invested in risky industries, especially if the bank went bankrupt. Two examples of these complaints can be found in the discourse around the Royal British Bank which collapsed in 1856 and the Aberdeen Banking company that failed in 1849, where depositors were far from happy how their funds had been lent.[275] Over the second half of the nineteenth century, UK banks gradually withdrew from their capital provision function[276] so that by the time of the 1930 Macmillan Commission banks had become disconnected from entrepreneurs. The lending flows and advice and nurturing of management evident in the work of the Praed bank had long gone, as demonstrated in the comment by Sir W. Guy Granet '*I do not see how you can secure a really effective connection that finds the money and the management ... It is not your function to supervise management, and when I am told that the German banks have done it I wonder if it is effective*' (Macmillan Evidence, 1931, p. 221).

The disconnection of banking from the capitalist motor that drives funds to the best entrepreneurs has, (as the Macmillan Committee found), constrained risk finance to entrepreneurs. Recent years have seen policy initiatives to address this gap with the formation of the British Business Bank; although, ensuring adequate funding is available for all types of entrepreneurship, especially in the early entrepreneurial growth remains a concern.

By contrast, Silicon Valley has ensured the continued 'capitalist' allocation of funds to entrepreneurs as it has grown its own venture capital ecosystem thereby mimicking the successful long forgotten example of Truro's Praed Bank in the late 1770's.

back and share buybacks return funds to shareholders; but in the long run without new products, R&D, applied innovation and associated capital and skills investment, competitiveness is lost and eventually returns to shareholders dry up. Box 22 presents a case study of such a situation.

Box 22. Electric Shock? The British Eveready Battery Company

For many over the age of 50, 'Eveready' batteries will conjure up memories of their childhood; buying batteries from local corner shops to power all manner of trinkets, but most especially torches and bicycle lamps. Some will also remember the colloquial joke of the 1980s and 1990s that the battery in this year's Christmas present would not last as long as Boxing Day. Unfortunately, this joke reflected an uncomfortable truth for Eveready; namely that their products did not move with the times, so they did not convert to the newer 'longer life' alkaline battery as manufactured by Duracell.

Towards the end of the 1960s, it is estimated that Eveready had over 90% of the UK battery market. It was investing in new technology and in 1973 was one of the pioneers in the new alkaline battery technology that became the backbone of Duracell. The company had recently opened the Tanfield Lea manufacturing plant in County Durham, which in addition to providing jobs for displaced miners, aligned to the company's goal to become the world's largest battery manufacturer. The plant and the company focused on manufacturing zinc carbon batteries most of which were exported globally. In the early 1970s, a rigid bureaucratic management refused to capitalise on the alkaline battery development at its large London-based laboratory and doubled down on manufacturing old technology zinc carbon products, notwithstanding that new electronic devices were coming to market that needed the longer lasting power of the alkaline battery. The company also failed to adapt its sales strategy and packaging to support supermarket sales, instead relying on the shrinking corner shop retail segment to give an outlet for its product. Making a product which was inferior to the competitor and was not available through one of the key sales channels was always likely to be a less than successful strategy.

Events started to take over. 1977 was a bad year for the company as the Monopolies and Mergers Commission forced them to sell their holding in Mallory Battery (maker of Duracell) to reduce their market dominance. At around the same time, Nigeria stopped buying batteries from Eveready, overnight removing nearly 50% of the demand from the Tanfield Lea Factory. The company tried to adapt by starting alkaline battery production in yet another factory and, introducing a zinc chloride battery at Tanfield Lea. The Zinc Chloride technology (which had been a local management 'skunk works' project undertaken away from the central R&D operation) had a better life than the Zinc Carbon product but crucially could be manufactured on the same equipment, so reducing the need for capital investment.

In 1981, Hanson Trust a US/UK conglomerate took control and started to slash costs and close central functions including the R&D operation. Overseas subsidiaries were sold and the company was focused on delivering short-term profits using the technology and assets that remained. Although Hanson attempted to reposition Eveready as a 'full range' producer by branding products as gold and silver seal, this distinction was too complex for consumers, who preferred Duracell's long-life association. A cycle of non-investment, staff redundancies and failures to prospect and open new markets followed, leading to Ever Ready's decline and eventual sale to US giant Ralston Purina, owner of global battery maker Energiser. Hanson made money with Eveready throughout its ownership; with for example a 1990 financial return on sales of 30%.[277] The final step in the story came with the 1996 announcement of the closure of Tanfield Lea, a factory recognised to have one of the best productivity records in the industry, but due to lack of appropriate investment no longer aligned to meeting global customer needs.[278] A case study in short-term financial gain, an entrepreneurial gap and with a consequence in the end of a business that had flourished for many years after its founding in 1914.

Silicon Valley, unlike Eveready, has constantly adapted itself to changes in its main markets. Why has Silicon Valley been so successful at constant reinvention?

INNOVATING NEW MARKETS IN THE FACE OF UNCERTAINTY

A key element in the Silicon Valley story has been how it has managed to keep re-inventing itself. One important contributor to both starting the entrepreneurial ball rolling and maintaining its momentum at crucial moments has been the positive influence of US Federal Government research and procurement programmes. In the 1950s much of the activity in Silicon Valley was enabled by both government contracts from the US Navy and its technology links with Stamford University. In the 1960s DARPA, and activities around the 1960s Space Program, became important growth engines. In the 1980s, it was networking and in the new millennium, it has been smart phone platforms that have served to spur the regions continued growth. Now, future growth engines may well include artificial intelligence, driverless cars and home and factory automation through the 'internet of things'.

Throughout these years of 'hothouse innovation', Silicon Valley companies have benefited from being a focal point for Federal development contracts, Federal funded pure scientific research and also from links into the 'Bay Area' (especially Stamford University) human capital repositories. One example of how these elements have come together is in the genesis of the Apple iPhone.[279] According to Mazzucato, the iPhone narrative is 'peppered' with innovation case studies where the Federal Government has had some nurturing role. In performing this catalytic function, the State has taken risks the market could not bear and become the *technical innovator of first resort*. At the early stages of developing new product paradigms, the technical actor of the first resort plays an essential anchor role thereby helping to nurture other ingredients for the entrepreneurial soup. By combining these various elements and adding its own venture capital capability, Silicon Valley has – over the years – evolved into a single self-sustaining entrepreneurial cluster. These dynamics involve a complex interrelation between the state, universities, firms and venture capitalists. The model is akin to a 'Triple Helix Innovation Model'[280] although with a fourth participant in Venture Capital.

The Triple Helix Innovation Model emphasises the role played and complexity of the multiple connections between different participants in the innovation system. Conversations can happen across all elements of this structure, and at any point, a connection may be made that leads to a new innovation or new product. A key feature of this model is the blurring of lines of individual competence and their recombination into a task focused deliverable. In a sense, this is another way to describe Mission Based Innovation where innovation becomes goal focused rather than organisation focused. Removing organisational barriers opens the way to 'objectives' rather than process driven connections. These ties allow novel resource combinations that then raise the chances of innovation success beyond the capabilities of any specific organisation.

Dealing with Uncertainty and Risk

All chances of innovation success are evaluated against an uncertain future and as a consequence, innovative products and service will always be associated with some risk profile as to whether or not they may succeed. This risk may be predictable (so testable against known statistics) or it may be in a sense unknown as it cannot be predicated by modelling and thereby in a sense random. This second type of risk links to "Knightian Uncertainty" that cannot be assessed by statistical paradigms, which makes it difficult for rational market actors to bear.

The state acting in a role as *'innovator of the first resort'* has a significant positive role to play in reducing this second type of risk and thereby making entrepreneurial innovations market fundable. In the USA, defence projects agency (DARPA) has played a key role in this respect.

Whether or not the risk is predictable, much time and effort has been spent over the past 40 years in creating 'risk models' to predicate risk incidence and impacts. These models combine extensive amounts of historic data with mathematical constructs (algorithms) and use computing power to try to predict outcomes. The models rely on having good and relevant data and assumptions. Events and experience have taught us such models are only as good as their assumptions, and by definition as our understanding of the world, which then introduces the concept of pure uncertainty.[281] 'Black Swan Events'[282] where the analyst has misread the impact of outlying observations as being irrelevant could also (if they had been recognised) have acted as the canaries in the coal mine warning that an assumption or view is in error. Even if modelled in the greatest of detail, innovation projects are always risky, and always open to the unexpected. An alternative or complimentary strategy to modelling is to network with others to test ideas and assumptions.

Even innovation networks that allow free interconnection and bring together different technologies to create new products and in some cases, new markets may not be enough to overcome the uncertainty barrier to moving forward. In these circumstances, innovators need an anchor risk taker to help bring the opportunity to market. For example, who could have guessed the market impact of GPS technology in say 1985, barely half way through the initial military project? The risks cannot be modelled or understood, so the market cannot bear them, and at that point the state needs to add a 'market creation' role to its existing tasks of addressing market failures.[283]

Part of innovation risk is reduced by combining the right resources for the goal, part of it is dealt with by studious modelling of known variables, and part of it is so great that it needs help from an external actor. In these cases (usually groundbreaking technologies), the uncertainty needs to be mitigated by sharing the risk with the State. The US Federal organisation DARPA is an example of how this 'market creation role' has successfully helped the Silicon Valley narrative from the late 1950s onwards, as DARPA started to transform direct armed services innovation procurement into a dynamic innovation system. This role is described in **Box 23** and exposes DARPA's role as *innovator of the first resort*.

Silicon Valley is not unique. Other clusters have grown in other industries in other countries. For example, South Korea moved from a 1960 GDP per

---

Box 23. DARPA – A State Venture Capitalist of the 'First Resort'

US agency DARPA contracts private companies to develop new technologies with maybe 250 programmes under way at any given time. In 'top drawer' private sector venture capital tradition it provides the SME's with both money and helps 'plug gaps' in technical expertise. Two key elements in its success are a willingness to contract SMEs (who may have the best innovation skills) whilst managing the programmes with programme managers rotated in from 'big' industry and research institutes on a three to five-year cycle (long enough to be effective, short enough to have up to date knowledge). This cross fertilisation brings together government, industry and research skills whilst embedding the innovation back into industry and research institutes. DARPA's budget is about US$2.5bn and it has had many successes including innovating the precursor to the Global Positioning System (GPS).

Prior to his inauguration as the 34th President of the USA, Dwight Eisenhower was president of Columbia University (1948–1953). Eisenhower's time at Colombia was not without controversy, punctuated as it was by his activity with the Council of Foreign Relations (CFR).[284] His work at the CFR focused on the implications of the Marshall Plan and the American Assembly; an area that he was particularly keen on and helped shape his later position on economic policies. Eisenhower saw the potential in the Council to become a great cultural centre where business and governmental leaders could meet to discuss and reach conclusions concerning problems of a social and political nature.[285]

Perhaps not as successful an academic administrator as his brother Milton (widely regarded as one of the most successful presidents of John Hopkins University) Dwight Eisenhower put his Colombia experiences to good use when, in 1958 as a direct response to the Soviet's success in launching Sputnik American President, Eisenhower, funded, the DARPA. He was acutely aware that the US was in danger of falling behind its Cold War rival in technological achievement, especially in the technologies of war fighting and defence. DAPRA's role was to fund and coordinate research programmes carried out by the military, private industry and academia to fulfil its mission of avoiding and creating technological surprise. Today, the agency claims that it has spearheaded initiatives that *changed the world* – a phrase frequently heard at DARPA to ensure a focus on trans-formative innovation as opposed to incremental improvements in existing technologies.[286]

DARPA's achievements include developing both technology and human capital. Its officers not only increase the flow of knowledge among research groups, but also engage in increasing the pool of scientists and engineers available to propel innovations into the market. The agency funded the establishment of computer science departments at universities across the USA; thereby acting as a catalyst for groundbreaking research and development undertaken by industry and academia.[287]

capita of US$944 to over US$24,000 by 2016[ix] thereby transforming itself economically from the bottom 25% of countries to being in the top 25%;[288] a radical and rapid transformation. The mix was different from Silicon Valley, possibly because South Korea focused on a sector by sector approach. The first phase in the 1960s saw private business forced to estab-lish companies (with part state ownership) to generate a heavy industry clus-ter. Capital controls were imposed and Foreign Direct Investment restricted to sectors where technology transfer could be obtained; the banking sector was nationalised and then directed to make available subsidised funds to industry for capital investment in incrementally higher value adding

---

[ix]All amounts in constant purchasing price 2010 US Dollars.

industries. Time limited import restrictions were used to provide short-term protection whilst competitiveness was raised to international levels. The second phase came in the 1980s as banks were privatised, and moves were made towards trade liberalisation. Government action moved from direct financing towards tax and grant incentives. The State's role was reduced as self-sustaining momentum had built up and the industrial cluster became capable of surviving alone.[289]

THE IMPORTANCE OF HUMAN CAPITAL

Areas that have built significant innovation clusters have combined research and development (and in cases such as South Korea industrial) policies with a focus on 'Up-skilling' local resources. High quality labour force skills are an important contributor to competitive advantage. These skills can be "home grown" and in some cases, such as for example in Silicon Valley imported through immigration.

STUDIO I: THE INNOVATION CANVAS

The first part of our journey was through a museum where we focused on revealing Brexits past and present. In doing so, we have now arrived at a new space that we refer to as an 'Art Studio.' It looks interesting and avoids the need to head for the transition corridor just yet.

We find ourselves in a sizable room with a number of huge canvases that are in a state of constant change. New brushstrokes appear as we study a particular canvas. The first one is the 'Innovation Canvas'. Now we have the freedom to draw our own picture, what do we want to create?

One immediate question is what is the connection between innovation and entrepreneurship and the current debate around Brexit. How does our fast changing global innovation canvas align to the outcomes of the debate about sovereignty, repelling foreigners from the beaches and re-establishing British Empire free trade?

Then, there is a hint of the connection as we recall the entrepreneurial characters we met on our travels through Elizabeth I's Brexit. Here are individuals, albeit in a different age, being empowered to drive success and solve problems by a State intent on working in partnership with them. What a different picture from the brilliant legal mind of Thomas Cromwell, or the instability of the Pilgrimage of Grace, or the bitter sectarian splits of the sixteenth century, or from the changes at the end of Roman Britain. Our Elizabethan age entrepreneurs are busy building business, making things better while working hand in hand with a State that wants to help and support them.

Then we see someone waving a napkin with the Laffer Curve drawn on it, and we hear another muttering that there is too much State and what's really needed is the Lawson Doctrine of *State Austerity*. We are prompted to ask what is the mechanism that will connect these seductive claims of low tax and a minimalist state to the innovators or tomorrow? We see the cuts in the State, but where are funds for entrepreneurs from the banks? Instead of reaching our entrepreneur they are diverted to funding house prices young people cannot afford, to funding large existing companies through bond issues that are sometimes used to fund share buybacks and so on and so forth.

And then we glance back at the innovation canvas, and we see how success comes from entrepreneurs who use capital to innovate new products and how these new innovations often require State and University support at their riskiest early stages. We are reminded that capitalism is not about whether business is in private or public ownership. Capitalism is about driving capital to entrepreneurs who deliver the innovations that customers want by offering entrepreneurs profits when they meet consumer needs.

Upon reflection, our Brexit Innovation Canvas needs to be filled with a picture showing how all the actors in the UK economic model can be mixed together to help build the UK into the top entrepreneurial innovation cluster in the world. In other words don't we need our Brexit Innovation Canvas to unlock UK Entrepreneurial Exceptionalism?

7

THE GENERATIONAL DIVIDE

The UK already has and will continue to have an ageing population; with numbers of old people rising as post second world war "baby boomers" age in the face of birth rates that are less than those needed to replace the existing population. This change in the population profile can be seen in Chart 1 below.

Chart 1. Forecast UK Population.

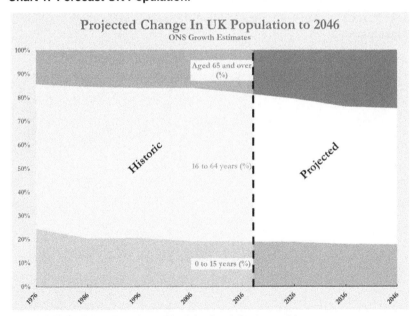

Source: ONS (2017a) contains National Statistics data © Crown copyright.

Note: UK Office of National Statistics population projections published in 2017 assume a continuing high rate of net immigration into the UK. These assumptions are reflected in Chart 1.

This rapidly changing population demographic has much in common with many other developed countries, as population ages in response to birth rate falls from the 1960's onwards and the dying off of the post war 'baby boomers'. In the millennium years these changes have to some extent been compensated for by immigration. Our two charts differ in the way we treat anticipated immigration. In Chart 1 we present forecast population trends on the assumption that pre- Referendum levels of net immigration continue. In our second chart (Chart 2) we take into account likely reductions in post Referendum immigration, thereby seeing a steeper fall in the 16−64 working age population from 63.1% in 2016 to 55.3% in 2036 than in Chart 1. Overall, the working population continues to fall until it reaches 53.9% in 2046. Less working age inhabitants mean less potential value adding inhabitants to generate national income to satisfy the aspirations of all. Box 24 indicates the extent of productivity improvements required to cope with this challenge.

Chart 2. UK Population Change Using Author-adjusted Net Immigration Estimates.

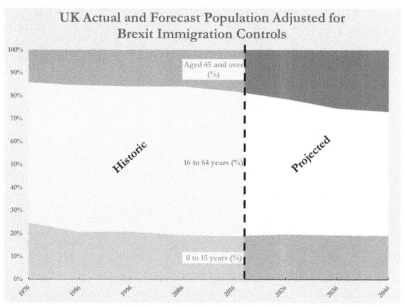

Source: ONS (2017a) contains National Statistics data © Crown copyright, Author Immigration adjustments.

Note: Net immigration patterns especially form the EU after the 2016 Referendum cast doubt on these assumptions. Chart 2 is produced under adjusted assumptions that see overall net immigration into the UK fall to 100,000 a year from 2016 forwards.

Box 24. How Will the UK Pay for Its Elderly?

Broadly speaking, we can estimate changes in living standards by looking at how GDP per person changes over time.[290] In 2016, each member of the UK workforce added US$85,783 (at 2010 prices) of GDP to the UK economy.[291] Additionally, the UK has a relatively high level of labour force participation at 77.3% of working age adults (ranking the UK at number 22 globally, just behind Germany at 77.9% and ahead of other global developed nations such as the United States at 73% or France at 71.4%).[292]

The authors suggest that if living standards stay exactly as today, then if the average increase in labour productivity (output per labour hour) from the last seven years is maintained for each year over the next 25 years. Projected GDP increases, in this scenario, will just about cope with the rise in elderly people, providing they do not consume any more resources such as health. Equally, the rest of the population will need to be prepared to accept that it will have no improvement in its standard of living over this period.

This projection seems unrealistic as we know the elderly consume more health care than young, that health care is innovating new and in many cases more costly treatments (that in turn can lead to more prolonged life spans) and that the English and Welsh health services are already believed to be underfunded.

An inevitable conclusion is that the overall rate of productivity will need to significantly rise if old people are to maintain their living standards and have access to the healthcare they have come to expect, let alone there being any rise in living standards for the working population whose efforts will be funding the retired.

Such a situation is likely to be unsustainable. If incomes need to grow faster than before, then, short of some magic windfall gain (such as happened with privateers seizing Spanish treasure ships in the 1580's), productivity will need to rise. This poses the question as to how challenging will it be to raise the rate of productivity growth? Overall growth in value adding (another way of viewing productivity growth) depends upon the productivity of all the firms in the economy. **Table 3** associates the UK productivity in each industry with the job creation capability of that industry. On a sector by sector basis, there are a total of 67 sectors; strikingly the UK has become good at creating jobs in lower productivity sectors.

Inevitably some sectors offer better opportunities to raise productivity than others. For example, someone working in a personal services business such as hairdressing may have less opportunity to raise productivity than a person working in advanced manufacturing. Even if labour force participation rises, strong improvements in per capita income need more people in work to be combined with improved productivity. The UK's tendency to create jobs in lower productivity sectors inevitably means per capital income growth will be lower than if the jobs were being created in sectors with better productivity records.

Table 3. Top 20 Job Creation Sectors and Associated Productivity Rank.

Rank	Industry	2015–2016		2016
		Jobs Created	% Workforce	Productivity Rank
1	Human health activities	109,000	5.1	45
2	Food and beverage service activities	68,000	4.2	60
3	Computer programming, consultancy and related activities	60,000	9.6	37
4	Land transport and transport via pipelines	59,000	11.3	53
5	Warehousing and support activities for transportation	47,000	10.0	54
6	Other professional, scientific and technical activities	46,000	27.4	47
7	Civil engineering	39,000	21.3	35
8	Office administrative, office support and other business support activities	39,000	8.4	50
9	Employment activities	36,000	3.9	64
10	Activities of head offices; management consultancy activities	35,000	4.8	55

Source: ONS 2018e and ONS 2018f contain National Statistics data © Crown copyright plus author analysis.

FUNDING RETIRED PEOPLE

For many people now in their 70s, retired and in receipt of a defined benefit company pension, a 'triple locked' state pension, free health care and owning valuable houses; it must seem inconceivable that their situation could in the event of severe economic difficulties, transform itself into becoming financially challenged. Yet the payments they receive are only as stable as the returns and tax revenues being generated in the economy.

Pensioners as a group have been the winners from the post-2008 crash years. Analysis suggests that average pensioner income is 13.5% above its 2007–2008 level, as compared to a 3.6% rise in non-pensioner incomes.[293] This increase has come partly from rising pensioner state benefits (a rise of 10.1%) and partly from an increase in investment income and associated private pensions (rising of 12.6%).[294] Additional indirect funding increases have also been flowing to pensioners via spending increases to the National Health Service to cope with the ageing population.

Pensioners owning a house, have done even better with the average UK house price (notwithstanding strong regional variations) rising around 21% from January 2008 to January 2018 to stand at £225,185.[295] **Table 4** indicates pensioner welfare costs at £120 + bn or 46% of the welfare budget in 2016/2017. £110bn of this, was for the old age pension and the rest for adult social care. This cost can be compared with the £16.7 billion estimated cost of student University Tuition Fees[296] or £2.2bn of unemployment support shown in 2017.

Welfare spending is paid for from general taxation and occupational pension flows come from pension fund returns on the investments (some of which come from interest payments on government debt and some from commercial rents, dividends and bond interest payments). With an estimated 53% of buy-to-let landlords aged over 55, it is likely that other assets a richer pensioner include one or more such properties.[297]

Table 5 analyses 2017 pensioner incomes, showing a total of 51% pensioners in the top half of the income distribution in 2017.[298] In summary, pensioners' lifestyles depend upon (1) the continued generosity of taxpayers to fund them in preference to their own personal priorities, (2) returns from financial markets and (3) the level of house prices and the housing market. **Box 25** explores the risks to private pension income sources for pensioners.

Table 4. UK Welfare Spending.

Rank	UK Gov. Spending Actuals £ Millions (Current Price)	£ Millions 2012–2013	£ Millions 2016–2017	£ Millions Change	% Change 2012–2013 to 2016–2017
1	Old age	112, 308	121,577	9,269	8.3
2	Sickness and disability	45,301	53,275	7,974	17.6
3	Working welfare (tax & universal credit)	32,373	32,151	−222	−0.7
4	Housing	26,361	25,390	−971	−3.7
5	Family and children	26,566	24,385	−2,181	−8.2
6	Social protection n.e.c.	3,808	4,131	323	8.5
7	Unemployment	5,939	2,227	−3,712	−62.5
8	Survivors	792	1,160	368	46.5
	Total social protection	253,448	264,296	10,848	4.3

Source: ONS (2016) contains National Statistics data © Crown copyright.
n.e.c., not elsewhere covered.

Table 5. Pensioner Incomes in 2017.

Gross Income	100 (%)
Benefit income	43
Occupational pension income	30
Personal pension income	4
Investment income	7
Earnings income	16
Other income	1

Source: ONS (2018g) contains National Statistics data © Crown copyright.

As firms allocate funds to make good pension fund deficits, the consequence can be a squeeze on other expenditure such as capital investment or wage increases. Unsurprisingly, over recent years, the labour share of national income has remained roughly constant whilst wages have been

Box 25. Pension Scheme Funding Risks

A total of 41% of pensioner incomes depend on returns from financial markets. This is made up of supervised defined benefit occupational schemes (30%) which are far more secure than the remaining 11% which relate to defined contribution schemes (that only pay out the investment returns they earn). For society as a whole the imperative of ensuring that pensioner income derived from defined benefit schemes is safe has had two significant negative impacts.

First a 'safety first' approach by regulators and accounting standards bodies has meant pension funds have increasingly avoided investing in higher risk assets. By definition, investments to fund capital investment or innovation are riskier than existing assets with known payment flows. Following the adoption of accounting standard IAS 19R[299] in 2013, pension funds started to pull away from risker assets like stocks and shares. Pension funds relating to 90 companies quoted on the German stock market were assessed for the impact of this change. Especially for less well funded and smaller pension funds, there was a shift from riskier assets (equities) into safer ones (bonds), thereby reducing overall fund volatility.[300] Whilst patterns may differ across countries and different fund managers, the effect seems to have been to restrict opportunities for pension saving flows to be used to fund capital investment in new technologies, products and growth. Instead these same funds ended up being invested in existing assets (such as stocks and shares) so that they benefit from payments existing company cash flows.[301] More demand for existing assets implicitly reduces the rate of interest on these assets so exacerbating needs for higher pension fund contributions to maintain pension fund solvency.

Depending upon existing assets for cash returns reduces the overall funding pool available for entrepreneurial projects. Funding flows that could be used to finance some forms of capital investment (such as large infrastructure projects) are to some extent diverted into existing lower risk assets. Paradoxically the desire to protect pensioners from short term risks depressess the financial flows that support their pensions in the long term.

The second negative effect is that as rates of return fall (resulting from the process described above), scheme sponsors are required to divert more resources to top up these schemes. These pension fund top ups put pressure on the firms available resources to fund operating costs (including wages), shareholder dividends, capital investment and innovation. In another paradigm, these resources could have been reinvested in innovation or used to increase real wages.

> In both cases, short-term regulatory imperatives to protect pensioners drive down the rate of return on pension assets and suck resources out of the productive sector to top up pension scheme deficits. This problem will go away in 20 or so years' time after most of the Defined Benefit Pension scheme beneficiaries have died off.

squeezed and pension contributions have risen. Inventive as ever, people look to see if they can perhaps raise their wealth in a different way.

Two other interconnected avenues exist to invest in the hope of making 'capital gains'. First, by investing in the housing market and second, by trading assets in financial markets. The logic in both these cases is that the value of the asset is determined in the market and thus reflects what someone will pay for it. When markets boom, everyone is richer and there is a belief that the higher asset values will be set in stone. Unfortunately, in asset markets, the traded price of an asset may sometimes not match its underlying direct or implied cashflows. Such mismatches are the raw material of the 'bubbles' and subsequent crashes discussed in **Box 26.**

ENTITLEMENT CULTURE

In the United States, key programmes that support the elderly are called 'entitlements' implying that access to the programme of benefits is a 'right' for someone of a specific age. The narrative then runs that old age support programmes as 'rights' cannot be cut, because these rights have been earned over each person's working life. The narrative around the UK payroll tax, National Insurance supports this concept, notwithstanding that old age benefits and health care are funded from current public expenditure and not from reserves in a ring-fenced National Insurance Pension Fund.

There are some early indications that there may beginning to be a recognition in the United States that balancing the Federal and State budgets will be very difficult without some change in 'senior entitlement' programmes. This is very challenging to politicians as this is an area where the 'newer old', (i.e. those just turned 65 and about to turn 65) are more politically engaged and vocally forceful than many older people in the generations before them.[308]

Box 26. Bubbles and Crashes

Financial markets can and do sometimes mis-price specific assets when the valuations are compared to the cash that will eventually flow to investors from these assets. It was the incorrect financial market valuation of sub prime mortgage bonds (that failed to reflect the recoverability of these mortgages) that led to the 2008 financial crash. One day, the market woke up and realised that these sub-prime bonds may not be worth what people were paying for them and their value crashed.

Markets relying on cash coming from companies that are not innovating and investing in the right long-term products and technologies are likely to see the value of their investment decline if products and technologies are not kept up to date. For example, the 2018 failure of outsourcing company Carillion Plc can be said to demonstrate how out of line its early 2017 market valuation was with its future realisable profits and associated cashflows. Owners of Carillion stock and bonds then lost the bulk of their money.

Some argue that market prices necessarily reflect the real underlying values of an asset, as markets are rational and efficient.[302] This does beg the question that if markets are so good at pricing perfectly, why are there financial bubbles and financial crashes? How could financial markets have missed some of the warning signals on the failure of UK contractor Carillion Plc?[303]

That markets can wrongly value assets in comparison to their long-term cash generating capability is synonymous with the 'Ponzi Stage' of a financial bubble described by Minsky in his narrative on Financial Instability.[304] In this scenario, assets are valued on compounded speculative hopes rather than cashflow. Unless cash and profit expectations are met, financial adjustment will eventually follow. This point underpins arguments that market values can diverge from underlying economic and societal values, and that price rather than reflecting underlying value can become disconnected from the underlying fundamentals.[305] Inflated asset values, otherwise known as 'bubbles' are the seed corn of financial crashes. This sets the stage for an assessment of UK housing wealth.

Housing markets depend upon a flow of buyers who can afford to buy. **Chart 3** shows how houses in the UK have become less affordable when compared to average incomes.

Chart 3. Housing Affordability.

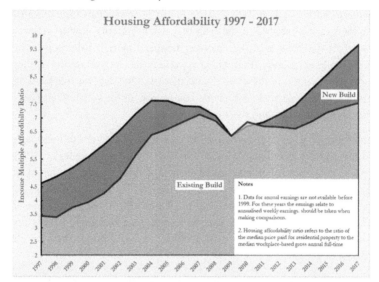

Source: ONS (2018h) contains National Statistics data © Crown copyright.

This chart shows how the multiples of average earnings to UK house prices have risen from around 3.5 times earnings to 7.6 times earnings in the 20 years from 1997. The 2017 ratio for newly built houses is even higher at 9.68, possibly reflecting the subsidy available to home buyers of new property from the governments 'Help to Buy' scheme. An investigation found that much of this subsidy has resulted in house builders raising prices by maybe as much as £8,500 per house and thereby improving their profit margins.[306]

Chart 4 shows how the over 65-year-olds' share of home ownership has risen from 24% to 35% from 2003 to 2017, while the later-middle-aged share of owner occupation (45–64 year olds) remained static at 41% and the under-45s' share has fallen from 35% to 24%. The falling share of young people owning their own homes has driven a fall in overall home ownership from 72% to 63% in 14 years.

Chart 4. Owner Occupation across Age Groups.

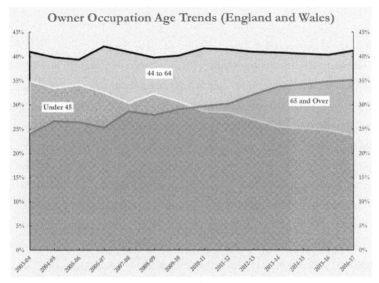

Source: National Statistics data © Crown copyright (ONS, 2018i).

Sustaining house prices depends on there being buyers who can afford to buy them. Stretched affordability ratios coupled with stagnant real wages are already leading to sharp declines in home ownership. Long term this mismatch is likely to challenge existing housing market paradigms.

Resolution can come via one of three avenues: first average working population real wages can rise strongly whilst house prices stay static and so adjust affordability ratios (which requires an implicit rebalance in the distribution of income, welfare system and benefits from economic growth to younger generations). Second the market stops where it is, and with minimal activity it maintains its current balance into the medium term whilst incomes gradually rise over time, so improving affordibilty ratios and third there could be a house price crash that adjusts the affordability ratio by a sharp downward shift in house prices whilst money wages stay at their current levels. In each of these scenarios or in a combination of them, adjustment will be both painful for existing home owners and require a shift in the intergenerational wealth to the younger generation.[307]

Could the same political dynamics regarding old age "entitlement" be at work in the UK?

The 2017 UK General Election saw a sharp intergenerational divide in the way votes were cast. The Conservative Party benefited from 58% of votes from the over 65's and 18% of the 18–24 generation, whilst the Labour party saw the reverse with 23% of pensioners and 66% of 18–24s voting for them. The major switch in voting behavior between the age groups for the parties seems to be around 45 years old, which is coincidently the point where the percentage change home ownership stabilises. Liberal Democratic Party support is broadly constant across all the generations.[309]

How divisive this intergenerational narrative may become, is likely to relate to how successful the UK is at raising productivity and economic growth. Sharing a growing pot of gold is less challenging than arguing over a shrinking one. In a world of low growth, low productivity improvements and relatively more wealthy pensioners, it would be unsurprising if younger generations seek to reduce pensioner entitlements over time. Non divisive solutions as to how an ageing population can be supported are likely to be much easier if the UK can raise growth levels and drive economic success. Pensioners, many of whom may have voted for Brexit on a nostalgic basis and an assumption that they will never lose out economically whatever impact Brexit has, could be in for a rather unwelcome surprise if Brexit decreases rather than raises economic growth rates.

STUDIO II: THE GENERATIONAL CANVAS

Our narrative has exposed a significant shift in both income and housing wealth to pensioners. Most pensioners are not working in paid employment although they may be making significant and important charitable or voluntary contributions to both their families (through caring for grandchildren whilst parents work) and society as a whole. This group are the winners economically of the period since the 2008 crash and they are one of the main groups that voted to leave the European Union. Over 50% of this group are in the top half of the income distribution. For those who are also home owners and are asset rich, their Brexit vote is likely to have been more nostalgic than economic.

The Leave campaign promised this group something for nothing via the pledge of an extra £350 million per week to be given to the National Health Service. The Leave Campaign also offered this group an implicit assurance that there was no risk to their wealth. Negative economic projections were 'Project Fear', and anyway they already owned their houses and pensions already being paid also appear rock solid safe. In summary, for this group voting to leave offered the prospect of combining a satisfaction of nostalgic desires, with a risk free potential bonus in the form of more money for the National Health Service at no cost or risk to them.

Yet this comfortable state of affairs may not be as stable as was advertised. We can see how the over valued housing market is already excluding younger buyers. How would retired property owners feel if their homes lose 30% of their value in a property crash? How would this group react if Brexit leads to economic disruption, reductions in capital investment and business relocations away from the UK that mean both their children and grand children are visibily less well off and their own 'triple locked state pension increases' could come under threat? What happens if the financial sector that is key to assuring their private pension payments faces a sharp adjustment, resulting in substantial losses that cannot be easily borne by the existing 'pensions lifeboat' structure or, where at the same time sponsoring firms cannot afford to make good pension fund deficits?

What happens if young people refuse to divert more of national income to pensioners and want the benefits of growth for themselves?

The canvas we see has some sense of a pensioner aspiring to an idyllic picture of an armchair in front of a warm fire, enjoying their years of rest yet, but superimposed over this picture are a number of large looking question marks. The question marks reflect the interdependency that the pensioners have on support from the younger generations, the generations who will directly face any negative economic consequences of Brexit. One part of this generally younger generation that did vote for Brexit is the 'Left Behind'. It is to the Left Behind of the working generation that we turn in our next chapter.

8

THE LEFT BEHIND

Success Breeds Success

Helps (1868)

Failure breeds Failure. The Seeds they have sown
We are expected to reap

Foundation (2015)

In an analysis of the 2016 Referendum results, part of the narrative behind the 'Leave Vote' is the 'tale' of the Left Behind. This group is statistically correlated to poor educational attainment, denoted by social attitudes aligned to economic insecurity and alienation from the successful.[310] While 59% of the Brexit vote came from the middle classes (albeit a substantial proportion of whom who were over 65) only 21% of the vote came from people identified as having 'routine' or 'semi-routine' jobs (which we take as a proxy to indicate the size of the Left Behind vote).[311] Although not the biggest group in the Leave Vote, the 'Left Behind' are an important, sizable, distinct group. The largest 'pro leave' group are the retired, many of whom are middle class home owners.

DEFINING THE LEFT BEHIND

Having identified there is a 'Left Behind' constituency, how it is defined? One proxy that is regularly used in statistical studies is to measure relative educational attainment in connection with sex and ethnicity. The argument runs that the 'Left Behind' are dominated by white working-class males of low educational attainment. This definition does not stand on its own as the

Left Behind can also be associated with a sense of place or rather a sense of having failed to migrate from a locality.[312] This helps explain the correspondence between strong Brexit voting towns and declining areas. Areas in decline are typically associated with a Leave vote that is around 20 points higher than elsewhere.[313] These areas can also anecdotally be associated with a relatively high deprivation index.[314] **Box 27** paints a picture of one such locality.

Box 27. From Herrings and a Golden Mile to Deprivation and Decay

A chronological record of Great Yarmouth from its founding date in AD 46 through to the nineteenth century paints a picture of a proud town, determined to protect its identity and economy. This was a local port with a substantial herring fishing industry (that it went to war with the fishermen of Kent over) and a keen supporter of the English navy. The town was the welcoming point for more than one Royal, with landings from the Princess of Orange (1795), George II (1737); and if one can count monarchs who were just off shore but were still feted by the town, Queen Victoria steaming nearby in 1844.[315] The town also has a history of independence dating back to a least Edward III[316] that it asserted on a number of occasions. Notwithstanding its loyalty to the Crown, it was often open to playing for its own independent advantage.[317] A proud, well to do town with a distinct and local economy.

Connection to the rest of the UK and the growth of a local tourist industry came with the completion of the railway on 1 May 1844.[318] By 1846, there were 80,000 tourists per annum. This led to a seafront building boom. Subsequently, the tourism industry developed over the next 130 years, with town-based facilities being augmented by the UK's first holiday camp and boating holidays on the nearby Norfolk Broads.[319]

Decline set in the 1970's as the combination of overseas package holidays and a lack of investment in the resort led to falls in visitor numbers. The population composition started to change at the same time, as a significant number of the town's property assets morphed from being hotels into hostel type houses of multiple occupation. Like many other seaside towns, Great Yarmouth started to attract many individuals who are individually challenged.

Great Yarmouth is now the 20th most deprived area in England, with the heart of the deprivation centred where the tourist industry used to rule supreme.[320] Whilst actions are underway to raise educational standards the area still significantly lags behind other places in England. Only 16.9% of residents have attained NVQ Level 4 compared to 36.8% for England as a whole, and GCSE grades are slightly behind the rest of the country. The population is mainly white, a little bit more concentrated on the over 45's than elsewhere and has only 3.2% ethnic minority inhabitants.

Locally, employment is more likely to be part-time than the national average, with 35% of employment related to the tourism industry, which can be seasonal and tends to have low productivity and low wages. The local unemployment rate is nearly double that of the surrounding areas. There is a significantly higher incidence of both substance abuse and mental health problems than the national norm and the town has a higher crime rate than the rest (with the exception of Norwich) of the county. About 18% of the shop units in the town centre are empty.[321] This description of Great Yarmouth is mimicked in an analysis of the economic and social situation in Blackpool.[322]

With 69% of the Great Yarmouth voters voting 'Leave', Great Yarmouth is the 5th most pro-Brexit constituency in the UK; by comparison Blackpool was 27th.[323]

No single measure uniquely defines someone as being a member of the Left Behind, although one has a sense the defining foot print of an area that is Left Behind is there is a tendency towards a lack of ambition and a feeling of mistrust and alienation, with perhaps a sense that their situation has resulted from the malign (be intentionally or unintentionally) actions of others. It is no surprise then that this group is very vocal in its condemnation of immigrants as taking jobs, wealth, housing and services they feel are theirs by right. For those trapped in this landscape, depression and pessimism have a higher currency than optimism and 'can do'.

THE IMPORTANCE OF AMBITION

But that aside, we can't pretend that Ofsted judgements are not lower in certain areas – many of them with a high proportion of white working-class children. But that shouldn't surprise us. [...]

> *We are having to grapple with the unhappy fact that many local*
> *working-class communities have felt the full brunt of economic*
> *dislocation in recent years, and, perhaps as a result, can lack the*
> *aspiration and drive seen in many migrant communities.*
>
> Spielman, (2018)

Barely a year into her new role as, Chief Inspector of OFSTED, Amanda Spielman spoke of the lack of aspiration in white working-class children in the education system.[324]

Spielman's predecessor, did not hold back blaming parents in white working-class communities. '*The reason why London schools are doing so well, apart from good head teachers and good teachers, is because a lot of the immigrant families care about education, they value education, they support their children.*'

Soon after Spielman and Wilshaw's interventions, a new report highlighted the key role that ambition plays in driving growth in young, high growth potential MSMEs.[325] Another strand has been identified in the Ambition Gap between UK and US firms.[326]

New firms in the UK are often formed to house the self-employed; whereas in the US, firms often facilitate a group of individuals with a common business idea and the ambition to drive it to success. Without ambition, success is challenging to attain.

A pilot project focused on white working-class children with few life chances '*run by the Transformation Trust under the* [Barclays] *Lifeskills programme*' Wright (2018), has focused on mentoring 14 and 15-year-olds from 'Left Behind' families to gain the confidence that they can achieve and succeed. Initial results are impressive both in improved exam terms (a rise of two grades against a control group that did not experience the intervention) and young people whose outlook on life has been transformed into 'can do'.[327] An earlier and unrelated study looked at the importance of building success as an enabler for further success, unsurprisingly it found that '*Success does breed success*'.[328]

THE IMPORTANCE OF STABILITY

Another key feature in dealing with 'Left Behinders' is like every other human being, they respond better when not faced with chronic instability.

A study of a car plant in the US looked at the impact of unstable work patterns on motivation, job satisfaction and crucially on physical health. It found that people in unstable work suffer from more health problems and (unsurprisingly) less job satisfaction.[329] Equally, housing stability makes an important contribution in generating confidence and successful societal skills. There are many studies supporting this point[330] although this subject is not a primary focus within out narrative, with the exception of the following observation; many people living in private rented accommodation on short term tenancies can feel constantly insecure in their home. Rising rents have become associated with some landlords terminating tenancies and re-letting at a higher rent; and, 71% of tenants living in private rented accommodation have moved within the past 5 years.[331] There is also some correlation between chronic instability in housing and work and negative self-impression.[332]

EARNINGS

One key feature we previously identified has been the squeeze on real incomes, especially in lower parts of the income distribution. Recent analysis of the period 2011–2017 shows that the bottom 20% (despite some at the very bottom showing a relative improvement since the recent increases in the minimum wage) of the income distribution has fallen behind income growth in the middle. (The top 10% were also squeezed notwithstanding the income gains made by the top 1%). A key factor in the squeeze impacting the bottom 20% has been the reductions in welfare benefits they receive. Further, significant benefit income losses (maybe four times greater than so far) are forecast based upon already announced policy changes. Rises in housing costs for lower income families have added to this squeeze. Households with children in the bottom 20% of the income distribution faced a 47% increase in housing costs from 2002–2017 whilst in the top 20% housing costs fell by 16% over the same period.[333]

Chart 5 shows rates of earnings growth across the age distribution. Younger people under 40 have (with the exception of a slight skewing after the introduction of the National Living Wage) had lower increases in earnings than those in elder generations.

In summary, with real income growth squeezed since 2008, the greatest pressures on earners have been borne by both, the working poor (who lost benefits and saw housing costs rise) and the under 40s who were the losers

Chart 5. Earnings Growth Across the Age Distribution.

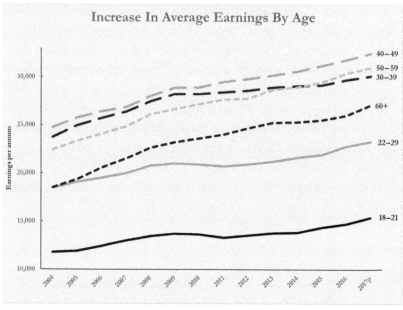

Source: National Statistics data © Crown copyright (ONS, 2018j).

in the earnings growth competition. The winners were those over 40, who own or are buying their home and are above the bottom 20% of the income distribution.

Our commentary has focused on those in work, but the picture is less than complete without some mention of those out of work for medical reasons. This group, which is in the lowest part of the income distribution has been income challenged by the benefit changes associated with austerity. There is an indication that more sick people are finding their way back to work as the disability employment gap is showing some modest narrowing. Whilst sickness rates have remained broadly level over the period since 2002/2003, there has been a significant rise in sickness due to mental health, especially in poorly qualified males.[334]

JOB SUBSIDIES

In-work benefits can act as a support for abnormal family circumstances or can act as a subsidy to employers that allow them to pay 'uneconomic wages'.

We define 'uneconomic wages' where a removal of general benefit subsidies to employees (such as working tax credit, housing benefit and the newer Universal Credit) would result in that firm not being able to find workers at the wages it is paying. In a pure capitalist economy, firms and entrepreneurs only supply goods and services from which they can make a profit and workers only work for these firms for earnings that allow them to live in the locality of the work. If firms underpay, they cannot find staff then they cannot produce their product or service and they go out of business, unless they can raise prices or productivity.

For standard family types (the word 'standard' is loaded with the potential for unhelpful value and political judgements and we consciously avoid defining it for this reason) in work, benefits become a subsidy for either uneconomically low earnings or for uneconomically high rents or both. In all cases, the payments of these benefits to 'standard families' distorts the market's role to optimally allocate resources to activities with the highest productive and profit generation potential. Where prices charged to buyers do not reflect the true underlying costs, firms are incentivised to provide things people are not prepared to pay the full price for. In addition to the negative effects that producing uncompetitive goods has on the overall economy (through implicitly misallocating resources, reducing export potential and limiting productivity increases), the same people who benefit from having these cheaper products or services then pay a levy through general taxation to fund the welfare payments that underpin the uneconomic wage structures. By paying the benefit to the earner rather than as a direct subsidy to the firms involved, the true dynamics are masked by mislabeling 'corporate welfare' as 'individual welfare'. Firms can still report they are profitable, notwithstanding that some or all of these profits may really come from the 'hidden' wage subsidy provided by income supplementing benefits. If the benefit was removed, the employees could not afford to work for these companies and these companies would either need to raise wages and prices to reflect true costs or go out of business. According to a recent British Social Attitudes Survey[335] there is significant public support (over 75%) for the notion that wages should be at a level that allows individuals without children to live without needing State Benefits; there is also strong support (58%) that families with children may need some additional help. The generational divide is again visible as older people are generally less sympathetic to welfare payments to people in work.

Looking at the size of the in-work welfare budget, a significant part of this is in effect a wage subsidy to firms paying uneconomically low wages. If this wage subsidy were to be repurposed into an appropriately allocated subsidy for firms to invest and innovate, the impact in terms of raising growth, real wages and productivity could be significant. Welfare costs for people in work currently stand at around £44.8 billion.[336] If one estimates that two-thirds of this is allocated to 'standard families' then the subsidy to their employers would be around £29.5 billion per annum. The individual cost of tax credits for a single earner married with two children on the minimum wage is estimated at £7,829 and the cost of housing benefit £2,898.[337] This makes an estimated total subsidy of £10,727 pa which put in an alternative way, is likely to be a supplement of more than 75% on this group's earned income.[338] It is unlikely that all the jobs that currently benefit from a 75% subsidy are going to be competitive if the subsidy is removed.

Could this subsidy be more effectively targeted at supporting innovative growth businesses to create jobs that will be in the long-term be self-sustaining? Such jobs may well generate higher value added per labour hour, so raise productivity and with higher productivity raise living standards. Could a switch in the current job supporting subsidies we have highlighted into helping to entrepreneurs to improve their skills be combined with programmes to raise skills in the Left Behind to offer a more effective ladder out of deprivation?

STUDIO III: THE LEFT BEHIND

Our canvas this time has its background painted with a sad and grey scene of decline and hopelessness, leading to a loss of aspiration and the nurturing of resentment by those Left Behind. In the foreground, we have a group of angry white working-class males. They have followed the rules they were given when they grew up. Maybe they did not do very well at school, but they wanted to work in a good well-paid job, buy a house, marry and bring up children. Of course, they wanted their earlier life to continue as it had done, with the friends, entertainment at the local pub and a holiday somewhere warm once a year.

What they found was house prices they could not afford, no available social housing and jobs and hours of work that come and go with the wind. Now when they want to improve themselves there seems to be no easily available ladder to climb, no big company to fund their training and no secure work. Instead they see the skilled jobs they could have aspired to, filled by Eastern Europeans with the necessary skillset.

Many in this group are angry with the system. The ones who are married with children face a continual pressure on their in-work tax credit benefits; but may have not benefited from recent rises in the minimum wage because they are already paid more than the minimum wage. These are the Left Behind Strivers who have been promised a Brexit that will give them steady well-paid jobs, remove the competition for housing (so they can find somewhere stable to live, and ideally "nice" to live). In a perfect world these are people who aspire to buying their own home. This is a group who want to improve themselves if only they had a ladder. They feel the dice are loaded against them and they don't have the confidence to reset the rules for themselves; so for many of them Brexit is as much about personal liberation as it is about national pride.

This group is expecting Brexit to improve their lives financially, socially and in status. They want to be able to hold their heads high that they have a secure roof over their head, a stable well-paid job and a country they can be proud of. For them Brexit is about bringing quality jobs with the associated pay back into their reach, so they can have the jobs and opportunities their parents told them they were entitled to.

A canvas with a grey background, an angry foreground and a big bag of gold on the horizon labelled Brexit Dividend. The delivery mechanism for this prospective dividend is claimed to be opening the UK to trading under World Trade Organisation Rules by leaving the UK; with the prospect of even more bonuses to come if new and substantial Free Trade Agreements can be struck. It is to this corner of the studio that we move next.

9

INTERNATIONAL DIMENSIONS

To Trump or Not to Trump – that is the question we must decide
Adapted from Bruni (2015)

June 2018 saw global headlines and world stock market adjustments as investors reacted to a prospective 'trade war' between the United States and many of its key trading partners; these included China, the European Union, Japan, South Korea, Canada, Mexico and South America. Even Rwanda (an impoverished African nation) is facing the wrath of the United States because it wants to increase tariffs on the imports of second hand clothes that have been undermining its attempts to create a domestic textile industry.[339] Again in 2018, the United States decided to bypass existing multilateral dispute mechanisms available at the World Trade Organisation and impose new tariffs on its trade partners via Section 232 of the Trade Expansion Act of 1962.[340] This law allows the US President to impose tariffs if *an article is being imported into the United States in such quantities or under such circumstances as to threaten or impair the national security*.[341] The legislation is at time of writing being used to impose a 25% tariff on steel imports and to threaten to impose a 20% tariff on automobiles.[342]

FREE TRADE DREAMS?

Free Trade Optimists argue that the greatest Brexit benefit will be the opportunity to strike independent Free Trade Agreements that can maximise the UK's competitive advantages. There is a belief that Free Trade will unlock entrepreneurial animal spirits as a swathe of EU 'vested interest' protectionist regulations are swept away.[343] An example of how sweeping away these regulations could help UK entrepreneurs is given by the struggle UK innovator James Dyson has had with the European Commission to establish a level playing field in electrical testing. Dyson whose vacuum cleaners are 'bagless' complained that the power consumption tests allowed specific German manufactures to test their cleaners (which are bagged) with no bag, thereby favourably misrepresenting their power consumption. Dyson won the appeal case at the European Court of Justice, in November 2018, (the judgment had the effect of canceling the testing regulation).[344] There are echoes in this case that resonate with the Volkswagen (and other car manufacturers) diesel emission scandal that again revolved around the exact permissible test conditions.

Brexit Free Trade advocates (typified by the group, Economists for Free Trade), argue that removing all UK trade barriers on Brexit day and relying on World Trade Organisation (WTO) rules will reduce prices for consumers by around 8% through tariff removal and raise productivity by 2% by removing EU regulations. In their scenario, these 'Free Traders' suggest that poorer households could be 15% better off as welfare spending on immigrants is stopped.[345] Downward wage pressures on unskilled and semi-skilled employees estimated to have led to a 1.8% fall in wage rates for each 10% increase in immigrants would also be reduced.[346]

In this view, rises in productivity can be anticipated by exposing industries to competition that will force them to adapt to survive. A fair trading environment can, it is argued, be enforced through the WTO, engendering a minimal impediment due to Non-Tariff Barriers (which include customs procedures, definition of goods origin and regulatory standards). Under this scenario, the UK will receive a boost of 4% to GDP from non-EU trade that may be offset by a 1% reduction with the EU when trading under WTO rules, rising to an incremental of 4% on GDP when a Free Trade Agreement is in place.[347] If this 'Free Trade Optimist' vision is realistic it could reposition the UK on a new productivity and income growth trajectory.

Others, including most mainstream economists, disagree with the Free Trade Optimists. A January 2018 UK Government provisional cross departmental briefing[348] looks at the same data and comes up with a very different set of conclusions. In this analysis, the WTO option sees a 15-year per capita GDP loss of 3.6%−8.9% which corresponds to a loss of GDP of between 5% and 10.3%. If there is a Free Trade Agreement in place with the EU, these losses are smaller with a loss of GDP of between 3.1% and 6.6% and a per capita GDP loss in the range of 2.4%−5.9%.

Why Are These Forecasts So Different?

The Free Trade Optimist view assumes that automated customs procedures that have not been specified or agreed at time of writing can lead to minimal customs processing delays. The Optimists also refuse to accept, as real, the anticipated £13 million annual increase in customs declaration costs as suggested by the current head of the UK Customs Authority.[349] The Free Trade Optimists also seemingly take the view that since regulations for current UK trade with the EU are aligned and will by definition remain so, there will be no need for additional EU regulatory checks. They cite the Swiss experience as an example as to why customs procedures should be straight forward after Brexit. Equally the optimistic assessment does not take into account how distance between a supplier and their customer impact transport costs whilst estimates such as those presented in the Government study do. It does feel unrealistic to suggest that the cost of shipping a product to Sydney is the same as say, to Amsterdam.

All forecasts are uncertain and so are prone to error, leading to cries that 'We have had enough of Experts' (Gove, 2016) that implicitly suggest if forecasts are inaccurate, perhaps we should ignore them (especially if they forecast an outcome we do not want).[350] It is challenging to forecast the 'unknown' in a new trade paradigm with a situation (a withdrawal from a single market and customs union rather than opening of a Free Trade process) that is different to the complex econometric model the Government projections uses. Inevitably this uncertainty is likely to make any forecast results somewhat speculative. As with so much in economics, assumptions drive the results. With Brexit, the only road maps we have come from either hundreds of years ago or more recently relate to completely different context's, such as the breakup of Comecon and the USSR in the early 1990s. We have already looked in detail at previous Brexits. It is now time to ask if the fall of the Soviet Union can give us any pointers as to whether the Free Trade case is overly optimistic? **Box 28** provides some pointers.

Box 28. Breaking Up Is Hard to Do – The End of Comecon and the USSR

Following the fall of the Berlin Wall and the collapse of the Soviet Union in the early 1990s, the economies of Eastern Europe undertook a rapid adjustment from the former Comecon arrangements into trading in the wider world. The economic shock was significant and seems to have been initially disruptive regardless of whether adaptation policies were gradualist or precipitate. In the first few years after the collapse of Comecon, all of its constituent countries (with the exception of Poland with a fall of only 28.3%) saw a fall in GDP of over 30%. The highest fall was over 60% in Lithuania.[351] This has been suggested as a *'transformational adjustment'* where the economy adapted to sharp changes in its market, new ways of managing its economy, a need to revise its macro-economic management to a non-Comecon world and changes to its financial system. The key factors in recovering from the adjustment were raising of both investment and exports.[352]

Sharp adjustments can occur when economies structurally change to align to different markets. The way in which the adjustment proceeds and how sharp and painful it is, is related to the way in which it is undertaken. Economist Joseph Stiglitz[353] contrasts deregulation in China to that in Russia, finding that in Russia, GDP fell by nearly 50% and in the more gradualist China, it nearly doubled. The differences between the Chinese and Russian adjustment pathways emphasise the importance of managing a structural adjustment through ensuring high levels of investment and innovation in export focused industries. This is likely to be one panacea for the output losses and associated social costs that retrenching and rationalising pre-existing industries will imply.

ADJUSTING TO A NEW INTERNATIONAL MODEL

In Chapter 2 we mentioned the *Lawson Doctrine* which assumes economic crises arise from governments mismanaging the public finances and that the private sector being 'perfectly rational' will always be in balance. This doctrine implicitly underlies the Free Trade Optimist arguments, as with this assumption, models of the economy suggest significant adjustment to significant structural shocks without a crisis or a crash. The implicitly assumed adjustment mechanism results from private sector players chasing new opportunities as old ones disappear. The efficacy of this mechanism is often associated with calls for a 'realistic personal and corporate tax regime' and removal of regulatory barriers. These measures are supposedly required to enable the 'Laffer Curve' growth mechanism to deliver growth. We have already seen that both the Lawson Doctrine and the Laffer Curve are poorly supported by real world evidence (notwithstanding both mechanisms are likely to be true in extreme conditions). We have also seen that the structural adjustment to new trading arrangements after the fall of Comecon was very painful and we have heard that recovery in this case depended upon new investment.

What Sort of Adjustment Can We Expect with Brexit?

Transition to the new post Brexit world will be determined by how complex and challenging are the changes being faced. If there is a no-deal situation, then large exporters, such as the aerospace and automotive industries have made clear, that they will adapt their operations by reducing their commitment to the UK. There have been a number of warnings from automotive companies such as Jaguar Land Rover, Honda and Toyota; but one of the starkest pointers that some Brexit cases would lead to current operations being relocated away from the UK was delivered by civil aerospace group Airbus.[354] Financial services companies are as this book is being written starting to open offices in, and move operations to, remaining EU Members. Major businesses have started to and will continue to adapt their operations to the new reality. The bulk of SME's are it appears still waiting for clarity before deciding how to adapt to a post Brexit world, although there are indications that some SME's are now starting to take action.[355]

During the UK industrial restructuring that took place in the 1980s, many industries retrenched. In some cases they shut down and in others they rationalised and changed. For example, the domestically owned automotive industry faded away and was replaced by inward investments from Japanese companies who built new and efficient facilities to obtain easy tariff free access to EU markets, utilising established skills and labour flexibility. Will a UK with different access to the EU be such an attractive investment location? Evidence suggests that this is unlikely, with 2017 data already showing a significant drop in direct investment flows into the UK.[356]

If inward investment is already showing a downturn, will domestic capital investment rise sharply? We have already seen that modern financial markets are largely disconnected from entrepreneurs and that big companies are driven by short-term earnings and share price considerations. This combination means that in the absence of any positive capital investment promoting measures it is unlikely (as things stand) the economy will respond to Brexit dislocation by steeply raising the rate of investment. Indeed, recent evidence from the small business sector shows that investment is falling in the face of Brexit uncertainty.[357]

Non EU Free Trade Agreements as a Growth Engine?

The Free Trade Optimist would argue that notwithstanding concerns to the contrary, the pull of Free Trade Agreements will be such that when combined and associated with de-regulation, that they will drive successful change. An analysis of the 447 Free Trade Agreements struck between 202 contracting parties between 1948 and 2015 (60% are still in force) registered at the WTO does not suggest that these will be a cure-all. The analysed Free Trade Agreements are biased in favour of the more powerful party, have grown more complex over time, mainly cover goods and not services and in the new millennium are increasingly reflecting regional clusters rather than bi-lateral country to country deals. It is true that the focus for new agreements is moving towards services or goods and services together; but these agreements tend to be very complex and take a long time to negotiate. Agreements also tend to be very similar for many industries whilst focusing on specific details for industries such as transport or agriculture with strong local lobbies.[358] A recent report from a group of Free Trade Optimist think tanks concedes that existing Free Trade Agreement structures are unlikely to be effective as engines of

Brexit economic change. They refer to these agreements as having successfully reduced tariffs over the past 80 years by establishing 'managed' rather than Free Trade. These groups argue for a radical break with the past and the establishment of true Free Trade, going on to propose a model agreement for future use.[359] Does anyone believe President Trump will offer the UK an instant preferential trade deal that will allow the UK to significantly raise its existing export surplus with the USA and by juxtaposition the US trade deficit with the UK?

That leaves the alternative adjustment mechanism, the one faced by Russia and the Comecon countries and the one used by Iceland in 2008 and Argentina in 2001/2002, namely GDP falls until the economy adjusts to its new situation. Although very painful, economic crises do reset the market playing field so that growth can start once again, albeit normally from a significantly lower starting point.

STUDIO IV: INTERNATIONAL TRADE

Our latest canvas has focused exclusively on international economic matters. We have not looked at how the UK's political role in the world may be impacted by Brexit. Whilst for the optimists, Brexit will enhance the UK's global role, there is a second dimension to raising the UK's role internationally. Success will require that there be a positive desire to project both 'soft' and 'hard' power in a coordinated and cohesive manner. From outside the UK, there is little understanding of both Brexit and Westminster and the UK focus of these narratives and discussions. Former Deputy UN Secretary General and former UK Foreign Office Minister Mark Malloch Brown talks of 2018 Britain with a foreign policy that *seems to have all but collapsed – and even to have disowned its past and its governing ideas* (Malloch Brown, 2018).

Much of the Brexit narrative has been met with bemusement by overseas observers. For example, Brexiteer rhetoric around the 2018 Commonwealth Heads of Government that suggested Brexit offers the opportunity to rebuild the previous UK Imperial trading system into something new and based upon the Commonwealth has not materialised into anything concrete. Rather it has been overshadowed by an immigration scandal (the 2018 Windrush scandal) as to how UK authorities treated long-standing Commonwealth immigrants to the UK over recent years.

The brush strokes according to Professor Patrick Minford's Brexit analysis and associated aspirations on this international economic canvas started by offering the hope of a rosy exciting new future as our journey commenced. His group has suggested there could be a 15% lift in the real incomes for the 'Left Behind' through Brexit restrictions on immigrants. Were such an anticipated impact to translate into reality, it would be a huge boost for such a disadvantaged group. Then as more brush strokes were added a picture emerged that outcomes could turn out to be far less rosy. For example the structural adjustments undertaken by the former Comecon states when Comecon broke up, resulted in sharp downward adjustments in overall economic activity.

No longer, could we see a sunny ocean, serene, calm and blue with the prospect of finding some hidden treasure in a long forgotten corner of the world. Instead our canvas was plunged into a darker vista, with remote countries erecting sea walls to keep storms and disruption from affecting them.

As we turn away from this canvas, perhaps we need reminding of how dams burst. At first, there may be a subtle creaking, and then maybe a trickle until crack! The dam bursts and nothing is the same again. Economic crises can be a bit like dams and take a long time to break. Then we are reminded of the Dornbush Law, *The crisis takes a much longer time coming than you think, and then it happens much faster than you would have thought.*[360]

If Brexit is going to result in a sharp adjustment to a new state of affairs could this involve another financial crash? History seems to suggest this is how adjustment has happened elsewhere. If this is the case, we need to wonder for a moment, what the social consequences could be. Which takes us to Chapter 10.

10

POPULARISM AND THE INTERNET

*In South Africa in 1856, the spirits of three ancestors visited a
15-year-old Xhosa girl called Nongqawuse requesting that the tribe
destroy their crops and cattle so their ancestors could then return
and drive the white settlers into the ocean. New, beautiful cattle
would appear and the sun would turn red. The Xhosa duly began
killing cattle and burning crops and of course the tribe went hungry
and starved.*

Adapted from Kuper (2017)

SIGNS OF AN OLDER NARRATIVE IN A MODERN AGE?

The year 2019 will mark the centenary of the signing of the 'Treaty of
Versailles' that formally ended the 1914—1918 World War I. It is unlikely
this event will be marked with Pan European jubilation, given that for many
it opened the pages of a new narrative in Germany that became associated
with the rise of National Socialism. In Germany, the signing of the Versailles
Peace Treaty in 1919 was seen by some as a 'Stab in The Back' by the then
Berlin Government.

The 'Stab in The Back' simile is particularly powerful in a Brexit context as
it transfers responsibility for difficulties to someone else. It is sometimes used in
a military context, where in the face of defeat, military leaders have sometimes
claimed (notably at the end of the World War I) that they were on the threshold of a great victory only, to be let down by the lack of resolve and weakness
of government and civil society.[361] One consequence of such an allusion is the

discrediting of established authority in a belief that failure has not come from either fighting the wrong war or, from fighting the right war in the wrong way (or both), but from a failure of resolve to meet the objectives at hand. Both elements were visible during the 1920s in Germany as National Socialism sought to put its foot firmly on the ladder to power.

The risk of a 'Stab in The Back' narrative being promulgated is significant if the Brexit outcomes do not meet the hopes and aspirations of the 'Leavers'. Already there are claims (valid or otherwise) that the EU is trying to turn the UK into a vassal state.

> *I have often pointed out that the problem with the sticking to the EU model and following it closely is you then need to ask what is the point of leaving? [...] If we just accept what the EU does from outside we must surely be the vassal state. (Rees-Mogg, 2018a)*

There are also the first indications of a 'Stab in the Back' type narrative. One recent intervention from Dominic Cummings, Director of the official Vote Leave campaign reads as follows.

> *The Government effectively has no credible policy [...] It now thinks its survival requires surrender [...], it thinks that the MPs can be bullshitted by clever drafting from officials, and that once Leave MPs and donors [...] will balk at bringing down the Government when you finally have to face that you've been conned. [...] their only strategy is to 'trust officials to be honest', which is like trusting Bernie Madoff with your finances. Brexit cannot be done with the traditional Westminster / Whitehall system as Vote Leave warned repeatedly before 23 June 2016. (Cummings, 2018)*

Despite potential for historical symmetry, no doubt all Brexiteers will want to avoid having the 2019 Brexit Exit Treaty being signed at Versailles with possible unfortunate centennial undertones. Even if the Treaty is not signed in Versailles there must be fears that if Brexit does not deliver its promised benefits, this new Treaty could, in the UK, become known as the '2nd Treaty of Versailles'.

NEW FAULT LINES

Although definitive understanding of today's Brexit will only be possible 50 or 100 years from now, it is beginning to look like the UK political fault lines may have been permanently changed by the 2016 Referendum, moving from class driven voting to one driven by attitudes to Brexit. Both Leave and Remain seem to have become entrenched camps, defined as much by the insults thrown at each other as by policy. About 40% of Leavers see Remainers as dishonest, selfish and close minded. Remainers are even more forthright with over 50% seeing Leavers as dishonest, selfish and close minded. More neutral observers see Leavers as patriotic and Remainers as optimistic, with both sides seen as expressing fear.[362] The split between Leave and Remain is also true on attitudes to ethnic issues. Over 80% of Leavers believe that sensitivity to, and, equal opportunities policy for minority ethnic groups has gone too far, whilst over 80% of Remainers think the opposite.[363]

With little evidence indicating that any significant number of people in either camp are about to change their opinion,[364] (although there have been some recent opinion poll shifts towards 'Remain' with a small majority suggesting Leaving the EU is a mistake), it would appear that the battle lines are now firmly drawn. Both sides have more than a passing resemblance to the religious sects of former centuries.

Today's Brexit divide in some senses, provokes deep echoes of the divides from the Brexits of Tudor years.

NIHILISM AS A MAINSTREAM POLICY

What if a regressive trait lurked in "the good man," likewise a danger, an enticement, a poison, a narcotic, so that the present lived at the expense of the future? Perhaps in more comfort and less danger, but also in a smaller-minded, meaner manner? [...] So that morality itself were to blame if man never attained the highest power and splendor possible for the type man? So that morality itself was the danger of dangers? (Nietzsche, 1887, p. 8)

The UK's irrepressible former Foreign Secretary, Boris Johnson, summed up some Brexiteer views on any possible commercial obstacles business may face if there is a 'no deal' Brexit in his widely reported comment 'F*** [Expletive Deleted] Business'.[365] Trampling over concerns from the wealth producing sector, with loud and strident rhetoric chimes with the sentiments of the 'Left Behind'. For some, this type of strident rhetoric acts as an inspiring rallying call that implicitly recognises their own alienation from civil society. This is symbiotic of the feelings of being undervalued, ignored and consequently demeaned by society that are synonymous with many of the Left Behind.

These feelings can be seen as an example of Nietzsche's herd psychology of resentment against superior individuals, classes and the state. These same elements are claimed to underpin much of President Trump's white working-class voter base. So, it comes as no surprise that President Trump claimed his victory would be Brexit Plus.[366] The white working-class movements that support both Brexit and President Trump, whilst in many respects different due to the different contexts, have much that is similar in the underlying sentiments of their voter bases.

Both movements reflect a disillusion with current ruling paradigms that seem to avoid giving respect to those indigenous nationals who deserve it, while showering both glory and help on non indigenous minorities. *Election 2016 was thus in part a whitelash against 'PC culture' (i.e., political correctness that criticizes racism, sexism, homophobia, and other forms of bias while advocating a more open, inclusive, and tolerant culture)* (Kellner, 2017, p. 138).

Both movements channel this dissatisfaction into nationalism identifying solutions with 'America First' or in the romantic echo of a lost Empire 'Global Britain'. For some it appears that all the dice are loaded against them, so what does it matter if making the omelette breaks a few eggs, all their eggs were smashed years ago. Indeed, for the British movement *The difficulty of Brexiting is part of the appeal: only a great tribe can renew itself through sacrifice* (Kuper, 2017).

For those involved, the perceived injustice against them can only be remedied by returning 'power to the people'; by removing it from 'out of touch' liberal elites who in the eyes of the Left Behind have 'fixed the rules' so the elites take the rewards and leave the scraps for the 'Left Behind'.

A new and defining feature of this elite is that it is global and not national, so in the eyes of those at the bottom, the elite is typified by a lack of moral responsibility and loyalty to their country. It becomes a natural step for some to feel that only by breaking the control of the foreign elite can power, respect and a fair share of wealth return to the citizen of a nation state. There is something altogether nihilistic in the suggestion that progress is only possible by removing (or for the more extreme destroying) the inter-loping foreigner.

Could some who support Brexit feel that by repelling the foreigner they will be reinstated to their rightful role as the heirs and torch bearers for the democracy of Magna Carta, the 'Mother of Parliaments' and the heroes of the Battle of Britain who kept alight the candle of liberty in its darkest hour?

Many may have held these views individually for years, but they have gained collective power as their holders have been given easier opportunities to come together. In 2018, no 'Munich Beer Hall' meetings are needed for groups to coalesce. Rather instant association is possible through a smart phone and social media.

IS SOCIAL MEDIA TODAY'S 'SMART' MUNICH BEER HALL?

In the early 1920's Germany unrest famously found one of its homes in the Beer Halls of Munich. These provided a gathering point for people of similar views to share thoughts and ideas. Today's virtual world of social media provides almost unlimited opportunity to join communities, but unlike beer halls where it is possible to feel shame and contrition the morning after, social media offers a 'remote viewing' experience, where human contact that can moderate more extreme human behaviour is lost in a world of nameless digital engagement.

Many of these communities have their own narratives and their own sources of news. One feature of the divide between Leavers and Remainers has been a tendency for each side to dismiss anything the other side says as 'fake' or false, and only believe things that reconfirm views already held by themselves.[367] An interim report by the UK Information Commissioner on *how political campaigns use personal data to micro-target voters with political adverts and messages, the techniques used, and the complex eco-system that exists between data brokerage organisations, social media platforms and political campaigns and parties* (ICO, 2018, p. 9), highlighted how both data and behavioural models can be combined to help target and personalise political and attitude forming advertising. Targeting advertising and information flows to reinforce existing prejudices risks dialogue and debate becoming informed by prejudice and filtered facts thereby creating a reinforcing circle of prejudice.

It's notable that this same trait is observable in tightly knit sects. Sustaining these groups is partly a function of 'shared' views, news and experiences that are held within the group and partly from the group perceiving it is 'under attack' from outside.[368] Unsurprisingly attempts to provide news or comment from a source that is associated with the other side of the Brexit divide is perceived as an 'attack' on the group and immediately discredited as 'worthless' as it must be biased, even if it is in fact true.

In sects the group can be further sustained if there is a core group of 'rabble rousers' who are loud and respected by the group. In a Brexit context, we have good examples of 'rabble rousing' in both newspaper headlines and speeches by key Brexiteers. Group affirmation is also visible by the stream of 'troll' comments made on internet news sites to any article that diverges from either side of the Brexit creed. The comments have two important group roles: first to expose the offending article as 'propaganda'/fake news from the opposing camp and second to reinforce the group's collective identity and its perception that it is under threat.

Without human interaction, aggressive comments from one group against another are perceived as costless; whereas with human interaction, the personal relationships and the element of listening serve to moderate behaviour. Face to face debate and interaction across divides breaks down barriers, provided theatrics and the spotlight of 'media face offs' are avoided. In the latter case, the role of the debate mutates into a platform for each side to reinforce the dynamics and loyalty of its own tribe or sect.

Matters are further complicated by search and selection algorithms in social media which have the effect of combining individual's previous internet behaviour with search algorithms to present personalised data results corresponding to that individuals pre-set preferences and prior behaviour.[369] Consequently, individuals unconsciously find their social interaction being determined by previous interactions, so reducing their opportunity to gain knowledge broadening debate. For many, especially in younger generations, social media news feeds such as Facebook help the individual to decide what they would like to 'dip into' and explore adding another element to information selection. The constant 'event feed' is complemented by using opinionated discussion programmes to explore subjects that may be of interest.[370] Information may flow, but it is less clear that balanced debate will follow.

New ways of communicating have bought new ways to refine and deliver specific social media messages to specific individuals. Concerns have been raised that data analytics can combine individuals perceived pre-ferences (from analysing some of their internet and especially social media interactions), with psychological insights and be used to deliver individu-ally or micro group tailored advertising to help solidify that individual's political views. Following media articles on data analysis firm Cambridge Analytica and its connection with the US Trump campaign, the spotlight also fell on AggregateIQ a company that undertook media placement work for the official Brexit Leave Campaign in the lead up to the 2016 Referendum. This company provided written evidence to the UK Parliamentary Committee investigating fake news in which they describe how they provided advertising platforms (for example Facebook) with details of the type of voter the advertiser is trying to contact, including the voter's demographics and interests. This information is then combined with tailored promotional content to allow each potential voter to be 'micro targeted' by the Platform's advertising delivery engine.[371] For some, this process is controversial as it allows advertisements to be microtargeted for specific individuals in a way that will best align to their personal interests.

This overall landscape opens the door to both unintentional and inten-tional manipulation of both the news message (fake news) and the emotional impact in the way the message is delivered (microtargeting). The impact has been summarised as follows.

> *Accounts of populism detailing the central tenets of popular resentment, disenfranchisement, anti-elite sentiment, and institutional distrust often focus either on its specific ties to local conditions and histories or its conceptual generality as an umbrella category of political behaviour [...] If new media technology has disrupted institutionalized politics, it has also afforded populism's restylization of the relations between digital social media and conventional forms of political power. In its alignment with [...] social media has served to normalize, broaden, and reframe extremist commitments, articulating them to longer histories of media technology and political identity. (Govil & Baishya, 2018, p. 68)*

POST-MODERN TRUTH?

False words are not only evil in themselves, but they infect the soul with evil. (Plato, c375BC:165)

If the news and information we receive becomes (to a large degree) the information that we may want to receive (based on analysing individual internet behaviour), how can we know what is true? In the sixteenth century, the proliferation of pamphlets from sundry printers led to a spread of new ideas and debates which eventually became one of the intellectual backdrops to the English Civil War. These pamphlets and associated local gossip often emphasised one viewpoint of the religious sectarian divide that had opened up since the 1530s.

In the 1920s, the 'Stab in the Back' narrative was broadened into an ethnic narrative, both by news media outlets, controlled and sympathetic to the Nazi's and by speeches and writings by Nazi theorists and leaders. In 1924, Hitler made a speech in which he stated of the Versailles treaty, *It was a filthy crime against the German People, a stab in the back of the German Nation* (Weaver, 2011) which very rapidly by 1925 had developed into *The state is only a means to an end. Its end and its purpose is to preserve and promote a community of human beings who are physically as well as spiritually kindred. Above all, it must preserve the existence of the race* (Weaver, 2011 from *Mein Kampf* p. 357).

In line with the research that shows sects are sustained if they have a strong rabble rouser and a strong perceived threat, the 1920's narrative moved rapidly from a Stab in The Back, onto racial superiority and then later onto scapegoating and all the atrocities associated with the genetic theme. The core groups (of which the 'Left Behind' of Weimar Germany were undoubtedly important support) unity and focus were sustained by an evolving message.

Nationalism coupled with distorted news, a lack of reasoned public debate and a nihilistic dimension are powerful fuel for the engines of hate, mistrust and discord. Removing this fuel from the UK Brexit engine requires a Brexit that above all delivers benefits and optimism for the Left Behind, for they have much more energy and many more years ahead of them than pensioners who are reaching the end of the line.

We will now embark on our final chapter as we have no more canvases to view; it is time to draw the threads together and try to put some substance as to what could lie behind the 'Opportunity / Challenge' door to end this leg of the Brexit journey.

11

WHICH BREXIT THIS TIME?

This year's referendum is more than a hands up for or against Europe. It is one aspect of a disintegrating political order.

The Guardian (21 May 1975)

The months since the 2016 Referendum have seen an endless narrative of twists and turns in the Brexit tale with a Shakespearian cast of characters and a Machiavellian litany of plots, counterplots, hidden loyalties and betrayals. If, having completed this rapid journey through a gallery of, at times, challenging pictures you feel as though this was the wrong gallery to be strolling though and you are asking where the sunny uplands of the Brexit dividend are; we have a simple answer. In the real world and in life, benefits must be earned. Only the past is set in stone and the past seems to repeat itself (albeit in slightly different guises) with monotonous frequency!

The theme of this final chapter is try to answer the question 'How can we make this work?' The future is not yet written and so it is available for us all to mould. If the slogan 'Take Back Control', (that was central to the Leave Campaign) has any meaning, it is in its emphasis that finding success will need policy and action to be driven by us all. Together we have the detailed knowledge to drive success. Brexit, as we have seen is a symptom and not a cause of the stresses and strains in our society. It needs to be the concern of everyone, not a few vocal commentators and politicians.

Like any great artwork Brexit is complex and made up of an untold number of brush strokes. For it to become a masterpiece, these brush strokes need orchestrating to create a work of art that is both simple for the eye to behold, yet complex under the microscope. Whilst conceptually simple; execution is hugely complicated. Acknowledging the past, we saw how Thomas Cromwell executed a near flawless legal Brexit in record time; however for his changes to 'stick', it required the pragmatic Elizabeth I to engage and work with all around her to effect a lasting transformation. The same will be true for this Brexit, one that in itself is far more complex than that of the 1530's and lacks the benefit of Cromwell's brilliant legal mind. Success will require the wisdom and patience of those in power to listen to and learn from the people who understand the detail and, to then modify their plans and ideas to match the realties they face.

Unlike earlier Brexits, this time it will be delivered in a 'goldfish bowl' for eyeryone to see. The prevalence of social media means that every detail will be open to instant exposure and debate; and that every debate risks being used to confirm pre-existing biases in both the Leave and Remain camps. Take for example, the warnings of potential supply chain disruption being made by some companies. Soon after one such warning, one of the authors started to receive emails from friends who are keen Brexiteers decrying the start of 'Project Fear Mark II'. For many Remainers, these company warnings were merely statements of the obvious, that putting new barriers in the way of complex supply chains is likely to cause problems. This tendency for every piece of news to be used to confirm existing views is combined for some with the sense of 'nihilism' we described in Chapter 10. The findings of the 2017 British Social Attitudes Survey confirm a Leave/Remain divide that is hardening rather than healing.[372]

In July 2018, a few days before a crucial cabinet meeting to agree the UK preferred option for post-Brexit customs arrangements, one leading Brexiteer wrote

> *The question for the Cabinet at Chequers is what to do with the freedom the British people want reinstated. Does it seize this great opportunity [...] or does it follow the managers of decline to place a once proud country in a tremulous state that sees Brexit as mere damage limitation? ... One former Tory leader, Sir Robert Peel, did decide to break his manifesto pledge and passed legislation with the majority of his party voting the other way so leaving him dependent on opposition votes. This left the Conservatives out of majority office for 28 years, 1846 to 1874. At least he did so for a policy*

*that worked. At Chequers the Prime Minister must stick to
her righteous cause and deliver what she has said she would.
(Rees-Mogg, 2018b).*

In the above narrative, managers of UK businesses are portrayed as implicit failures; as *managers of decline* (thereby speaking to a deeply held Left Behind view that they have been left behind because of decline, whilst pandering to a sense of 'loss of Empire' among the nostalgic elderly). Rees-Mogg goes on to threaten the Prime Minister that if the Brexiteer view is not adhered to, she will split her party so causing her government to fall. By combining a nihilistic element with a 'flag' wrapped in the spirit of 'Custer's Last Stand', a key Brexiteer metaphor is revealed. This metaphor is the allusion to a strong and hearty English preparing to fight on the beaches to repel the foreign invader. This very clever and powerful article speaks directly to the dynamics of the Brexiteer sect.

Both Leave and Remain repackage the same facts into completely different messages that reinforce each group's own support, and increase the divide in the country. Divide and mistrust makes it less likely that people will work together to find smart answers to the very many challenges a change this substantial will inevitably create.

IS THERE AN UNRECOGNISED ELEPHANT IN THE BREXIT ROOM?

Could this highly polarised dialogue mean that so much time is spent arguing through megaphones that there is danger of missing key factors that could contribute to a making Brexit success? The focus on divide, rather than listening and learning through dialogue, has happened before. In Henry VIII's break with Rome, there are places where we can sense a disconnection between the standoff between Church and State and ordinary people's lives. This disconnect starts to transform into a deeper divide in 1536 thereby leading to the Pilgrimage of Grace insurrection as the changes start to touch many people's lives.

Probably the biggest visible changes for most people in the 1530s came from (i) the dissolution of the monasteries in 1536 and (ii) the new orders of worship. The monasteries had provided the welfare system, so a religious revision became a change in a welfare system that affected everyone as there are always people in need. The changes to worship affect all church goers across the country and these changes also threatened many local memorials that related to family bequests. It's likely that at the point of both these changes ordinary people started to feel the depth of the change. A more modern analogy could be taken from the winter of 1940, during a period called the 'phoney war'. Although the country was on a war footing; in January 1940 no one could have imagined the military disasters that were to happen during the forthcoming May. Disaster had to happen before the existential risk to nationhood that the war represented became real. It was (as always) reality that forced both the leadership and practical policy to change and rise to the challenges.

Today, we are told that great momentous things are happening; but in reality, the only visible thing that has changed is the fall in the pound and associated price rises. Companies may be starting to relocate some of their operations but these moves take time so the effects are not yet visible to the general population and are yet to be felt by the general public. This sense of unreality leaves some Leavers frustrated and holding a sense of a possible conspiracy to slow down or stop Brexit. 31% of Leavers don't trust the current political leaders to negotiate Brexit, many people (55%) are bored with Brexit and a sizable group of Remainers (48%) fear a 'Hard Brexit' no deal, so also do not trust any of the current leaders to negotiate a deal.[373]

If the end Brexit deal has a strong negative impact on the UK economy we can expect that views on both sides of the divide are likely to rapidly change. History suggests, that barring great wisdom in public leaders, the likely reaction will be as in the late 1540s to harden divisions. Within our historical narrative, that story changes as the country goes through the chaos of the late 1540s and the early 1550s, setting the stage for Elizabeth's pragmatic 'People's Brexit' that occurred in the second half of the sixteenth century.

Elizabeth, unlike Thomas Cromwell, spotted the elephant in the room. What her people desired was to feel safe, better off, respected and have a sense of national pride. Elizabeth's genius was to recognise that to achieve these objectives she needed a series of (often colourful) characters in her looser circle who were the entrepreneurs with the ability and connections to translate ideas into action. These people both formulated policy and financially invested in them personally to help deliver her own goals.

In today's Brexit, where is the open and engaged narrative with business and entrepreneurs about how to make Brexit work? Elizabeth knew that if she was to preserve the cloth trade, then she had to work with and support the London Company of the Merchant Adventurers as they wrestled with trading difficulties that both the Regent of the Netherlands and the Dutch Revolt caused to the key Antwerp cloth market, during the 1560s and 1570s. Without a partnership between merchant and state, it is likely that the vital English cloth export trade would have been deeply damaged by this instability, as almost overnight its main export market location closed on more than one occasion.

Elizabeth was in some sense following a much older precedent that can be traced back to the days when the Roman colony Britannia was at its height. The Romans created supply chains, markets and a monetary economy as they colonised different lands. By acting as a major customer, by guaranteeing market stability and by underpinning the investing activities of the great Roman families in the earlier years of the Empire, Rome acted as the state partner of the local entrepreneur. Rome had its fair share of colourful Emperors such as Nero and Caligula, but for centuries their shenanigans were not allowed to disturb the stability of the Empire. It was only in the later third century that the model started to break down and even then, Britannia seems to have avoided the worst consequences until the closing decades of the fourth century. Whilst other colonies such as Gaul had significant difficulties during the third century, Britannia still had a functional and Entrepreneurial State. Elizabeth unknowingly replicated this previous success by establishing the Elizabethan State as the entrepreneur's partner. The policies and their execution were different, but the principle was the same, namely that the state underpinned and partnered entrepreneurial activity.

This brings us to today's unrecognised elephant in the room. The state needs to be the entrepreneur's partner. In many cases, where the technology and market are known and sufficient capital is already allocated, the state can and should be a 'silent partner', but where the technology and market are evolving and the risk finance is yet to enter the sector, the State needs to wake up and become a more active partner.

Success in changes as momentous and complex as Brexit can only come through everyone working together. This means there has to be an open and frank dialogue, productive understanding and joint working between the state and the individuals (entrepreneurs) who make change happen on the ground. Elizabeth I understood the primary goal was to improve what could be improved. Her Brexit was not about her trying to prove she was more virulent than the other rulers of Europe; Elizabeth's

Brexit was about making things work. Amongst all the arguments between all today's protagonists, where is partnership and associated quiet listening learning space that allows people to communicate, solve problems and make things work?

THE LEFT BEHIND NEED ECONOMIC SUCCESS

We have identified the importance of engaging and supporting the 'Left Behind' to give them realistic hope of attaining success and inspire aspiration in them to achieve it. Hope and aspiration for Left Behind white males will not come from creating more zero-hours contract jobs that pay minimum or just above minimum wages. The Left Behind need a ladder that is feasible for them to climb and to feel affirmed as they step on the first rung. Central to this ladder are access to quality stable affordable housing, stable employment and predictable working hours required to start solving some of the issues they face.

If the economy is failing to create the jobs that they need, then they need to be empowered to create their own. Entrepreneurs come in all shapes and sizes and work across all types of commercial activity. The entrepreneur starting a computer repair business or a motorcycle refurbishment business is in some sense just as significant to the economy as the entrepreneur creating the next Google; it is just the scale of the impact that is different. The economy needs them all; with the implication that many of the start-up and growth initiatives focused on the IT sector need expanding and adapting to fit other less obvious sectors. For the 'Left Behind' (and indeed probably for most aspiring entrepreneurs), such measures need to be combined with specific actions that embrace them into entrepreneurship. This raises three questions.

(1) First, how can the Left Behind (and indeed anyone else who thinks they have a smart idea to innovate a new business) be constructively engaged as to both if it is worth doing and if so how to do it?

(2) Second, where is the start-up capital and working capital finance going to come from to support these budding entrepreneurs? Currently banks don't generally lend to start ups and early stage businesses unless there

are either guarantees against personal assets or access to a state guarantee; venture capital is not necessarily targeting all sectors.

(3) Third, how will these budding entrepreneurs be given the skills that they need to succeed?

In a 2018 survey of 605 aspiring entrepreneurs by the authors,[x] the respondents identified that entrepreneurs feel that they need support to connect them to markets and customers, deal with regulatory challenges and to obtain finance. The bulk of these entrepreneurs were looking to build businesses in sectors such as personal services or car repair and many had a fairly low level of educational attainment. They knew, they needed to raise their skill levels, but could not see the route to doing this. It is unlikely that a 35-year-old would be happy to go back to school!

Whilst not all entrepreneurs are looking to build businesses in the 'Tech Super Star Sectors', there is an opportunity to "cross-fertilise" understanding garnered from how the Silicon Valley entrepreneurial cluster evolved as a series of self-reinforcing interactions between the entrepreneurs, the state and Stamford University. This model can be adapted into one of an *'Entrepreneurial University'* where a nominated local university acts as the focal community point in a locality to orchestrate entrepreneurial activity and integrate itself with both the local business community and the wider academic scientific communities.

To help potential entrepreneurs assess the validity of their idea, space can be created where groups of potential entrepreneurs share ideas with established entrepreneurs and academics to see if the idea looks like it can fly and if so, what help they need. The rest follows from this initial interaction.

For those with ideas that are considered worthwhile; a tailor made 'action learning plan' can be created, targeted at building the entrepreneur's skills, whilst concurrently helping the aspiring business formulate its business plan that is "entrepreneurial university" certified as to its quality before it is presented for funding. If someone attends the screening session and then decides their idea is not good enough, they still win as

---

[x]The survey was undertaken in the Western Balkans for the British Council and Swedish Institute.

they will have gained self-esteem and confidence that their ideas are being listened to.

The UK needs to unlock a burst of innovation to create new products and services that are competitive globally (trade agreement or no trade agreement). As with the first industrial revolution, success needs entrepreneurs to be able to access sufficient risk capital to create products and services that can dominate their chosen markets globally. Free Trade Agreements can help and certainly borderless trade with a single set of market access regulations is much easier to work with than a labyrinth of different restrictions dependent upon which market one is entering. Such benefits are however illusory if the businesses that need to grow cannot access the capital, the skills and the science they require. Without the financial support from the Praed Bank in the last quarter of the eighteenth century, it is unlikely that the Boulton–Watt steam engine (a foundation technology of the industrial revolution) would have survived its commercialisation.

Capitalism is not a system that is defined by private or public ownership, rather a capitalist society is one where the market drives risk finance to budding entrepreneurs who need the capital to invest and, innovate to grow their businesses. In a capitalist society, capital flows into profitable projects and shares the profits in recognition of the risks it has taken to attain this position. The entrepreneur largely does not care if the capital comes from a bank, an individual or the state; they just care that they have access to quality long term affordable capital. It is an ironic quirk of history that both the right wing and left wing mistakenly associate ownership of the means of production as the distinguishing mark of capitalism.

A successful Brexit needs to be an authentic capitalist Brexit where risk capital reaches the entrepreneurs that need it.

THE BREXIT OPPORTUNITY

Just like Elizabeth I, and long before her the Roman Empire, we can see the commanding importance of supporting innovating entrepreneurs and breaking the boundaries holding them back. There are many different ways to do this. For example, we can see with what the Japanese did in the 1960s and 1970s, the South Koreans did in the 1970s and 1980s and the Chinese have been doing more recently, that by focusing on providing capital, market access and innovation, they open the opportunity to grow the industries of tomorrow. This is a recipe for economic success. Their focus has been on achieving growth. Another example is Mauritius, which by 2018 had 37 years without a recession, and raised per capita GDP from US$4,529 in 1980 to US$20,404.[374] This is a very current example of how the State working with entrepreneurs can build success.[375] Mauritius focused on supporting manufacturers that export a significant part of the output to attain this growth without a balance of payments crisis. Other countries that have focused their economies on investment driven export led growth have also succeeded in driving stable growth over a number of years. Their problems (such as the 1997 Asian Financial Crisis) have come later, when they relax their growth and investment focus and allow consumer and asset markets to find their own head.

Blockbuster disrupting and micro disrupting businesses leap frog their competitors to change the markets they are in, by providing customers with next generation products and services. To achieve this requires capital flows and support resources are made available to innovating entrepreneurs. It is also essential to ensure that high growth businesses have a level playing field with big companies. These companies need the finance to access the legal wherewithall to defend their innovations and inventions should some bigger companies try to poach them. They also need to develop their workforce and their own entrepreneurial skills to align them with what is needed to drive market success.

Entrepreneurs come in all shapes and sizes and from all sorts of backgrounds. An 'entrepreneur first' policy gives the 'Left Behind' the opportunity that they too can succeed. Help mentoring and nurturing their success to become beacons in their local communities helps inspire confidence to those around them. Some may not be looking to build a Google, but they can still build sustainable businesses. Empowered by the success of others, these potential entrepreneurs may have spotted either a new or 'Scale Up' opportunity that they can seize and develop, if they have access to the capital resources and the skills support to take it. Nothing transforms like success.

THE BREXIT ADJUSTMENT

For these changes to happen there will need to be three quite distinct and different adjustments.

The first adjustment will be to adapt the many existing and perhaps larger companies that are integrated into complex Pan European supply chains to a post-Brexit environment. In making this adjustment there will be a need to minimise damage that could be inflicted by Brexit through non-tariff barriers and associated customs procedures, impacting existing business operations. The ideal adjustment for this group of businesses is, (from their perspective) zero adjustment, that is to keep things as they are. If there must be change, then these businesses need it to occur at a pace and a cost that they can absorb within their day-to-day operations. The July 2018 Brexit White Paper (discussed in Appendix 3) recognises the need to minimise disruption in complex supply chains by proposing that goods movement is kept within the EU's rule book and, both the single market and customs union.

Avoiding unnecessary damage to these companies is emerging as a priority, not least as they employ (directly and indirectly) a large number of people and export large amounts. Many of these firms are also very efficient with good productivity growth records. Much the same can be said regarding the need to avoid damage to the UK's globally important financial sector. The July 2018 proposals look to preserve existing regulatory relationships through a process of 'regulatory equivalence'. Equivalence regimes are less flexible than 'mutual recognition' and not as robust as 'single market' rights.[376] The UK is proposing sophisticated joint governance arrangements over the equivalence regime to ensure its stability.

There is a second significant adjustment that is a necessary condition to raising UK productivity and growth rates. This change requires mechanisms to ensure that resources flow to entrepreneurs, enabling them to grow, invest, innovate and undertake necessary workforce reskilling. Third, entrepreneurial support will need to be combined with measures that enable stable and cost effective housing for the many younger people for whom locating affordable acceptable housing is so challenging. Successful entrepreneurs and quality workers share the need to be aspirational, and aspirational people need stability at home.

It is implicit to these adjustments that there will need to be an inter-generational shift to take wealth and income from the old and, flow these resources to both entrepreneurs to fund entrepreneurial investments and to younger generations to improve their standards of living and give them access to long term stable housing. This adjustment can (but is unlikely to) happen voluntarily through richer pensioners accepting reductions in their benefits, possibly needing to contribute more towards their health costs and accepting higher taxes on their wealth, especially property. More likely is that adjustment in the housing market will result from a market driven adjustment that restates housing values to where houses become affordable to younger generations on average incomes. There may also need to be a market adjustment (in terms of confidence related to funding long term UK state debt) that forces government to prune welfare and health spending to richer pensioners. Such an involuntary adjustment could be very painful and very sudden. When asset markets adjust, past adjustments tell us that markets do so rapidly and without mercy.

In practical terms, such a Brexit adjustment may be related to a 'Sudden Stop' financial event. The risk of such a sharp adjustment happening rises if the challenges facing larger companies and the financial sector are not handled with great skill. We should anticipate that Brexit, will by definition impact some financial flows that currently pass through London and it is likely there could be significant disruption to service exporters operations through loss of market access, if they are excluded from any trade deal.

Inevitably, if there is disruption it is likely that some companies will relocate away from the UK and others reduce their capital investment. The implications – especially if the UK experiences significant outflows of financial capital from the City of London – could be a significant further fall in sterling that then becomes the trigger for a significantly challenging financial shock. Such a shock would almost inevitably, adjust markets and asset values, including house prices, to a point where they correspond with the income streams and cashflows that support them, meaning houses once again become affordable for younger people to buy. The juxtaposition of this process is that such an adjustment is likely to wipe out a significant pro-portion of the elder generation's wealth.

THE BREXIT RISK

Both Britain and within it England have in the past been as divided as they are now. For example, there were deep divides after the changes of the 1530s. England had a Civil War in the seventeenth century that in a sense reflected many of the deep divides that date back to the splits of the 1530s.

In a world of social media and fake news, with nihilist politicians breathing hyperbole and untruth, the story of Germany in the 1920s and 1930s provides a chilling warning of how unrealism and disappointment can mutate into a Stab in The Back narrative, and how such a narrative can mutate into finding and punishing scapegoats. Politicians, editors, bloggers and those with the strongest views need to stop, draw a deep breath and ask if what they are doing is wise. Putting the hate genie back in the bottle is much more difficult than letting it out.

OUR SHARED CHALLENGE

As a nation, as a community and as individuals we will all add our own brush strokes onto the canvas of how Brexit will unfold. In AD 410, there was the hardest of hard Brexits and one hopes that even the most avid Leaver will want to avoid some aspects of what happened then. In the 1530s much as today, the focus was legal and on keeping the various 'power players' at court happy. Then in the latter half of the sixteenth century there was a collaborative and entrepreneurial Brexit led by pragmatist Elizabeth I.

Today's specific challenges are different, but many of the risks are very similar. If one key to the future is to raise living standards, then Brexit is currently missing a narrative as to how it enables a return to entrepreneurial capitalism. Indeed, perhaps both Leavers and Remainers could unify if the focus can be tweaked from nostalgia for 'English Exceptionalism' into aspiration to grow 'Exceptional Entrepreneurs'.

Threat or opportunity, which Brexit will we choose and which door will be one of the defining choices of this generation.

Which Brexit do you want?

APPENDIX 1: THE EUROPEAN UNION TODAY

The European Union (EU) is both a legal form in itself and an affiliation of nation states. The EU is governed by a series of Treaties which have created its institutional framework as a supra national institution and its legal persona. This EU legal persona enables the EU to sign bi-lateral treaties with non-EU Countries and register for membership at bodies such as the WTO; binding all EU Member States to the terms of these treaties and memberships.

The EU's operations are restricted to areas where it has 'Competence' under the Treaties, although there is continual 'niggling' at the edges by the EU to extend its authority and by the Member States to limit its powers. A concept of 'Subsidiarity' has been embedded into recent Treaties to assure Member States of the limits to the EU's powers. This concept is discussed separately in Appendix 2.

The role of the Member State (and intergovernmental dimension) is implemented via the decision making European Council and in the Member State origins of appointments of Commissioners in the policy setting European Commission. The EU 'corporatist' aspects are visible in both the EU Commission's policy-making functions, as the sole initiator of legislation and its monitoring role as 'guardian of the treaties', together with the European Parliament's legislative functions. These are in many cases, competing institutions, with the Parliament and Commission seeing themselves as guardians of the 'Community Method', as opposed to the 'intergovernmental' method favoured by the Member States.[377] Since the ratification of the Lisbon Treaty (2007), the European Parliament has become increasingly assertive. For example, although there is no 'Treaty' basis for it, the EU Parliament has asserted its right to nominate the candidates for the Presidency (the *spitzenkandidaten*) on the basis that the Parliament has to confirm the appointment.[378] In a counter move, leading EU politicians such as Frau Merkel have proposed the Community Method should be replaced by the 'Union Method' that blends institutions and Member States into a single framework.[379]

Institutional competition is complemented by national rivalries, sometimes reflecting historic narratives that percolate the political levels of the European Council. At a more functional level, many detailed issues are resolved at a diplomatic level through the 'Committee of Permanent Representatives' and associated working groups. Political rivalries between member states are paradoxically mirrored by 'thick trust' between diplomats in the EU Permanent Representations of each Member State allowing for a dynamic process of give and take.[380]

Notwithstanding the changes of recent years, France has always had a belief that the European Union (following the work of Monnet and Schumann in the late 1950s) is a French construction founded on a mutual alliance between France and Germany. A 2004 report[381] to the French National Assembly on French influence in Europe opens by declaring *'France [an EU] founding country, has its stamp over the European construction. In a golden age this was typified by its triple influence: policy, administrative and linguistic'*[xi] One can sense the notion of the *grande project* in many of the French attitudes to the EU, representing an underlying belief of a French leadership that is embedded into the structure of in European decision making.[382] This sense of entitlement has been progressively eaten away as new member states have joined, Germany has reunified and became the visibly senior partner and English has become the working language of the EU.

Germany's post-reunification role is a paradox. It is militarily weak, (with for example, only nine out of 44 tanks intended for use in the NATO rapid intervention force for the Baltics operational in 2018),[383] yet economically dominant. Germany has become the main political power in the European Union, most especially in the Eurozone, where it drives the monetary union in a manner that protects its own national interest at the expense of other members.[384]

[xi]Author sense translation of *'La France, pays fondateur, a marqué la construction européenne de son empreinte. Ce que l'on peut qualifier « d'âge d'or » de la présence française est ainsi le fait d'une triple influence: politique, administrative et linguistique'* (from Floch, 2004).

APPENDIX 2: COULD SUBSIDIARITY BE 'PRAEMUNIRE' IN SHEEP'S CLOTHING?

Under current EU Law, both of the supranational legislative bodies (The European Commission and The European Parliament) are restrained in what they can do by the principle of 'subsiduarity', which is set out in the Governing Treaties and is interpreted by the European Court of Justice.[385] The EU framework for the 'Subsidiarity Principle' was formally adopted in the Maastricht Treaty, further codified in the Amsterdam Treaty and embedded into the Lisbon Treaty.[386] In practical terms, this mechanism acts by challenging the right of the European Institutions to be the first and right place to legislate. The 'subsiduarity' principle suggests there should always be a preference to take action at a Member State level rather than EU level unless the competence is specifically assigned to the EU in the Governing Treaties.

This "Principle" has been tested in the European Courts. For example, in the 2010 Fundación Gala-Salvador Dalí case, the court recused itself on the basis that the issue as to whom royalties on copied artworks should be paid is not within EU competence as [the];

> preamble to Directive 2001/84 [...] did not, in accordance with the principle of subsidiarity, consider it appropriate to take action through that directive in relation to Member States' laws of succession, thus leaving to each Member State the task of defining the categories of persons capable of being considered, under national law, as those entitled. (ECJ, 2010)

Importantly, the decision was based on how the preamble in the Directive was worded and not upon the Treaty Article governing 'Subsidiarity' itself. Although the Treaty grants an absolute right, in practice, the court restricted this Principle to determine if the principle of subsiduarity applies by reviewing how the Preamble has interpreted the right. This is consistent with other European Court of Justice decisions in cases such as the 1996 judgement on UK v. the European Council on the Working Time Directive (C-84/94) in which the Court held that internal market needs for harmonisation (in this case of health and safety regulations) took precedence over the treaty obligation of subsidiarity. Again in 2001, the Court found that the needs of harmonisation and the internal market took precedence over subsidiarity (ECJ, 2001).

In practical terms, the European Court of Justice has been keen to avoid incorporating the subsidiarity issue into its judgements,[387] preferring to leave this as a political issue for the other European Institutions (Parliament, Council and Commission) to deal with. It is notable that one of the UK's highest profile successes in the European Court (the 2011 action against the European Central Bank's proposed regulation to prohibit Euro Clearing outside the Euro area) was not decided upon the fundamental decision-making rights of Member States under the Treaties (ECJ, 2015b), but rather on the basis that the European Central Bank had not been granted specific competence to make the decision.

APPENDIX 3: JULY 2018 BREXIT WHITE PAPER

In July 2018, the UK Government issued a White Paper (HMGOV, 2018) that outlined its detailed vision for the post-Brexit relationship with the UK. This document (colloquially known as the 'Chequers Proposals') has become the negotiating blueprint for the UK, despite its rejection by both ardent Brexiteers and by the European Union. In summary, the UK is looking to sign an 'Association Agreement' under Article 217 of the Treaty of the Functioning of the European Union (EU). Association Agreements can be broad in scope and are defined as *involving reciprocal rights and obligations, common actions and special procedures* (EU, 2008, p. 98). Typically, these have been signed with EU border states such as the Ukraine to give them some privileged access to EU markets without requiring full membership.

The UK proposal extends previous uses of this instrument to include economic and political relationships and to propose a new governance relationship.

PROPOSED GOVERNANCE RELATIONSHIP

Three governance streams are proposed, economic, security and 'cross cutting' that then come together into a joint UK/EU Governing Board/Committee structure that is empowered to make the decisions on the relationship's future direction that are then to be ratified by each Parliament. The framework if agreed would give the UK a formal consultation role on new EU Regulations at both a political and a technical level. The stated aim is to maintain same level of consultation and pre-decision access for matters where the UK accepts EU rules as a Member State has despite the UK not being a member and not having a vote. The White Paper envisages maintaining a common rule book for goods and formal recognition for rules being treated as 'equivalent'. This process sets in place a fixed and certain relationship for goods, services and security and is described as follows:

> *By making firm commitments, the UK and the EU would agree to establish a new free trade area for goods; the access that should be provided to firms and individuals to provide services in each other's markets; provisions related to socio-economic cooperation; and the arrangements for how the UK and the EU will jointly combat security threats. (HMGOV, 2018, p. 89)*

ECONOMIC STREAM

The economic stream proposes a free trade area in which goods from the UK will freely circulate across the EU (as if the UK were still in the EU Single Market); in return the UK will be committed to following all the EU rules and regulations for these 'goods' markets. Free circulation under this proposal will mean that UK goods in the 'Single Market' do not require certificates of origin or customs procedures and, that cross EU movement reported through the EU 'Intrastat' VAT declaration linked system. In summary, for goods moving between the UK and EU, the proposal is for no change from today.

Supporting this and allowing the UK to sign non-EU trade deals is a proposal for a 'Facilitated Customs Arrangement' whereby the UK operates a 'dual customs regime'. For goods known to be destined for Europe, the UK operates its customs procedures in accordance with EU rules, and for goods known to not be going to the EU, the UK will operate its own tariff and customs procedures. If there is doubt as to where the goods will go, the higher tariff will be payable and any difference can be reclaimed later, if the goods are proven to have entered the lower tariff destination. The UK is seeking mutual recognition of key regulators with EU so that UK certifications would have validity in the EU along with continued, but non-voting affiliation membership of various EU regulators such as air safety, medicines and chemicals. In essence, the proposal is to establish new arrangements that at a practical level maintain the current status quo.

Trade in services is proposed to rely upon regulatory equivalence between the UK and the EU, with this 'equivalence' managed through the governance regime. Taking equivalence and the governance regime together suggests the UK is looking for the same sort of regulatory certainty that would be available under 'mutual recognition'. Fast growth markets such as, digital and ecommerce are singled out for developing new accords, the aim of which seems to be to preserve unrestricted UK/EU data transfers but allow the UK to adopt pioneering regulations.

In generality, the UK is proposing that it aligns with and works with EU regulators and rules on competition and state aid issues.

SECURITY STREAM

The UK is looking to maintain its current security and information exchange links (in summary its operational capabilities) with the EU, while removing itself from any automatic joint political foreign policy actions.

CROSS-CUTTING ISSUES

The UK is looking to keep close links and shared working on data protection, classified information and international research and development efforts.

ENDNOTES

(1) Andrews and Beer (2013).

(2) A recent example of how uncertain today's global landscape is seen in the continual policy changes and evolutions under US President Donald Trump. For example January 2018, there were fears of a new war on the Korean Peninsula, yet by June 2018 there had been a summit between the two halves of divided Korea and between the North Korean leader and the US President leading to talk of de-nuclearisation of the Korean Peninsula.

(3) Mazzucato (2018).

(4) Abstracted from Ramsey (1979).

(5) The Brexit Museum (https://www.museumofbrexit.uk/) is the brainchild of Dr Lee Rotherham, former Director of Special Projects at Vote Leave.

(6) Hingley (2016).

(7) Clery, Curtice and Harding (2016).

(8) Becker, Fetzer and Novy (2017).

(9) Dorling (2016).

(10) Swales (2016).

(11) Seventy per cent of Leave voters reported that they had read *The Sun* and 66% the *Daily Mail* (Swales, 2016).

(12) Menon and Wagner (2018).

(13) Ford and Goodwin (2014).

(14) Kaufmann (2016).

(15) Clarke, Goodwin and Whiteley (2017).

(16) The British Social Attitudes Survey has taken place each year since 1983. It is the United Kingdom's longest running survey with over 90,000 citizens having participated, so far. The survey is a critical gauge of public opinion, and is used by the Government, journalists, opinion formers and academics, due to the rigorous techniques employed in collecting the mood of the nation. In 2016, the survey shone a spotlight on the opinions of Brexit Leavers.

(17) Becker et al. (2017).

(18) Kenny (2015). Rival perspectives on the national identity of the English have become increasingly salient during the last two decades. They include radical-democratic, restorationist and Anglo-British forms of patriotic discourse. This trend has rendered other circles of attachment – to the UK and Europe – more tenuous and distant.

(19) Camden (1695) ed intro iii.

(20) Surtees (1886, p. 165).

(21) Clarke, Whiteley, Borges, Sanders and Stewart (2016).

(22) EUaud (2014, p. 5).

(23) Sobolewska, Galandini and Lessard-Phillips (2017).

(24) Swales and Tipping (2018, p. 22).

(25) Swales and Tipping (2018).

(26) YouGov (2017a).

(27) Clery et al. (2016, p. 131).

(28) Phillips, Curtice, Phillips and Perry (2018).

(29) Metropolitan Police (2016).

(30) UN (2018).

(31) Hingley (2016).

(32) Hirsch (2018).

(33) Link and Hornburg (2016).

(34) King, Rosen, Tanner and Wagner (2008); Childers (1985).

(35) Curtice (2016b).

(36) Curtice (2016a).

(37) Maffesoli (1988).

(38) Knapton (2015).

(39) Cunliffe (2005); Moore (2011).

(40) Phillips et al. (2018).

(41) BBC (2018).

(42) Bank of England (1971).

(43) Bowen, Hoggarth, and Pain (1999).

(44) CMA (2016).

(45) Muellbauer and Murphy (1997, p. 1701).

(46) Barton (2017).

(47) Sufi and Mian (2014).

(48) Intergenerational Commission (2018).

(49) Daily Mail (2016).

(50) Lisbon Treaty (2007).

(51) May (2017a).

(52) The notification was submitted in accordance with the procedure set out in 1969 Vienna Convention on the Law of Treaties (Vienna, 1969).

(53) De La Baume (2016).

(54) Vienna (1969).

(55) Eden (2017).

(56) Scotcourt 'Opinion and Referral' (2018, September 21).

(57) May (2017b).

(58) EU (2018a).

(59) Miller (2017).

(60) Von Der Burchard (2018).

(61) Parliament (2017).

(62) FT (2018a, 2018b).

(63) Elton (2012).

(64) Ollivaud and Turner (2015).

(65) Crawford, Jin and Simpson (2013).

(66) Crawford et al. (2013).

(67) The relative importance to productivity growth of lower capital intensity, in combination with an increasing labour force (as older workers have sought to stay in work and not retire early) and a lack of trade union bargaining power, has been questioned. Although conventional economic theory suggests that if you lower the relative price of labour in comparison to labour, more labour will be used (Blundell, Crawford & Jin, 2014).

(68) Cribb and Johnson (2018).

(69) Krugman (2008).

(70) The 2018 Migration Advisory Committee Study (MAC, 2018) recommends (with the exception of establishing a seasonal worker scheme for agricultural workers) restricting post Brexit low skill immigration. The report finds that low skilled immigration only has a modest impact on low skill wage rates. They calculate that low skilled migration led to just under a 5% reduction in wage rates in the bottom 10% of the earnings distribution over the period 1993 – 2017. They also present alternative estimates that suggest this loss could be as high as 7+% over this 14 year period. The study makes clear that the negative impact on wage rates of the 2008 financial crash was far higher than migration.

(71) Pessoa and Van Reenen (2013).

(72) Riley and Bondibene (2016).

(73) Machin (2015).

(74) Machin (2011; 2015).

(75) Blundell, Joyce, Norris Keiller and Ziliak (2018).

(76) Hood and Waters (2017).

(77) Manacorda, Manning and Wadsworth (2012).

(78) The September 2018 Migration Advisory Committee's own estimates suggested a fall of just under 5% in the wages of the lowest 10% of the income distribution in the period 1993–2017 (MAC, 2018).

(79) Wadsworth (2010).

(80) The increase in self-employment did not represent an increase in the proportion of people taking second jobs, which has stayed broadly stable over the past decade.

(81) Miller, Pope and Cribb (2018).

(82) Miller et al. (2018).

(83) ONS (2018b).

(84) ONS (2018c).

(85) O'Connor (2018).

(86) Schumpeter (1934).

(87) This is strictly the split of 'value added' where we define value added as the value received minus the costs of the material inputs, not including labour. The word 'profit' is used in the main text to make the picture easier for the reader to relate the concepts into everyday language.

(88) The distribution of income and associated value creation issues is historically controversial, the subject of much scholarly literature that includes contributions from Smith, Ricardo, Marx, Schumpeter, Sraffa, Piketty and Mazzucato to name a few.

(89) OECD (2015).

(90) Ark and Jäger (2017).

(91) Haldane (2017).

(92) Bloom et al. (2007).

(93) Centre for Cities (2018).

(94) Verdoorn's Law suggests that productivity gains are derived from economies of scale in manufacturing. The original 1949 paper that assumed a static level of technology was later modified to reflect technical changes embedded in new capital expenditure to give a more dynamic view of the relationship (Verdoorn, 1980). Both variants of the relationship were tested against growth dynamics in Spain over the period 1962–1991 with mixed findings. Scale productivity effects (productivity rising as output rises) are visible in manufacturing but unexpectedly they are also found in the service sector. They are not found in the construction or agricultural sectors (Léon-Ledesma, 2000).This suggests that whilst in late 1980's level of technology manufacturing was still a key sector driving productivity growth (as output rises), services can make productivity improvement contributions, whilst other sectors such as construction and agriculture will not see productivity rise as output rises.

The policy consequences of this are that unless there is substantial surplus under utilised labour employed in industries such as construction, (unlikely in the UK's open labour market), policy interventions that include large increases in house building will not raise overall productivity. Whilst it is likely that this relationship holds true in construction; technological advances in information processing (including emerging Big Data and Artificial Intelligence technologies) both explain why some service industries see productivity increases related to the scale of output, and may thereby require a re think of Verdoorn's Law for some parts of the service sector. The service sector may in the near future, because of new technologies, and most especially moves towards artificial intelligence and smart alogrithms, have the capacity to deliver rising productivity in response to rising volumes.

Anecdotally, this view seems to be supported by the experiences of 'Platform' technology companies, such as Google. Two key features of the 'Google' search platform are that as it becomes more predictive the more people use it, and second, there are high fixed costs to provide the search function in the first place but very low incremental costs for each additional search. Raising productivity in service sectors in this context may require helping companies reach sufficient size where they can become 'Platform' companies rather than niche players. Inevitably, such Platform companies will be supranational in character as once the Google's and Amazon's reach scale, they start to command competitive advantage over potential competitors as their fixed costs are spread over higher volumes.

(95) Kenya (2018).

(96) Monks (2017).

(97) Mazzucato (2013).

(98) OECD (2018).

(99) Powell (2018).

(100) Buchmann and Pyka (2012).

(101) Knibb, Gormezano and Partners (2009).

(102) Automotive Council UK (2017).

(103) BEISC (2018).

(104) Thompson (2018).

(105) Giles (2018).

(106) ONS (2018d).

(107) Export composition, capacity restrictions and import and export elasticities may mean modest falls in sterling will not correct the UK trade deficit. Kristin Forbes, a former member of the UK's Monetary Policy Committee, demonstrated the impact of Sterling's upward revaluations as widening the trade deficit, in a speech entitled, *'The economic impact of sterling's recent moves: more than a midsummer night's dream'*. In her model, imports rise faster than exports fall (Forbes, 2014). The Marshall/Lerner condition that underlies predictions that currency devaluations will improve the current balance of payments, (by comparing sensitivity to import prices with overseas demand sensitivity to export prices) has seemingly not been fulfilled. Bahmani, Harvey and Hegerty (2013) argue that for the UK, *a priori* devaluation is ineffective in reducing the trade deficit. In essence according to this research, the appreciation of sterling can lead to falls in UK export performance (widening the trade deficit) and falls in sterling seem to little if any impact on export volumes. Some specific business export track records have tended to challenge this statistical finding by citing specific cases where a fall in the currency has improved a specific company's export ability.

(108) Carney (2017).

(109) Summers (1995).

(110) Eichengreen and Gupta (2016).

(111) Sufi and Mian (2014).

(112) Obstfeld (2012).

(113) Obstfeld (2012).

(114) Corden (1994).

(115) Efremidze and Tomohara (2011).

(116) Eichengreen and Gupta (2016).

(117) *'Significant economic changes did occur but these affected the most visible parts of the economy most catastrophically. The biggest slice of Romano − British GDP, the largely invisible agricultural economy, remained resilient and may even have prospered once the burdens of the Roman Empire had been lifted. This allowed diversification and a move to a less efficient pastoral economy, which manifested itself in the way landscapes were managed and perhaps increased calorific intake [...] rural economy actually rested upon relatively small blocks of land, [...] connected in some cases by ownership tenurial obligations and kinship [...] Together [with] [...] other forms of social practice, as well as economic linkages, defined so called "small words"'*
(Gerrard, 2013).

(118) Euparl (2016).

(119) Khan (2018).

(120) FT (2018a, 2018b).

(121) AFME (2017).

(122) FCA (2017).

(123) Investment Association (2016).

(124) UNCTAD (2018).

(125) Borio and Disyatat (2015).

(126) Spufford (2006; 2010).

(127) Centre for Cities (2018).

(128) OECD (2015).

(129) Davies, Haldane, Nielsen and Pezzini (2014).

(130) The argument that the public sector 'Crowds Out' investment in the private sector can be summarised as: *'In short, if the combined ratios of private consumption and non-market spending rise and current account balance of payments equilibrium must be maintained, the ratio of market sector investment must inevitably become lower. Hence, in these conditions 'crowding-out' of market sector investment is inescapable'* (Bacon & Eltis, 1979, p. 411). This statement holds true when a country is on the 'Gold Standard' (or today is a member of the Eurozone) but it does not correspond with the modern reality of endogenous credit creation in the banking system as described by the Bank of England (2014). In today's economy banks can create unlimited credit subject to liquidity and risk weighted asset ratios. UK Government bonds are fully discountable for cash at the Central Bank and carry a zero-risk weighting, thereby having no impact on credit creation for the private sector.

The modern limitation to overall credit growth is hinted at by Bacon and Eltis (1979), namely, overseas confidence in the currency. In this context, both private and public credit volumes matter. To be long term effective, the credit being raised must be invested in future productive capacity that will increase wealth, otherwise the credit raised (both public and private) will have been 'frittered' on current consumptions with no long term economic benefit.

(131) National Museum of American History (2013).

(132) Goolsbee, Hall and Katz (1999).

(133) Friedman (1962).

(134) McKinnon (1973).

(135) Mussa (1982).

(136) Gavin (1996).

(137) Aghion and Blanchard (1994).

(138) Dehejia (1996).

(139) Minford et al. (2017).

(140) Knight (1921).

(141) Amoroso, Moncada-Paternò-Castello and Vezzani (2017).

(142) DARPA (2018).

(143) Fraunhofer (2018).

(144) CIA (2012).

(145) Cleary (1989).

(146) Fulford and Bird (1975).

(147) Mazzucato (2013).

(148) Campbell (2004).

(149) Cleary (1989).

(150) Temin (2006).

(151) Andreau (1999).

(152) Yerxa (2006).

(153) Cleary (1989).

(154) Rogers (2010).

(155) Cleary (1989).

(156) Erdkam (2016).

(157) Walton and Moorhead (2016).

(158) The main sources for hoards are Robertson (2000), the Coin
Hoards from Roman Britain Series (Vols. I–XIII), Coin Hoards
I–VII (Royal Numismatic Society 1975–95) and summaries in

the Numismatic Chronicle (1994–2011) and British Numismatic Journal (2012 onwards), the Treasure Annual Reports (1997–) and for Wales, Guest and Wells (2007). A thorough listing and analysis of gold hoards is in Bland and Loriot (2010).

(159) Sixty-two per cent of early fifth-century precious metal treasures and 58% of all hoards containing silver coins from the period AD 300–500 come from Britain; Britain also had 24% of all bronze hoards from the period (Guest 2005, p. 28); 80% of all known silver coin hoards from the period 388–410 come from Britain (Abdy, 2002, p. 62; Bland, 1997a; Guest, 2005, note 33; Guest, 1997, p. 411 and Hobbs, 2006).

(160) Guest (2005); Johns (2010); Inscker and Orna-Ornstein (2009) and Robertson (2000, pp. 405-6, pp. 1621).

(161) Walton and Moorhead (2016).

(162) Bergstrand (1985).

(163) Tinbergen (1969).

(164) Yerxa (2006).

(165) Gibbon (1909).

(166) Lane (2014) and Lyne (2016).

(167) Brown (1894).

(168) For example, it can be argued that the theatrical splendour of the Field of the Cloth of Gold Meeting between Henry VIII and Francis I (of France) in 1520 was an early attempt at 'summitry' intended to cement the 1518 Universal Peace (Richardson, 2014).

(169) Sixteenth-century rulers were always looking for more prestige than their rivals. In 1521, Henry VIII produced a book *Assertio Septem Sacramentorum* that challenged Martin Luther's theses and which opened the opportunity for the Pope to confer the title 'Fidei Defensor' or Defender of the Faith on him. (Cardinal Wolsey had been lobbying for Henry to receive a special title for some time). Brown (1894) describes how Pope Leo X balanced rivalries between different states, by awarding Henry a prestigious title that was not

hereditary, whilst other European Sovereigns already had titles that were hereditary, so were able to feel superior to Henry. Pope Leo X died shortly after issuing the title, so there was immediate opportunity to press his successor Pope Clement VII to make the title hereditary. Clement acted in 1523 using the words *'Considering all these things, we also, the successors of St. Peter, in the plenitude of the apostolic power, of our own sure knowledge and free will approve, confirm and grant to you the title and name of Defender of the Faith, to be your own for ever'*. The words 'for ever' being an early example of a classic 'European' fudge.

(170) Lisbon (2007).

(171) ECJ (2015).

(172) Garcia-de-Andoain, Heider, Hoerova and Manganelli (2016).

(173) Slavin (1986).

(174) Erasmus (1514).

(175) Butler (2012).

(176) Gaston and Harrison–Evans (2017).

(177) Butcher (2018).

(178) Leake (2018).

(179) Clark (2007).

(180) Costa and Machin (2017).

(181) In 1512, Parliament passed an Act restricting clerical immunity from secular prosecution for 'minor holy orders' (to prevent junior orders such as acolytes from being able to claim immunity from prosecution if caught for a crime) without criticism from the Church. By 1515, when the Act was due for renewal, the political climate had changed and Richard Kidderminster, Abbot of Winchcomb, made a full political attack on it. The 'matter' progressed into a public dispute with the King. Subsequently Parliament's advocate Henry Standish won the argument. The Church reacted by accusing Standish of Heresy (Skousen, 2008). The case mirrors the civil case of Richard Hunne in 1515, when Hunne challenged mortuary fees for his dead

infant from his (likely absentee) parish priest in London. Hunne was arraigned in the church courts and lost, so sued the church for Praemunire. Hunne was arrested for heresy and then found hanged in the Bishops jail (McBride, 1969). Both cases led to ecclesiastical apologies to the King, but both cases reinforced the sense of alienation of the senior clergy from their parishioners and the state. Overall in reformist circles, the Roman Curia in the early sixteenth century was seen as intrusive, corrupt and remote. '*Reformers complained also about the quid-pro-quo patronage system that rewarded family and friends, who were often unworthy of the positions bestowed upon them. Even more irritating to many bishops and rulers was the growing centralisation of authority in the Holy See and the imposition by the papacy of ever more taxes and other financial exactions to fund an ever more ostentatious papal court'* (O'Malley, 2013).

(182) Having tried to solve this through both negotiation and threats, there seems to have been a pause during which Henry sought ways to delay the calling of the third session of the Reformation Parliament, that was postponed from October 1531 until January 1532.

(183) Elton (1988).

(184) Starkey (1988).

(185) Elton (2012).

(186) The importance of 'Common Law' was reinforced by Norman initiatives to separate Church Law from State Law in 1070 (Moore, 1980). The workings of the law also evolved over time, for example in 1150 there was not much of a legal profession anywhere, yet by 1250 almost all European Countries including England had professional lawyers (Brundage, 2008). Early sixteenth-century competition between secular and Roman Law was mirrored by competition between 'Common Law' lawyers at the Inns of Court (versed in English Common Law) and the 'Doctors Commons' who were advocates trained in Admiralty and Ecclesiastical Law and thereby following in the tradition of Roman Law (Brundage, 1993). Unsurprisingly, competing legal systems led to competing lawyers.

(187) Helmholz (1996).

(188) Waugh (1922).

(189) This is demonstrated by a 1515 case, where a goldsmith Ryecroft who was being summoned to the Roman courts attempted to sue for Praemunire. His case was refused by the English court on the basis that his case was spiritual and not secular (Waugh, 1922). Elton (1991) spoke of a revival of English Common Law in the 1490's, which occurred at the expense of Church or Canon Law. For example, in 1504, Bishop Nykke complained that attempts were being made to press the 'Praemunire' boundary by aggressive secular litigants in cases of 'breach of trust' (Cavill, 2011). Perhaps this reflected heightened anti-clerical feeling at that time, or given that such events were very localised, it reflected some specifically aggressive local litigants. Ironically, a much later use of Praemunire was postulated in 1923, when the UK Attorney General and possibly Home Secretary faced the risk of Praemunire for violating a Habeus Corpus decision (Chandler, 1924).

(190) Bell (2018).

(191) Broman (2014).

(192) Thornton (2009).

(193) Bernard (2011).

(194) Bush (1991).

(195) Hoyle (1994).

(196) Elton (2012).

(197) Stephens (2004).

(198) Broman (2014).

(199) Broman (2014).

(200) Ellacombe (1852).

(201) Clark (2007).

(202) For example, Evans Pritchard (2016).

(203) Fletcher and MacCulloch (2015, p. 125).

(204) Wyatt spent three days in Southwark where his supporters looted Bishop Gardiners house, before moving on to Kingston and dispersing.

(205) Associated by some with a desire to make Mary Queen of Scots the sovereign of England.

(206) Contemporary writings concerning them are rather limited and as an the chronicling work of John Stow has shown, tended to be very sensitive to the issues of the moment and change over time (Beer, 1988).

(207) Kett's 'Campmen' have been described as being somewhat 'utopian' in their vision and aims, looking to change the economic model, rather than who was in charge of running it (Holstun, 2008).

(208) Booth (2014).

(209) Throughout the period cloth was the most important export being about 78% of the total export sales (Stone, 1949).

(210) Fisher (1940).

(211) Fisher (1940).

(212) Stone (1947).

(213) Ashton (1967).

(214) Bisson (1987).

(215) Aston (1967).

(216) HOC (1604).

(217) The 1604 dispute had deep roots, some of which lie in a struggle between two licensed merchant companies, the Staplers and the London Company of the Merchant Adventurers that goes back to Henry VII's reign (and before). An example of the protagonists being at loggerheads is available in the Star Chamber proceedings of 1504, subsequent proceedings in 1512, a prohibition on the Staplers trading cloth into the Low Countries in 1561 (relaxed in 1564) and a further ban in 1581 (Bisson, 1987).

(218) Minford et al. (2017).

(219) The classic Free Trade vs Mercantilism debate is mirrored in the Brexit arguments being made by Minford et al. (2017) who assert that unilaterally removing tariffs will give the highest benefits as consumers and industry benefit from cheaper food and goods from non EU sources. They argue that removing tariffs reduces the price of imports, notwithstanding that this price reduction may not reach the consumer, as it can be pocketed by the importer or the supermarket to raise their profits. There will no doubt be some cases when the consumer benefits and others when the exporting nation raises its prices to the UK to improve its own earnings. Minford *et al.* explicitly assume the pound sterling will not fall and that it will rise to its pre-Brexit Referendum value within 10 years. They also do not explain how 'non-tariff' barriers will be compensated for despite their suggesting that these could in some cases be equivalent to a tariff of 18%–20% of the products price.

(220) Iyer et al. (2018).

(221) Nef (1937).

(222) Stone (1947).

(223) Fisher (1940).

(224) O'Brien and Pigman (1992).

(225) Lampe (2011).

(226) Bairoch (1976).

(227) Hakluyt is an historian of many of the early entrepreneurial voyages and he believes it was his son Sebastian.

(228) Hakluyt and Purcas (1830).

(229) The Tsar introduced Jenkinson to the Persian Ambassador at a dinner in 1562.

(230) Personal experience of one of the authors.

(231) Jenkinson had been previously been briefed to criticise the Ottoman Sultan because of his trading links with England's competitor Venice.

(232) Meshkat (2009).

(233) Çeliktemel (2012).

(234) Brotton (2016).

(235) Stone (1949).

(236) Investors came together to finance these expeditions, which could be quite costly. Andrews (1959) found that costs could range from £500 for a small privateer to £3000 for a large well-equipped vessel.

(237) Hillman and Gathmann (2011).

(238) Stone (1965).

(239) Dietz (1932, pp. 321–330).

(240) The document itself appears to have been presented to the Queen much later in 1582, when the political climate was ripe for informers to report customs fraud. Around that time there appears to have been an Elizabethan 'whistle-blowers' campaign to encourage action against fraud.

(241) Nef (1933).

(242) Ramsey (1979).

(243) Stone (1949).

(244) Adapted from an epigram by Photios I of Constantinople (AD 820–AD 893) commenting on the *Bibliotheca of Pseudo-Apollodorus* mentioned in Fowler (2013, p. 384). The *Bibliotheca* is a compendium of the legends of Ancient Greece that includes the legend of the 12 labours of Hercules. The epigram of Photios is not visible in the 1921 Frazer translation. More comments are available in wikipedia https://en.wikipedia.org/wiki/Bibliotheca_(Pseudo-Apollodorus)

(245) Whilst the word challenge can be associated with thrill seekers and dare devils for some, it can also be associated with uncertainty, disruption and difficult hurdles.

(246) Roper and Hart (2018).

(247) Vise (2005).

(248) Davies et al. (2014).

(249) Roper and Hart (2018).

(250) Roper, Hart, Bourke and Hathaway (2018).

(251) Facebook (2018).

(252) Gartner (2008).

(253) Downes and Nunes (2013).

(254) Facebook, Amazon, Netflix and Google.

(255) 'FAANG' as an acronymn was first suggested by CNBC host Jim Cramer.

(256) Reillier and Reillier (2017, p. 23).

(257) Lewis (2017).

(258) Examples of these companies innovating first and facing the regulator second can be seen in the details of the anti-trust competition actions taken by the European Commission against companies such as Google, in the various hearings in both the United States and Europe into Facebook's privacy policies and in the 2018 Amazon reaction to internet sales tax changes in Australia.

(259) EU (2018b).

(260) EU (2016).

(261) Google has recognised the importance of the data held by the National Health Service (NHS) though the arrangements its UK artificial intelligence subsidiary Deep Mind has with the NHS (Deepmind, 2016).

(262) Babylon Health (2018).

(263) Ginzton and Varian (1999).

(264) Fairchild (2018).

(265) Kenney (2017).

(266) Mazzucato (2013).

(267) Usher (1954).

(268) Schumpeter (1934).

(269) Scherer (1965).

(270) Brunt (2006).

(271) Vise (2005).

(272) Smith (1776).

(273) Krippner (2005).

(274) Minsky (1986).

(275) Davis (1966).

(276) Brunt (2006).

(277) Bowen (1993).

(278) Hansard (1996).

(279) Mazzucato (2013).

(280) As described by Etzkowitz and Leydesdorff (2000).

(281) Knight (1921).

(282) Taleb (2007).

(283) Mazzucato (2016).

(284) Jacobs (2001).

(285) Wiesen Cook (1981).

(286) National Research Council (2009); Mehra (2013).

(287) Mazzucato (2013, p. 77).

(288) World Bank (2017).

(289) Seguino (1999).

(290) Using GDP per capita as a measure of living standards is a rough indicator; for strict comparison, discrete groups should be identified (possibly by quintiles of the income distribution) and the figures should be adjusted to reflect purchasing power in each group in respect of its own circumstances (earnings, benefits and the goods that that group buys).

(291) ILO (2018b).

(292) ILO (2018a).

(293) In this context we mean 'Median' income pensioner.

(294) Cribb, Norris Keiller and Waters (2018).

(295) LREG (2018).

(296) Belfield, Britton, and Hodge (2017).

(297) Faulkner (2016).

(298) ONS (2018g).

(299) IAS 19R, stopped pension funds smoothing actuarial gains and losses forcing these to be booked immediately leading to higher volatility, particularly for pension funds dependent upon equity holdings (stocks and shares).

(300) Barthelme, Kiosse and Sellhorn (2018).

(301) Pension funds end up investing in assets like bonds with guaranteed interest-based repayment cash flows that come from either governments borrowing money and repaying it over time or from companies and individuals doing the same thing. The interest rate balances the two flows and can be seen in market terms as being the 'neutral rate of interest' where monetary markets are in balance and where central bank monetary policy is neutral (Archibald & Hunter, 2001).

There is an important confusion between the 'natural rate of interest' definition (Wicksell, 1898) and the 'neutral rate' which has been falling for the last 50 years (Wynne & Zhang, 2018). Wicksell's 'Natural Rate' is set at the point where the risk adjusted return on cash from savers matches the returns on new capital investment projects. Wynne and Zhang measure the 'neutral rate' (not the natural rate as they claim) as when monetary policy actioned through financial markets is in equilibrium (the Archibald and Hunter definition). In a world that has perfect markets, no uncertainty and no regulatory distortion the 'neutral rate of interest' should equal the 'natural rate of interest'. It is clear that we do not live in such a world.

These semantics matter as the capitalist system requires savings to be channelled to entrepreneurs. The capitalist system comes into a sense of 'dynamic equilibrium' when the returns on savings match the risk adjusted returns on entrepreneur's new projects. Both the structure of financial markets and their associated regulation mean that nowadays primary savings flows are disconnected from entrepreneurs and mainly go to fund either government deficits or give an upfront payment against companies future cash flows for things such as share buybacks.

(302) The Efficient Markets Hypothesis favoured by some suggests that asset pricing markets are perfectly efficient at pricing all known information to give accurate values, whilst the Adaptive Markets Hypothesis suggest markets tend to the same point but through behavioural learning over time (Lo, 2007).

(303) Ford (2018).

(304) Minsky (1992).

(305) Mazzucato (2018).

(306) Shelter (2015).

(307) There is an implicit assumption in this analysis that 'buy to let' investors will not maintain house price momentum and thereby replace younger generations as starter property owners. There are three limits to possible growth in this sector: first, the affordability of rents against average incomes, and second, the appetite of investors and third, public policy. There are recent indications that investment is falling in this sector.

(308) Hudson and Gonyea (2012).

(309) Ashcroft (2017).

(310) Goodwin and Heath (2016).

(311) Menon and Wager (2018).

(312) Jónsson (2011).

(313) Jennings, Stoker and Warren (2018).

(314) HCLG (2015). The "deprivation index" looks at a number of statistical variables that are associated with deprivation in a specific local district and uses these to compile a composite index for each local area. The local areas can then be ranked to establish which ones show the highest level of deprivation. Specific issues reviwed in the

compilation of the index include income and employment levels, education and skills attainment, health and crime metrics, housing local services and measures concering the local environment. The index is published by the UK Government.

(315) Finch Crisp (1884).

(316) Otherwise known as the Hammer of the Scots (1312−1377).

(317) Wood (2016).

(318) Finch Crisp (1884).

(319) GYBC (2018).

(320) HCLG (2015).

(321) GYBC (2017).

(322) O'Connor (2017).

(323) Electoral Commission (2016).

(324) Wilshaw (2018).

(325) Roper and Hart (2018).

(326) Levie (2014).

(327) Wright (2018).

(328) Van de Rijt, Kang, Restivo and Patil (2014).

(329) Heaney, Israel and House (1994).

(330) One recent one in Australia is Johnstone, Parsell, Jetten, Dingle and Walter (2016).

(331) Shelter (2016).

(332) Evidence for this is available in the studies already referenced as support for this chapter.

(333) Cribb et al. (2018).

(334) Cribb et al. (2018).

(335) Phillips et al. (2018).

(336) ONS (2016).

(337) Ashton, MacKinnon, and Minford (2016).

(338) No precise estimation can be made as Aston et al. (2016) take data from different years to perform their calculation. Some data is from 2015 and some from 2016; the estimates will have changed due to changes in both the benefits system and the introduction of the National Living Wage.

(339) Pilling (2018).

(340) This long enacted statute bypasses the multilateral dispute resolution procedure available at the World Trade Organisation (WTO).

(341) Mercer and Kahn (2018).

(342) The use of national security as a justification for these tariffs is being challenged by the EU at the WTO, the remedy for which would be to allow the EU to raise compensating duties.

(343) See for example Ikenson et al. (2018). A group of liberterian think tanks in both the United States and the UK combined to publish what they regard to be the ideal free trade agreement post Brexit between the US and the UK. They propose an agreement that allows free movement between the US and UK based upon a job offer and the removal of regulatory barriers between the two nations.

(344) ECJ (2018).

(345) Minford (2018b).

(346) Nickell and Saleheen (2015).

(347) Minford (2018a).

(348) BRSC (2018).

(349) Thompson (2018). Thompson who as head of Customs and Excise was confirming potential Brexit Customs issues to the Chairperson of the UK Parliament Treasury Select Committee has explained that the costs estimate is the result of a 'bottom up' study that has been undertaken by HM Customs and Excise.

(350) Gove (2016).

(351) Winiecki (2002).

(352) Kornai (1994).

(353) Stiglitz (1999).

(354) Airbus (2018). Airbus issued a direct warning to the UK that it would need to relocate its operations from the UK in the event of certain Brexit scenarios.

(355) Bounds et al. (2018).

(356) UNCTAD (2018).

(357) Roper and Hart (2018).

(358) Alschner, Seiermann and Skougarevskiy (2017).

(359) Ikenson et al. (2018).

(360) Dornbusch (2001: PBS Interview Jan 31).

(361) Abenheim (2003).

(362) Hobolt, Leeper and Tilley (2018).

(363) Sobolewska and Ford (2018).

(364) YouGov (2018).

(365) Times (2018).

(366) Kellner (2017).

(367) Hobolt et al. (2018).

(368) This study by Short, McCalla & D'Orsogna (2017) looks at competing sects and analyses their behaviour through a mathematical model based on 'game theory'. One important finding is that each sect has a tendency to 'self-moderate' behaviour unless it either (1) perceives it is under external attack and/or (2) there is an extremist caucus at the centre of the group that is large enough, loud enough and strong enough to incite the overall group to maintain or deepen an extreme position. This feels a good fit to much of the Nazi narrative and clear signs of this process feel visible in both the US Alt Right and Trumpism and Brexit.

(369) Just and Latzer (2017).

(370) Marchi (2012).

(371) HCCMS (2018, p. 5).

(372) Phillips et al. (2018).

(373) YouGov (2018).

(374) Amounts are in constant 2011 purchasing parity dollars.

(375) Johnson (2018).

(376) In an environment of regulatory equivalence, the UK will be forced to adapt its regulations to changes in the EU environment as those regulations change, as opposed to a mutual recognition regime in which the EU would recognise that the UK regulations provide the same standard of protection as the EU.

(377) Eijsbouts and Reestman (2015).

(378) EUparl (2018).

(379) Merkel (2010).

(380) Lewis (2000).

(381) Floch (2004).

(382) Drake (2006).

(383) Tooze and Vallée (2018).

(384) Bibow (2018).

(385) Horsley (2012).

(386) Lisbon (2007).

(387) Moens and Trone (2015).

GLOSSARY

Adverse Selection Adverse selection occurs when pre-ordained circumstances determine a group to select at a higher rate than the normal statistical population. Such selections are often associated with "Asymmetric Information", where one group has access to different and better information than another. In the "perfect markets" that underline economic theory adverse selection and asymmetric information cannot happen, whereas both are a normal feature of the real world.

Article 50 Article 50 of the Lisbon Treaty sets out how a state can leave the European Union.

Big Bang Disruptions Products or services that restructure and disrupt entire industries. For example, the digital camera vs the film-based camera.

Bilateral Treaty A treaty signed between two contracting bodies as opposed to a 'multi-lateral' treaty that has many signatories.

Brexit Day Brexit Day is at 11 p.m. on 29 March 2019 when the UK leaves the European Union and ceases to be a Member State.

Citadels of Remain Geographic areas with a high concentration of voters who wish to stay within the European Union.

Crowding Out The crowding out effect stipulates that rises in public sector spending drive down private sector spending. Though the 'crowding out effect' is a general term, the common usage that we follow is in reference to the stifling of private spending by government expenditure.

Entrepreneur	An individual or group of individuals who identify a market opportunity and then orchestrate resources to realise it with the objective of earning a profit.
European Council	The European Council is the EU decision making body made up of heads of government of the Member States and their associated delegations. It works in partnership with the European Parliament and the European Commission to establish European Legislation.
European Court of Justice	The court responsible for making sure that (1) European Law is consistent with the EU treaties, (2) that Member State transcription and interpretation of EU Law is consistent with the EU Law in question, (3) the European Institutions act within the EU Treaty framework and (4) detailed points of the operation of EU Law are interpreted where these are unclear. This court does not have jurisdiction and does not hear cases relating to Human Rights; these cases are heard separately in the European Court for Human Rights.
Euratom	The collective European body for handling civilian nuclear issues that is the counterparty to the United States Economic Energy Authority in the bilateral treaties with the United States governing nuclear matters.
Firm	A firm is a business organisation, such as a corporation, limited liability company or partnership, that sells goods or services to make a profit.
Great Debasement	This episode between 1544 and 1551 was intended to improve state finances by reducing the amount of gold and silver in the coinage. Debasement devalued the currency for overseas trade and led to inflation at home (Gould, 1964).
Innovation	Product or service changes to embed new technologies, features or designs.
Internet of Things	A term used to describe items (e.g. consumer products such as refrigerators or industrial products such as plant sensors or cars or heating/cooling systems) where the product has imbedded sensors that send monitoring

data to a controlling host, that then adjusts how the device performs based on data received.

Leave Voter   A voter who voted to leave the European Union in the 2016 Brexit Referendum.

Lisbon Treaty   EU Consolidating Treaty of 2007 adopted in place of the previously proposed European Constitution. Official Title *'Treaty of Lisbon Amending the Treaty on European Union and the Treaty Establishing The European Community (2007/C 306/01)'*.

Kett's Revolt   Kett's Revolt sometimes known as Kett's Rebellion of 1549 is seen as a rebellion against large landowners enclosing common land.

Market-Facing Innovation   Where the market, customer and potential customer drive the 'needs statement' to innovate a new product or service as opposed to where the innovation idea *either* is a product idea that comes from within the firm and looks for a customer to need it *or* is an idea that improves firm internal efficiency and does not touch the customer. Otherwise defined as a *Customer Active Paradigm* or a *Manufacturer Active* Paradigm (Hippel, 1978).

Member State   A nation state that is a full member of the European Union.

Mercantilism   A state-enforced regulatory framework designed to support business interests especially in foreign trade.

Mutual Recognition   A treaty-regulated process that allows two states to recognise each other's regulators, rules and regulations as 'in effect' acceptable to each other. This avoids 'dual regulation' and allows each treaty party to establish their own rules within the overall parameters of the mutual recognition treaty.

Natural Rate of Interest   The "natural rate of interest" is where the overall rate of interest matches the financial return on the least profitable project being funded. More formally, Wicksell (1898) based his theory on a comparison of the marginal product of capital with the cost of borrowing

	money. If the money rate of interest is below the natural rate of return on capital, entrepreneurs borrow to purchase capital (equipment and buildings).
Neutral Rate of Interest	The "Neutral Rate of Interest" is defined as the interest rate that balances savings and investment flows, thereby indicating that monetary markets are in balance. A precondition is that central bank monetary policy is neutral (Archibald & Hunter, 2001). Crucially this rate is a reflection of the financial economy and has no automatic linkage to rates of return available on new capital investments.
Overseas Territories	A legal definition used by the EU to denote countries that were or continue to be colonies or territories of EU Member States and, for whom special provision has been collectively made in the European Treaties. By these provisions they are neither a Member State nor a Third Country but are affiliated to the EU and thereby have special access arrangements to EU markets.
Pilgrimage of Grace	The 1536 uprising in Northern England.
Praemunire	An English mid-to-late medieval judicial process that allowed the state to block church courts having jurisdiction on matters the state felt were not the church's concern.
Referendum	The 2016 Referendum on whether the UK should leave the European Union.
Regulators	Regulators are official bodies established under legalisation to issue and monitor rules and regulations that control corporate behaviour. Regulators can be at the nation state level or the supranational level such as, regulators established by the European Union.
Regulatory Equivalence	This occurs when Regulators in different countries accept that rules on a specific set of issues have the same impact at that point in time. Because this concept is time related, equivalence can be withdrawn at very short notice making for an uncertain long-term business environment.

Remainer	Someone who believes that the UK should stay as a member of the European Union.
Royal Succession	The formal list of who will be the next King or Queen.
Single Market	A unified regulatory and customs free area that allows goods to be seamlessly traded across borders (internal or external) without barriers.
Supply Chain	A group of firms and individuals linked and orchestrated together to design, manufacture and deliver finished product or service to end customer.
Third Country	A country that is not a member of the European Union.
Transition Period	The period after the UK leaves the European Union (Brexit Day) until the date that its stops generally applying European Union Regulations.
Vienna Convention of Treaties	The international convention that governs how treaties between states work, including how such treaties can be cancelled.
Welfare	Payments in cash and benefits in kind made to those in need from the UK state (both central and local authority) social support system.
Western Revolt	Sometimes known as either the Western Rebellion or Prayer Book Rebellion of 1549, a grassroots revolt against the imposition of a new Protestant Prayer Book. The revolt had multiple aspects including Catholic sympathies, Cornish nationalist undertones, and economic dimensions. It was suppressed by Edward Seymour, 1st Duke of Somerset.
Wyatt's Rebellion	Starting in Kent, this 1554 rebellion against Queen Mary I taking Philip II as her husband marched on London to overthrow the Queen. London failed to rise against the crown and the rebellion failed.
Zero-hours contracts	Employment contracts that bind an employee to working for an employer, but that do not guarantee how many hours per week that employee will be required to work for the employer.

BIBLIOGRAPHY

Abenheim, D. (2003). War, military leadership, and democratic civil-military relations: 'The Stab in the Back' – The endurance of a dubious Idea, Calhoun: The Naval Postgraduate School Institutional Archive, Calhoun: California. Retrieved from https://calhoun.nps.edu/bitstream/handle/10945/47136/Abenheim_War_Military_2003.pdf?sequence=1

AFME. (2017). Bridging to Brexit: Insights from European SMEs, corporates and investors. AFME: London, study by Boston Consulting Group. Retrieved from https://www.afme.eu/globalassets/downloads/publications/afme-bcg-cc-bridging-to-brexit-2017.pdf

Aghion, P., & Blanchard, O. J. (1994). On the speed of transition in Central Europe. *NBER Macroeconomics Annual, 9*, 283–320.

Airbus. (2018). Brexit risk assessment, Airbus: Toulouse. Retrieved from http://www.airbus.com/company/worldwide-presence/uk.html#Economy. Accessed on June 21, 2018.

Alschner, W., Seiermann, J., & Skougarevskiy, D. (2017). Text-as-data analysis of preferential trade agreements: Mapping the PTA Landscape. Retrieved from http://unctad.org/en/pages/PublicationWebflyer.aspx?publicationid=1838

Amoroso, S., Moncada-Paternò-Castello, P., & Vezzani, A. (2017). R&D profitability: The role of risk and Knightian uncertainty. *Small Business Economics, 48*(2), 331–343.

Andreau, J. (1999). *Banking and business in the Roman World.* Janey Lloyd (Trans.). Cambridge: Cambridge University Press.

Andrew, J. A., & Beer, B. (2013). *Rebellion and riot: Popular disorder in England during the reign of Edward VI.* Ashland, OH: The Kent State University Press.

Andrews, K. R. (Ed.). (1959). English privateering voyages to the West Indies: Documents relating to English voyages to the West Indies from the defeat of the Armada to the last voyage of Sir Francis Drake, including Spanish documents contributed by Irene A. Wright. Cambridge: Cambridge University Press.

Annio, V. (1498). Commentaria super opera diversorum auctorum de antiquitatibus loquentium Rome.

Archibald, J., & Hunter, L. (2001). What is the neutral real interest rate, and how can we use it?, Reserve Bank Of New Zealand: *Bulletin 64*(3), Sept 2001. Retrieved from https://www.rbnz.govt.nz/-/media/ReserveBank/Files/Publications/Bulletins/2001/2001sep64-3archibaldhunter.pdf

Ark, B., & Jäger, K. (2017). Recent trends in Europe's output and productivity growth performance at the sector level, 2002–2015. *International Productivity Monitor*, Number 33, Fall 2017. International Productivity Monitor: Ottawa, Canada. Retrieved from http://www.csls.ca/ipm/33/vanArk_Jager.pdf

Ashcroft. (2017). General election day poll 2017, Lord Ashcroft polls. Retrieved from https://lordashcroftpolls.com/wp-content/uploads/2017/06/GE-post-vote-poll-Full-tables.pdf

Ashton, P., MacKinnon, N., & Minford, P. (2016). The economics of unskilled immigration, economists for free trade: London. Retrieved from http://www.economistsforfreetrade.com/the-economics-of-unskilled-immigration/

Ashton, R. (1967). The Parliamentary agitation for free trade in the opening years of the reign of James I. *Past & Present, 381*, 40–55.

Automotive Council UK. (2017). Rise in amount of British parts used in British car production as manufacturers boost UK automotive supply chain investment, finds new research, Press Release, Automotive Council: London. Retrieved from https://www.automotivecouncil.co.uk/wp-content/uploads/sites/13/2017/06/170620-Auto-Council-release_Rise-in-British-parts-used-in-British-car-pr...pdf. Accessed on June 20, 2017.

Babylon Health. (2018). We believe it is possible to put an accessible and affordable health service in the hands of every person on earth, Babylon Health blog: London. Retrieved from https://www.babylonhealth.com/blog/

health/we-believe-it-is-possible-to-put-accessible-and-affordable-healthcare-in-the-hands-of-every-person-on-earth. Accessed on May 3, 2018.

Bacon, R., & Eltis, W. (1979). The Measurement of the growth of the non-market sector and its influence: A reply to Hadjimatheou and Skouras. *The Economic Journal*, *89*(354), 402–415.

Baglieri, D., Cinici, M. C., & Mangematin, V. (2012). Rejuvenating clusters with 'sleeping anchors': The case of nanoclusters. *Technovation*, *32*(3–4), 245–256.

Bahmani, M., Harvey, H., & Hegerty, S. W. (2013). Empirical tests of the Marshall-Lerner condition: A literature review. *Journal of Economic Studies*, *40*(3), 411–443.

Bairoch, P. (1976). *Commerce extérieur et développement économique de l'Europe au XIXe siècle* (Vol. 53). Mouton: École des hautes études en sciences sociales.

Bank of England. (1971). Competition and credit control, consultation paper, Bank of England London. Retrieved from https://www.bankofengland.co.uk/-/media/boe/files/quarterly-bulletin/1971/competition-and-credit-control-text-of-a-consultatice-document-issued-on-14-may-1971

Bank of England. (2014). Money creation in the modern economy. *Quarterly Bulletin Q1* 2014. Retrieved from http://www.bankofengland.co.uk/publications/Documents/quarterlybulletin/2014/qb14q1prereleasemoneycreation.pdf

Barro, R. J. (2001). Economic growth in East Asia before and after the financial crisis (No. w8330). National Bureau of Economic Research. Retrieved from http://www.nber.org/papers/w8330

Barthelme, C., Kiosse, P. V., & Sellhorn, T. (2018). The impact of accounting standards on pension investment decisions. *European Accounting Review*, *35*, 1–33.

Barton, C. (2017). Home ownership & renting: demographics. House of Commons Briefing Paper CBP 7706 9 June 2017, Parliament: London. Retrieved from http://researchbriefings.files.parliament.uk/documents/CBP-7706/CBP-7706.pdf

BBC. (2018). History of the BBC. Retrieved from http://www.bbc.co.uk/
historyofthebbc/birth-of-tv/coronations

Becker, S. O., Fetzer, T., & Novy, D. (2017). Who voted for Brexit?
A comprehensive district-level analysis. *Economic Policy, 32*(92),
601–650.

Beer, B. L. (1987). Bernard G.W. war, taxation and rebellion in early tudor
england: Henry VIII, wolsey and the amicable grant of 1525. New York,
NY: St. Martin's Press. 1986. *Albion, 19*(2), 226–228.

Beer, B. L. (1988). John Stow and Tudor rebellions, 1549-1569. *Journal of
British Studies, 27*(4), 352–374.

BEISC. (2018). The impact of Brexit on the automotive sector, House of
Commons: London, HC379 1 March 2018, House of Commons Business,
Energy and Industrial Strategy Committee. Retrieved from https://
publications.parliament.uk/pa/cm201719/cmselect/cmbeis/379/379.pdf

Belfield, C., Britton, J., & Hodge, L. (2017). Options for reducing the
interest rate on student loans and reintroducing maintenance grants', IFS
Briefing Note BN221. Retrieved from https://www.ifs.org.uk/publications/
10154

Bell, J. (2018). Sources of law. *Cambridge Law Journal, 77*(1), 40–71.

Bergstrand, J. H. (1985). The gravity equation in international trade:
Some microeconomic foundations and empirical evidence. *The Review of
Economics and Statistics, 67*(3), 474–481.

Bernard, G. W. (2011). The dissolution of the monasteries. *History,
96*(324), 390–409.

Béteille, A. (1998). The idea of indigenous people. *Current Anthropology,
39*(2), 187–192.

Bibow, J. (2018). The case for Germany leaving The Euro #Gexit, 18 May
2018, Social Europe: London. Retrieved from https://www.socialeurope.eu/
the-case-for-germany-leaving-the-euro-gexit

Bisson, D. R. (1987). *The merchant adventurers and the Tudor
commonwealth: The formulation of a trade policy,* 1485–1565 Doctoral
dissertation, The Ohio State University.

Bland, R. (1997). The changing patterns of hoards of precious-metal coins in the late empire. *L'Antiquité tardive, 5,* 29−55.

Bloom, N., & Reenen, J. V. (2007). Measuring and explaining management practices across firms and countries. *The Quarterly Journal of Economics, 122*(4), 1351−1408. doi:10.1162/qjec.2007.122.4.1351

Blundell, R., Crawford, C., & Jin, W. (2014). What can wages and employment tell us about the UK's productivity puzzle? *The Economic Journal, 124*(576), 377−407.

Blundell, R., Joyce, R., Norris Keiller, A., & Ziliak, J. P. (2018). Income inequality and the labour market in britain and the US. *Journal of Public Economics, 162,* 48−62. doi:10.1016/j.jpubeco.2018.04.001

Booth, T. W. (2014). Elizabeth I and Pope Paul IV: Reticence and reformation. *Church History and Religious Culture, 94*(3), 316−336.

Borio, C., & Disyatat, P. (2015). Capital flows and the current account: Taking financing (more) seriously. Retrieved from http://www.bis.org/publ/work525.pdf

Bounds, A., Tighe, C., & Parker, G. (2018). *British businesses plan to move overseas amid Brexit fears.* Financial Times, London, September 28, 2018. Retrieved from https://www.ft.com/content/ee7d7a1c-c264-11e8-95b1-d36dfef1b89a

Bowen, A., Hoggarth, G., & Pain, D. (1999). The recent evolution of the UK banking industry and some implications for financial stability. In BIS (1999), The monetary an regulatory implications of changes in the banking industry, BIS Conference Papers (Vol. 7). Retrieved from https://www.bis.org/publ/confp07l.pdf

Bowen, D. (1993). Assault and battery: The fall of the Ever Ready empire: A classic tale of British decline. *Independent Newspaper.* London. Retrieved from https://www.independent.co.uk/news/business/assault-and-battery-the-fall-of-the-ever-ready-empire-a-classic-tale-of-british-decline-by-david-1494225.html. Accessed on June 27, 1993.

Broman, T. (2014). *Thomas Cromwell. The untold story of Henry VIII's most faithful servant.* London: Hodder & Stoughton.

Brotton. (2016). *This orient isle: Elizabethan England and the Islamic World*. London: Allen Lane.

Brown, J. M. (1894). Henry VIII.'s book, "Assertio Septem Sacramentorum," and the royal title of "Defender of the faith". *Transactions of the Royal Historical Society, 8*, 243–261.

BRSC. (2018). Cross department Brexit briefing, parliament: UK, House of Commons Select Committee on Exiting the EU, Jan 2018. Retrieved from https://www.parliament.uk/documents/commons-committees/Exiting-the-European-Union/17-19/Cross-Whitehall-briefing/EU-Exit-Analysis-Cross-Whitehall-Briefing.pdf

Brundage, J. A. (1993). The early modern legacy of medieval canon law the medieval canon law: Teaching, literature, and transmission. The Sandars Lectures in bibliography by Dorothy M. Owen. Cambridge: Cambridge University Press, 1990. Roman canon law in Reformation England. Cambridge studies in English legal history. by R. H. Helmholz. Cambridge: Cambridge University press, 1990. Fundamental Authority in late medieval English law. Cambridge studies in English legal history. by Norman Doe. Cambridge: Cambridge university press, 1990. God and the moneylenders: Usury and law in early modern England. by Norman Jones. Oxford: Basil Blackwell, 1989. *The Journal of British Studies, 32*(3), 285–290.

Brundage, J. A. (2008). *The medieval origins of the legal profession: Canonists, civilians, and courts*. Chicago, IL: University of Chicago Press.

Bruni, F. (2015). To Trump or not to Trump. *New York Times*: New York, July 22 2015. Retrieved from https://www.nytimes.com/2015/07/22/opinion/frank-bruni-to-trump-or-not-to-trump.html

Brunt, L. (2006). Rediscovering risk: Country banks as venture capital firms in the first industrial revolution. *Journal of Economic History, 66*, 74–102.

Buchmann, T., & Pyka, A. (2012). The evolution of innovation networks: The case of the German automotive industry. *Economics and Management*, 2012. Retrieved from https://pdfs.semanticscholar.org/1d8a/ce3cab9be322e6492aa2d7379449f5e7498d.pdf

Bush, M. L. (1991). 'Up for the commonweal': The significance of tax grievances in the English rebellions of 1536. *The English Historical Review, 106*(CCCCXIX), 299–318.

Butcher, L. (2018). Access to transport for disabled people, House of Commons Briefing Paper Number CBP 601, 5 March 2018 House of Commons Library: London. Retrieved from http://researchbriefings.files. parliament.uk/documents/SN00601/SN00601.pdf

Butler, S. M. (2012). Sacred people, sacred spaces: Evidence of parish respect and contempt toward the pre-reformation clergy. *Canadian Journal of History*, 47(1), 1–27.

Camden, W. (1695). Britannia, E. Gibson (ed.). London. reprinted: David and Charles, 1971, Newton Abbot.

Campbell, B. (2004). Economics of the Roman Army; P. Erdcamp (ed.): The Roman army and the economy. Amsterdam: J. C. Gieben, 2002. *Classical Review*, 54(1), 198.

Camus, A. (1956). *The rebel*. A. Bower (Trans.). New York, NY: Vintage Books.

Carney, M. (2017). A fine balance. Retrieved from http://www. bankofengland.co.uk/publications/Documents/speeches/2017/speech983.pdf

Cavill, P. R. (2011). 'The enemy of God and his church': James Hobart, Praemunire, and the clergy of Norwich Diocese. *The Journal of Legal History*, 32(2), 127–150.

Çeliktemel, B. (2012). *A Study of the Third English Ambassador Henry Lello's Report on the Ottoman Empire* (1597–1607). Master's thesis. Retrieved from http://openaccess.bilgi.edu.tr:8080/xmlui/bitstream/handle/11411/68/celiktemel_A%20Study%20of_2012.pdf?sequence=1

Centre for Cities. (2018). The wrong tail. Centre for Cities: London. Retrieved from http://www.centreforcities.org/wp-content/uploads/2018/05/2018-06-05-The-wrong-tail.pdf

Chandler, P. R. (1924). Praemunire and the Habeas Corpus act. *Columbia Law Review*, 24, 273.

Childers, T. (1985). *The Nazi voter. The social foundations of facism in Germany 1919–1933*. Chapel Hill, NC: University of North Carolina Press.

Churchill, W. S. (1940). Fight them on the beaches speech, 4 June 1940. House of Commons: London, Hansard HC Deb 04 June 1940 vol 361 cc787-98. Retrieved from https://api.parliament.uk/historic-hansard/commons/1940/jun/04/war-situation

CIA, The. (2012). CIA's impact on technology. Retrieved from https://www.cia.gov/about-cia/cia-museum/experience-the-collection/text-version/stories/cias-impact-on-technology.html

Cicero. (51BC) On the commonwealth (trans. Sabine), Indianapolis, IN: The Bobbs-Merrill Company, Inc. 1929, (pp. 51–56).

Clark, G. (2007). The long march of history: Farm wages, population, and economic growth, England 1209–1869. *The Economic History Review*, *60*(1), 97–135.

Clarke, H. D., Goodwin, M., & Whiteley, P. (2017). Why Britain voted for Brexit: An individual-level analysis of the 2016 Referendum Vote. *Parliamentary Affairs*, *70*(3), 439.

Clarke, H., Whiteley, P., Borges, W., Sanders, D., & Stewart, M. (2016). Modelling the dynamics of support for a right-wing populist party: The case of UKIP. *Journal of Elections, Public Opinion and Parties*, *26*(2), 135–154.

Clery, E., Curtice, J., & Harding, R. (2016). British social attitudes: The 34th Report, London: NatCen Social Research. Retrieved from http://www.bsa.natcen.ac.uk/downloads/bsa-34-downloads.aspx

CMA. (2016). Addendum to provisional findings. The capital requirements regulatory regime. Competition and Markets Authority: London. Retrieved from https://assets.publishing.service.gov.uk/media/5710dc73ed915d117a00006d/addendum-to-provisional-findings-with-appendices.pdf

Corden, W. M. (1994). *Economic policy, exchange rates and the international system*. Oxford: Clarendon Press.

Costa, R., & Machin, S. (2017). Real wages and living standards in the UK, LSE Centre For Economic Performance: London. Retrieved from http://cep.lse.ac.uk/pubs/download/ea036.pdf

Crawford, C., Jin, W., & Simpson, H. (2013). Productivity, investment and profits during the great recession: Evidence from UK firms and workers. *Fiscal Studies*, *34*(2), 153–177.

Cribb, J., & Johnson, P. (2018). *10 years on — have we recovered from the financial crisis?* London: Institute of Fiscal Studies. Retrieved from https://www.ifs.org.uk/publications/13302 Accessed on September 12, 2018.

Cribb, J., Norris Keiller, A., & Waters, T. (2018). Living standards, poverty and inequality in the UK: 2018, Institute of Fiscal Studies: London. Retrieved from https://www.ifs.org.uk/uploads/R145%20for%20web.pdf

Cummings, D. (2018). On the referendum #25: A letter to Tory MPs & donors on the Brexit shambles, Dominic Cummings blog:London May 23 2018. Retrieved from https://dominiccummings.com/2018/05/23/on-the-referendum-25-a-letter-to-tory-mps-donors-on-the-brexit-shambles/

Cunliffe, B. (2005). *Iron Age communities in Britain* (4th ed.). London: Routledge.

Curtice, J. (2016a). Brexit: Behind the referendum. *Political Insight*, 7(2), 4−7.

Curtice, J. (2016b). Remain in light: What do Labour's many Remain supporters want to happen next? *Juncture*, 23(3), 209−212.

Daily Mail, The. (2016). Enemies of the people. Retrieved from http://www.dailymail.co.uk/news/article-3903436/Enemies-people-Fury-touch-judges-defied-17-4m-Brexit-voters-trigger-constitutional-crisis.html

DARPA. (2018). About us. Retrieved from https://www.darpa.mil/about-us/about-darpa

Davies, R., Haldane, A. G., Nielsen, M., & Pezzini, S. (2014). Measuring the costs of short-termism. *Journal of Financial Stability*, 12(1), 16−25. doi:10.1016/j.jfs.2013.07.002

Davis, L. (1966). The capital markets and industrial concentration: The US and UK, a comparative study. *The Economic History Review*, 19(2), 255−272.

De La Baume, M. (2016). Greenland's exit warning to Britain, Politico blog: Brussels. Retrieved from https://www.politico.eu/article/greenland-exit-warning-to-britain-brexit-eu-referendum-europe-vote-news-denmark/

Deepmind. (2016). DeepMind Health and the Royal Free, Deepmind: London. Retrieved from https://deepmind.com/applied/deepmind-health/

working-partners/how-were-helping-today/royal-free-london-nhs-foundation-trust/

Dehejia, V. H. (1996). Shock therapy vs. gradualism: A neoclassical perspective. *Eastern Economic Journal*, *22*(4), 425–431.

Dhanasai, C., & Parkhe, A. (2006). Orchestrating innovation networks. *The Academy of Management Review*, *31*(3), 659–669.

Dietz, F. C. (1932). *English public finance 1558–1641*. London: Century Company.

Dorling, D. (2016). Brexit: The decision of a divided country. *British Medical Journal*, *354*, i3697. doi:10.1136/bmj.i3697

Dornbusch, R. (2001). Dornbusch Law: PBS: USA Interview Jan 31 2001 Transcript. Retrieved from https://www.pbs.org/wgbh/pages/frontline/shows/mexico/interviews/dornbusch.html

Downes, L., & Nunes, P. (2013). Big-bang disruption. *Harvard Business Review*, (March), *91*(3), 45–56.

Drake, H. (2006). France: An EU founder member cut down to size? *European Integration*, *28*(1), 89–105.

Ecclesiastical Appeals Act. (1532) (24 Hen 8 c 12) Act of Parliament. Retrieved from http://www.reformationhenryviii.com/1532-act-of-appeals-preamble.html

ECJ. (2001). C-377/98 Netherlands *et al* C-377/98 vs EU Parliament *et al*. re Biotechnology. Retrieved from http://curia.europa.eu/juris/showPdf.jsf?text=&docid=46255&pageIndex=0&doclang=en&mode=lst&dir=&occ=first&part=1&cid=604805

ECJ. (2010). Case C-518/08 Fundación Gala-Salvador Dalí et al. vs Société des auteurs dans les Arts Graphiques et Plastiques (ADAGP) *et al*. Judgement. Retrieved from http://curia.europa.eu/juris/liste.jsf?language=en&num=C-518/08#

ECJ. (2015a). Case T-368/15 R Alcimos Consulting SMPC vs European Central Bank Sept 2015. Retrieved from http://curia.europa.eu/juris/document/document_print.jsf;jsessionid=9ea7d2dc30dd438182efb89b4d52ac59a65d837a2cbb.e34KaxiLc3qMb40Rch0SaxyNch10?doclang=EN&

text=&pageIndex=0&part=1&mode=DOC&docid=166781&occ=first&
dir=&cid=224483

ECJ. (2015b). Case T-497/11 UK vs European Central Bank in matter of
euro clearing, judgement. Retrieved from http://curia.europa.eu/juris/celex.
jsf?celex=62011TJ0496&lang1=en&type=TXT&ancre=

ECJ. (2018). Judgment in Case T-544/13 RENV Dyson Ltd v Commission,
The General Court annuls the regulation on the energy labelling of vacuum
cleaners, General Court of the European Union: Luxembourg, Press Release
8 November 2018, Retrived from: https://curia.europa.eu/jcms/upload/docs/
application/pdf/2018-11/cp180168en.pdf

Eden, P. (2017). Can a notification under Article 50 TEU be unilaterally
withdrawn? Sussex University & Chatham House: UK, UK Trade Policy
Observatory blog. Retrieved from https://blogs.sussex.ac.uk/uktpo/2017/03/
17/can-a-notification-under-article-50-teu-be-unilaterally-withdrawn/

Efremidze, L., & Tomohara, A. (2011). Have the implications of twin
deficits changed?: Sudden stops over decades. *International Advances in
Economic Research*, 17(1), 66–76.

Eichengreen, B., & Gupta, P. (2016). Managing sudden stops. Retrieved
from http://documents.worldbank.org/curated/en/877591468186563349/
Managing-sudden-stops

Eijsbouts, W. T., & Reestman, J. H. (2015). In search of the union method.
European Constitutional Law Review, 11(3), 425–433.

Electoral Commission. (2016). EU referendum results, Electoral
Commission: London. Retrieved from https://www.electoralcommission.org.
uk/find-information-by-subject/elections-and-referendums/past-elections-and-
referendums/eu-referendum/electorate-and-count-information

Ellacombe, H. (1852). Executions in Henry VIII.'s reign, etc. *Notes and
Queries*, 6(161), 508.

Elton, G. (Ed.). (1983). Politics and the Pilgrimage of Grace. In *Studies in
Tudor and Stuart politics and government* (pp. 183–215). Cambridge:
Cambridge University Press.

Elton, G. (1991). Roman canon law in Reformation England. by R. H.
Helmholz. (Cambridge studies in English legal history.) pp. xxiv + 209.

Cambridge: Cambridge University Press, 1990. *The Journal of Ecclesiastical History*, 42(1), 120–122.

Elton, G. R. (1988). Tudor government: The English court from the Wars of the Roses to the Civil War, ed. David Starkey. *Historical Journal, 31*, 425–434.

Elton, G. R. (2012). *England under the Tudors* (3rd ed.). Hoboken, NJ: Taylor & Francis.

Eparl. (2016). Brexit: The United Kingdom and EU financial services, EU Parliament: Brussels Briefing. Retrieved from http://www.europarl.europa.eu/RegData/etudes/BRIE/2016/587384/IPOL_BRI(2016)587384_EN.pdf

Erasmus, D. (1514). Julius exclusus e Coelis. tr Pascal, P., & Sowards, J. K. (1968). Bloomington, IN: Indiana University Press.

Erdkamp, P. (2016). Economic growth in the Roman Mediterranean World: An early good-bye to Malthus? *Explorations in Economic History, 60*, 1–20.

Esmonde Cleary, A. S. (1989). *The ending of Roman Britain*. New York, NY: Routledge.

Etzkowitz, H., & Leydesdorff, L. (2000). The dynamics of innovation: From national systems and "Mode 2" to a Triple Helix of university–industry–government relations. *Research Policy, 29*(2), 109–123.

EU. (2008). Consolidated version of the treaty on the functioning of the European Union, Official Journal of The European Union C115/47 9 May 2008. Retrieved from https://eur-lex.europa.eu/resource.html?uri=cellar:41f89a28-1fc6-4c92-b1c8-03327d1b1ecc.0007.02/DOC_1&format=PDF

EU. (2016). Commission implementing decision (EU) 2016/125 protection provided by the EU-U.S. Privacy Shield, Official Journal I 207/1 1 Aug 2016, EU Commission: Brussels. Retrieved from https://eur-lex.europa.eu/legal-content/EN/TXT/PDF/?uri=CELEX:32016D1250&from=EN

EU. (2018a). Notice to stakeholders: Withdrawal of the United Kingdom and EU aviation safety rule, EU Commission DG mobility & transport: Brussels, April 13 2018. Retrieved from https://ec.europa.eu/transport/sites/transport/files/legislation/brexit-notice-to-stakeholders-aviation-safety.pdf

EU. (2018b). Notice to stakeholders withdrawal of the United Kingdom from The Union And Eu rules In the field of data protection, DG justice and consumers 9 Jan 2018. Retrieved from https://ec.europa.eu/info/brexit/brexit-preparedness/preparedness-notices_en

EUaud. (2014). *EU funded airport infrastructures: Poor value for money.* Special report. Luxembourg: European Court of Auditors. Retrieved from www.eca.europa.eu%2FLists%2FECADocuments%2FSR14_21%2FQJAB14021ENC.pdf&usg=AOvVaw15nHa7V7XgNMImkD9HIfBj

Euparl. (2016). Brexit: The United Kingdom and EU financial services, EU Parliament: Brussels Briefing 9 Dec 2016. Retrieved from http://www.europarl.europa.eu/RegData/etudes/BRIE/2016/587384/IPOL_BRI(2016)587384_EN.pdf

Euparl. (2018). "Spitzenkandidaten" process cannot be overturned, say MEPs." Retrieved from http://www.europarl.europa.eu/news/en/press-room/20180202IPR97026/spitzenkandidaten-process-cannot-be-overturned-say-meps

Evans Pritchard, A. (2016). Did Henry VIII's Tudor 'Brexit' lead to England's trading glory, or a century of depression? *Daily Telegraph*, 25 Sep 2016. Retrieved from https://www.telegraph.co.uk/business/2016/09/25/did-henry-viiis-tudor-brexit-lead-to-englands-trading-glory-or-a/

Evans, G., & Mellon, J. (2016). Working class votes and conservative losses: Solving the UKIP puzzle. *Parliamentary Affairs*, 69(2), 464–479.

Facebook. (2018). Statistics. Retrieved from https://newsroom.fb.com/company-info/

Fairchild. (2018). Fairchild semi conductor history and heritage. Retrieved from //www.fairchildsemi.com/about/history-heritage/

Faulkner, K. (2016). Who are the individual landlords providing private rented accommodation? TDS Charitable Foundation: Hemel Hempsted, July 2016. Retrieved from https://www.designsonproperty.co.uk/downloads/20160704

FCA, The. (2017). Asset management market study final report market study. Retrieved from https://www.fca.org.uk/publication/market-studies/ms15-2-3.pdf

Finch Crisp, W. (1884). Chronological retrospect of the history of Yarmouth and neighbourhood from A.D. 46 to 1884, 3rd ed., J Haddon & Co: London, Retrieved from https://www.gutenberg.org/files/41618/41618-h/41618-h.htm

Fisher, F. (1940). Commercial trends and policy in sixteenth-century England. *The Economic History Review*, *10*(2), 95–117.

Fisher, F. (1957). The sixteenth and seventeenth centuries: The dark ages in English economic history? *Economica*, *24*(93), new series, 2–18.

Fletcher, A., & MacCulloch, D. (2015). *Tudor rebellions* (6th ed.). London: Routledge Ltd.

Floch, J. (2004). Rapport d'information sur la présence et l'influence de la France dans les institutions européennes (Assemblée nationale, 12 May 2004, rapport no 1594).

Forbes, K. (2014). The economic impact of sterling's recent moves: More than a midsummer night's dream. Retrieved from http://www.bankofengland.co.uk/publications/Documents/speeches/2014/speech760.pdf

Ford, J. (2018). Carillion's troubles were shrouded in a fog of goodwill, FT: London June 18 2018. Retrieved from https://www.ft.com/content/765fc482-68db-11e8-b6eb-4acfcfb08c11

Ford, R., & Goodwin, M. (2014). Understanding UKIP: Identity, social change and the left behind. *The Political Quarterly*, *85*(3), 277–284.

Foundation, The. (2015). *Failure Breeds Failure*, Lyrics to track on Album Turncoat, Jawk Records.

Fowler, R. L. (2013). *Early Greek mythography*. Volume 2: Commentary. Oxford: Oxford University Press, 2013.

Fraunhofer. (2018). The Fraunhofer-Gesellschaft continues its successful course. 16 May 2018, Fraunhofer: Munich. Retrieved from https://www.fraunhofer.de/en/press/research-news/2018/May/presentation-of-the-2017-annual-report.html

Friedman, M. (1962). *Capitalism and freedom*. Chicago, IL: Chicago University Press.

FT. (2018a). Brexit raid on a British financial success story. London: *Financial Times*. Editorial 4 Jan 2018. Retrieved from //www.ft.com/content/62a6ff4c-f15c-11e7-b220-857e26d1aca4

FT. (2018b). UK to apply to stay in European standards system after Brexit, *Financial Times*: London, 11 June 2018. Retrieved from https://www.ft.com/content/94ef2bb0-6b31-11e8-b6eb-4acfcfb08c11

Fulford, M., & Bird, J. (1975). Imported pottery from Germany in late Roman Britain. *Britannia*, *6*, 171–181. doi:10.2307/525999

Garcia-de-Andoain, C., Heider, F., Hoerova, M., & Manganelli, S. (2016). Lending-of-last-resort is as lending-of-last-resort does: Central bank liquidity provision and interbank market functioning in the euro area. *Journal of Financial Intermediation*, *28*, 32–47.

Gartner. (2008). Gartner says worldwide mobile phone sales increased 16 per cent in 2007, Gartner Group. Retrieved from https://www.gartner.com/newsroom/id/612207

Gaston, S., & Harrison – Evans, P. (2017). *Nothing to fear but fear itself?* London: Demos. Retrieved from https://www.demos.co.uk/project/nothing-to-fear-but-fear-itself/

Gavin, M. (1996). Unemployment and the economics of gradualist policy reform. *The Journal of Policy Reform*, *1*(3), 239–258.

Gibbon, E. (1910). *Decline and fall of the roman empire*. London: Dent.

Giles, C. (2018). *The Brexit myth of no-strings frictionless trade*. London: *Financial Times*. 7 June 2018, Retrieved from https://www.ft.com/content/6dca820a-6979-11e8-b6eb-4acfcfb08c11

Ginzton, E., & Varian, R. (1999). *Varian associates: An early history*. Silicon Valley, CA: Varian Associates. Retrieved from http://www.cpii.com/docs/files/Varian%20Associates%20-%20An%20Early%20History.pdf

Glazier, A. (1980). Review of Commerce extérieur et développement économique de l'Europe au XIXe siecle by P Bairoch. *The Journal of Modern History*, *52*(3), (Sep., 1980), 489–491.

Goodwin, M., & Heath, M. (2016). *Brexit and the left behind: A tale of two countries*. London: LSE blog. July 22nd 2016, Retrieved from http://blogs.lse.ac.uk/brexit/2016/07/22/brexit-and-the-left-behind-a-tale-of-two-countries/

Goolsbee, A., Hall, R. E., & Katz, L. F. (1999). Evidence on the high-income Laffer Curve from six decades of tax reform. *Brookings Papers on Economic Activity, 1999*(2), 1–64.

Gove, M. (2016). Britain has had enough of experts. Retrieved from http://www.telegraph.co.uk/news/2016/06/10/michael-goves-guide-to-britains-greatest-enemy-the-experts/

Govil, N., & Baishya, A. K. (2018). The bully in the pulpit: Autocracy, digital social media, and right-wing populist technoculture. *Communication Culture & Critique, 11*(1), 67–84.

Guest, P. (1997). Hoards from the end of Roman Britain. In R. Bland & J. Orna-Ornstein (Eds.), *Coin hoards from Roman Britain* (Vol. X, pp. 411–423). London: British Museum Press.

Guest, P. (2005). *The late Roman gold and silver coins from the Hoxne treasure*. London: British Museum Press.

GYBC. (2017). Great Yarmouth Borough Profile 2017 (Draft), Great Yarmouth Borough Council: Norfolk. Retrieved from file:///C:/Users/Richard/Documents/Lecture%20New/Book%202%20research/Yarmouth%20profile%202017.pdf

GYBC. (2018). The history behind your holiday, Great Yarmouth Borough Council: Norfolk. Retrieved from https://www.great-yarmouth.co.uk/things-to-do/seaside-holiday-history.aspx

Hakluyt, R., & Purcas, S. (1830). The origin and early history of the Russia or Muscovy company taken from Hakluyt (1553–1616) and S Purchas (1575–1626) etc. Marchant: London. Retrieved from https://archive.org/details/originandearlyh00unkngoog

Haldane, A. (2017). Productivity Puzzles, Speech at LSE 20 March 2017, Bank of England: London. Retrieved from https://www.bankofengland.co.uk/-/media/boe/files/speech/2017/productivity-puzzles.pdf?la=en&hash=708C7CFD5E8417000655BA4AA0E0E873D98A18DE

Hansard. (1996). Ever Ready Factory, Tanfield Lea, House of Commons Debate 21 Feb 1996, Hansard: London. Retrieved from https://api. parliament.uk/historic-hansard/commons/1996/feb/21/ever-ready-factory-tanfield-lea

HCCMS. (2018). Submission to enquiry on fake news from aggregate IQ, Parliament Commons select committee on culture, media and sport: London, written submission from Jeff Slivester CEO aggregate IQ 16 May 2018. Retrieved from https://www.parliament.uk/documents/commons-committees/culture-media-and-sport/Written-evidence-AIQ.pdf

HCLG. (2015). English indices of deprivation 2015, Ministry of Housing, Communities and Local Government: London. Retrieved from https://www. gov.uk/government/statistics/english-indices-of-deprivation-2015

Heaney, C. A., Israel, B. A., & House, J. S. (1994). Chronic job insecurity among automobile workers: Effects on job satisfaction and health. *Social Science & Medicine*, *38*(10), 1431–1437.

Helmholz, R. H. (1996). The learned laws in 'Pollock and Maitland'. *Proceedings of the British Academy*, *89*, 169.

Helps, S. A. (1868). *Realmah*. London: Macmillan & Co.

Hillmann, H., & Gathmann, C. (2011). Overseas trade and the decline of privateering. *The Journal of Economic History*, *71*(3), 730–761.

Hingley, R. (2016). Early studies in Roman Britain: 1610 to 1906. In *The Oxford handbook of Roman Britain* (pp. 3–21). Oxford handbooks. Retrieved from http://dro.dur.ac.uk/21214/1/21214.pdf?DDD6+DDO65 +drk0rh+d700tmt

Hippel, E. v. (1978). Successful industrial products from customer ideas. *Journal of Marketing*, *42*(1), 39–49.

Hirsch, A. (2018). *Why Britishness as an identity is in crisis*. Washington, DC: National Geographic. 19 April 2018, Retrieved from https://www. nationalgeographic.co.uk/history-and-civilisation/2018/04/why-britishness-identity-crisis

HMGOV. (2018). *The future relationship between the United Kingdom and the European Union, UK Government*. London: White Paper. Retrieved from https://assets.publishing.service.gov.uk/government/uploads/system/

uploads/attachment_data/file/724982/The_future_relationship_between_the_
United_Kingdom_and_the_European_Union_WEB_VERSION.pdf

Hobbs, R. (2006). Late Roman Precious Metal Deposits, c. AD 200-700
Oxford: BAR International Series 1504 (Doctoral Dissertation: University of
London).

Hobolt, S., Leeper, T., & Tilley, J. (2018). Emerging Brexit identities, in
Brexit and public opinion, compendium report with various authors. The
UK in a changing Europe: London. Retrieved from http://ukandeu.ac.uk/
research-papers/page/3/

HOC. (1604). House of Commons Journal Volume 1: 06 June 1604
(2nd scribe), free trade bill. Retrieved from http://www.british-history.ac.uk/
commons-jrnl/vol1/06-june-1604-2nd-scribe#h3-0012

Holstun, J. (2008). Utopia pre-empted: Kett's rebellion, commoning, and the
hysterical sublime. *Historical Materialism, 16*(3), 3−53.

Hood, A., & Waters, T. (2017). Incomes and inequality: The last decade
and the next parliament. London: IFS. 5 May 2017. Retrieved from://www.
ifs.org.uk/publications/9192

Horsley, T. (2012). Subsidiarity and the European Court of Justice: Missing
pieces in the subsidiarity jigsaw? *JCMS: Journal of Common Market Studies,
50*(2), 267−282.

Hoyle, R. W. (1994). Crown, parliament and taxation in sixteenth-century
England. *The English Historical Review, 109*(434), 1174−1196.

Hudson, R. B., & Gonyea, J. G. (2012). Baby boomers and the shifting
political construction of old age. *The Gerontologist, 52*(2), 272−282.

ICO. (2018). Investigation into the use of data analytics in political
campaigns. Investigation update, Information Commissioners Office:
London, July 2018. Retrieved from https://ico.org.uk/media/action-weve-
taken/2259371/investigation-into-data-analytics-for-political-purposes-
update.pdf

Ikenson, D., Lester, S., & Hannan, D. (2018). *The ideal US−UK Free Trade
Agreement: A free trader's perspective, initiative for free trade: London.*
Washington, DC: Cato Institute. Retrieved from https://www.cato.org/

publications/white-paper/ideal-us-uk-free-trade-agreement-free-traders-perspective Accessed on September 18, 2018.

ILO. (2018a). Labour force participation rate by age and sex, ILO: Geneva, Statistical Down Load. Retrieved from http://www.ilo.org/ilostat/

ILO. (2018b). Output per worker (GDP constant 2010 US $) – ILO modelled estimates, May 2018. Retrieved from http://www.ilo.org/ilostat/

Inscker, A., & Orna-Ornstein, J. (2009). Haynes, Bedfordshire. In R. Abdy, E. Ghey, C. Hughes, & I. Leins (Eds.), *Coin hoards from Roman Britain* (Vol. XII, pp. 379–388). Wetteren: Moneta.

Intergenerational Commission. (2018). A new generational contract: The final report of the Intergenerational Commission, Resolution Foundation: London. Retrieved from https://www.intergencommission.org/publications/a-new-generational-contract-the-final-report-of-the-intergenerational-commission/

Investment Association, The. (2016). Asset Management in the UK 2015 – 2016. Retrieved from https://www.theinvestmentassociation.org/assets/components/ima_filesecurity/secure.php?f=research/2016/20160929-amsfullreport.pdf

Iyer, K., Quest, L., Hunt, P., Gladstone, J., Poulton, M., & Souta, P. (2018). *The "Red tape" cost of Brexit*. London: Oliver Wyman & Clifford Chance. Retrieved from http://www.oliverwyman.com/content/dam/oliver-wyman/v2/publications/2018/march/Oliver-Wyman_Clifford-Chance-The-Red-Tape-Cost-of-Brexit.pdf

Jacobs, T. B. (2001). *Eisenhower at Columbia*. New Brunswick, NJ: Transaction Publishers.

Jennings, W., Stoker, G., & Warren, I. (2018). "Towns and cities" in Brexit and public opinion, compendium report with various authors, The UK in a changing Europe: London. Retrieved from http://ukandeu.ac.uk/research-papers/page/3/

Johns, C. M., (2010). *The Hoxne late Roman treasure: Gold jewellery and silver plate*. London: British Museum Press.

Johnson, S. (2018). *Mauritius 'miracle' puts Australia in the shade*. London: *Financial Times*. Retrieved from https://www.ft.com/content/5b047cb8-6f03-11e8-852d-d8b934ff5ffa. Accessed on June 15, 2018.

Johnstone, M., Parsell, C., Jetten, J., Dingle, G., & Walter, Z. (2016). Breaking the cycle of homelessness: Housing stability and social support as predictors of long-term well-being. *Housing Studies, 31*(4), 410–426.

Jónsson, G. (2011). *Non-migrant, sedentary, immobile, or 'left behind'?* Oxford: International Migration Institute. Retrieved from https://ora.ox.ac.uk/objects/uuid:ecaf96f8-caa0-4421-8ec6-107992e33c96/download_file?file_format=pdf&safe_filename=WP39%2BNon-migrant%2BImmobile%2BSedentary.pdf&type_of_work=Working+paper

Just, N., & Latzer, M. (2017). Governance by algorithms: Reality construction by algorithmic selection on the internet. *Media, Culture & Society, 39*(2), 238–258.

Kaufmann, E. (2016). It's NOT the economy, stupid: Brexit as a story of personal values, LSE Blog: London. Retrieved from http://eprints.lse.ac.uk/71585/1/blogs.lse.ac.uk-Its%20NOT%20the%20economy%20stupid%20Brexit%20as%20a%20story%20of%20personal%20values.pdf

Kellner, D. (2017). Brexit plus, whitelash, and the ascendency of Donald J. Trump. *Public Culture, 13*(2), 135–149.

Kenney, M. (2017). Explaining the growth and globalization of silicon valley: The past and today. Working Paper. University of California Berkeley, CA. Retrieved from http://www.brie.berkeley.edu/wp-content/uploads/2015/01/BRIE-Working-paper-2017-1.pdf

Kenny, M. (2015). The return of 'Englishness' in British political culture – The end of the unions? *JCMS: Journal of Common Market Studies, 53*(1), 35–51.

Kenya. (2018). World GDP per capita ranking 2017, (base on IMF World Economic Outlook Data April 2018). Retrieved from http://kenya.opendataforafrica.org/sijweyg/world-gdp-per-capita-ranking-2017-data-and-charts-forecast

Khan, M. (2018). *Swiss lessons on life outside the EU*. London: Financial Times. 25 Jan 2018. Retrieved from https://www.ft.com/content/f2a13ff4-0192-11e8-9650-9c0ad2d7c5b5

King, G., Rosen, O., tTanner, M., & Wagner, A. F. (2008). Ordinary economic voting behavior in the extraordinary election of Adolf Hitler. *The Journal of Economic History, 68*(4), 951−996.

Knapton, S. (2015). Blood of Britain's ancient tribes still runs in our veins after 1,400 years. *Daily Telegraph* (London, England).

Knibb, Gormezano, & Partners. (2009). Mapping of the East Midlands automotive industry and identifying the main innovation drivers. Retrieved from https://docuri.com/download/mapping-automotive_59c1ea9cf581710 b286dd86a_pdf

Knight, F. (1921). *Risk, uncertainty and profit*. Boston, MA: Hart, Schaffner & Marx.

Kornai, J. (1994). Transformational recession: The main causes. *Journal of Comparative Economics, 19*(1), 39−63.

Krippner, G. R. (2005). The financialization of the American economy. *Socio-Economic Review, 3*(2), 173−208.

Krueger, A. O. (2016). A tale of two crises: Greece and Iceland. Working Paper No. 574. Stanford Centre for International Development. Retrieved from http://scid.stanford.edu/sites/default/files/publications/574wp_0.pdf

Krugman, P. R. (2008). Trade and wages, reconsidered. *Brookings Papers on Economic Activity, 2008*(1), 103−154.

Kuper, S. (2017). *Beware the Tory cult that's steering Brexit*. London: Financial Times. Nov 2 2017. Retrieved from https://www.ft.com/content/c276ed98-be8e-11e7-9836-b25f8adaa111

Lampe, M. (2011). Explaining nineteenth-century bilateralism: Economic and political determinants of the Cobden−Chevalier network. *The Economic History Review, 64*(2), 644−668.

Lane, A. (2014). Wroxeter and the end of Roman Britain. *Antiquity, 88*(340), 501−515.

Leake, J. (2018). Foreigners to net UK fish after Brexit. *The Sunday Times*. Retrieved from https://www.thetimes.co.uk/article/foreigners-to-net-uk-fish-after-brexit-hpf6njhvt. Accessed on March 25, 2018.

Lendering, J. (2002). Stad in marmer Gids voor het antieke Rome aan de hand van tijdgenoten (p. 141). Amsterdam: Athenaeum − Polak & Van Gennep.

Léon-Ledesma, M. A. (2000). Economic growth and Verdoorn's Law in the Spanish regions, 1962-91. *International Review of Applied Economics*, *14*(1), 67−69.

Levie, J. (2014). State of small business Britain conference 2014: The ambition gap. Enterprise Research Centre. Retrieved from http://strathprints. strath.ac.uk/59371/

Lewis, D. (2017). *China's global internet ambitions: Finding roots in ASEAN*. Delhi: Institute of Chinese Studies. Retrieved from http://www. icsin.org/uploads/2017/08/03/5daba78af515cb7bc67e43ae7c1d4ba1.pdf

Lewis, J. (2000). The methods of community in EU decision-making and administrative rivalry in the Council's infrastructure. *Journal of European Public Policy*, *7*(2), 261−289.

Link, F., & Hornburg, M. W. (2016). "He who owns the trifels, owns the reich": Nazi medievalism and the creation of the volksgemeinschaft in the palatinate. *Central European History*, *49*(2), 208−239.

Lisbon. (2007). Signed 2007 and effective from 2009. Retrieved from https:// eur-lex.europa.eu/legal-content/EN/TXT/?uri=celex:12007L/TXT

Lo, A. W. (2007). Efficient markets hypothesis. In L. Blume & S. Durlauf (Eds.), *The New Palgrave: A dictionary of economics* (2nd Ed.). Basingstoke: Palgrave Macmillan Ltd., Retrieved from at SSRN https://ssrn.com/abstract= 991509

LREG. (2018). Land registry house price data dataset. Retrieved from www.gov.uk/government/statistical-data-sets/uk-house-price-index-data-downloads-april-2018

Lyne, M. (2016). The end of Roman pottery production in Southern Britain. *Internet Archaeology*, *41*. doi:10.11141/ia.41.7

MAC. (2018). *EEA migration in the UK: Final report.* London: UK Government Migration Advisory Committee. Retrieved from https://www. gov.uk/government/publications/migration-advisory-committee-mac-report-eea-migration

Machin, S. (2011). *Changes in UK wage inequality over the last forty years.* Oxford: Oxford University Press. doi:10.1093/acprof:osobl/ 9780199587377.003.001

Machin, S. (2015). Real wages and living standards. Paper EA024, LSE: London. Retrieved from http://cep.lse.ac.uk/pubs/download/EA024.pdf

Macmillan Evidence. (1931). *Committee on finance and industry & appendices of evidence.* London: HMSO.

Maffesoli, M. (1988). Jeux de masques: Postmodern tribalism. *Design Issues, 4*(1&2), 141–151.

Malloch Brown, M. (2018). The end of global Britain. London: Social Europe Blog. 3 July 2018. Retrieve from //www.socialeurope.eu/the-end-of-global-britain

Manacorda, M., Manning, A., & Wadsworth, J. (2012). The impact of immigration on the structure of wages: Theory and evidence from Britain. *Journal of the European Economic Association, 10*(1), 120–151. doi:10.1111/j.1542-4774.2011.01049.x

Marchi, R. (2012). With Facebook, blogs, and fake news, teens reject journalistic "objectivity". *Journal of Communication Inquiry, 36*(3), 246–262.

Marcuss, R. D., & Kane, R. E. (2007). US national income and product statistics. *Survey of Current Business, 87,* 2–32.

May, T. (2017a). Letter to European Union Giving Article 50 Notification, 10 Downing St: London. Retrieved from http://www.consilium.europa.eu/ media/24079/070329_uk_letter_tusk_art50.pdf

May, T. (2017b). The government's negotiating objectives for exiting the EU, January 17th 2017 speech at Lancaster House updated on 3rd February 2017 to match delivery. UK Government: London. Retrieved from https:// www.gov.uk/government/speeches/the-governments-negotiating-objectives-for-exiting-the-eu-pm-speech

Mazzucato, M. (2013). *The entrepreneurial state*. London: Anthem Press.

Mazzucato, M. (2016). From market fixing to market-creating: A new framework for innovation policy. *Industry and Innovation, 23*(2), 140–156.

Mazzucato, M. (2018). *The value of everything*. London: Allen Lane (Penguin Random House).

McBride, G. K. (1969). Once again, the case of Richard Hunne. *Albion: A Quarterly Journal Concerned with British Studies, 1*(1), 19–29.

McKinnon, R. (1973). *Money and capital in economic development*. Washington, DC: The Brookings Institution.

Mehra, V. (2013). ARPA-E is here to stay. Retrieved from https://scienceprogress.org/wp-content/uploads/2013/01/ARPA-Ebrief.pdf

Menon, A., & Wagner. (2018). "Analysing the Referendum" in Brexit and Public Opinion, Compendium Report with various authors. The UK in a Changing Europe: London. Retrieved from http://ukandeu.ac.uk/research-papers/page/3/

Mercer, S. T., & Kahn, M. (2018). *America trades down: The legal consequences of President Trump's tariffs*. Washington, DC: The Lawfare Institute in association with Brookings. Mar 13 2018. Retrieved from https://www.lawfareblog.com/america-trades-down-legal-consequences-president-trumps-tariffs

Merkel, M. (2010). 'Rede von Bundeskanzlerin Merkel anlässlich der Eröffnung des 61. Akademischen Jahres des Europakollegs Brügge', Bruges, 2 November 2010. Retrieved from https://www.coleurope.eu/speeches

Meshkat, K. (2009). The journey of Master Anthony Jenkinson to Persia, 1562-1563. *Journal of Early Modern History, 13*(2), 209–228.

MetPolice. (2016). *Hate crime flagged offences, freedom of information request October 2016*. London: Metropolitan Police. Retrieved from https://www.met.police.uk/globalassets/foi-media/disclosure_2016/november_2016/information-rights-unit—statistics-in-regards-to-the-number-of-hate-crimes-committed-from-before-and-after-the-brexit-vote

Miller, H., Pope, T., & Cribb, J. (2018). *Tax records show that people working for their own business have much lower profits and are investing less than before the recession.* London: IFS. 4 June 2018, Retrieved from https://www.ifs.org.uk/publications/13022

Miller, V. (2017). Legislating for Brexit: EU external agreements. House of Commons Briefing Paper Number 7850. Retrieved from http://researchbriefings.files.parliament.uk/documents/CBP-7850/CBP-7850.pdf

Minford, P. (2018a). *How the civil service has misled us on the costs of Brexit and the customs union.* London: Economists for Free Trade. Retrieved from https://www.economistsforfreetrade.com/wp-content/uploads/2018/05/EFT-How-the-Civil-Service-has-misled-us-on-costs-of-Brexit-and-the-customs-union-May-2018.pdf

Minford, P. (2018b). *The economics of Brexit.* London: Politeia. Retrieved from http://www.politeia.co.uk/wp-content/Politeia%20Documents/2018/The%20Economics%20of%20Brexit%20-%20Minford/Patrick%20Minford%20The%20Economics%20of%20Brexit%20FINAL.pdf

Minford, P., Bootle, R., Bourne, R., Congdon, T., Lightfoot, W., Lyons, G., Mackinnon, N., & Matthews, K. (2017). The economy after Brexit. Retrieved from ://www.economistsforfreetrade.com/wp-content/uploads/2017/08/Economists_for_Brexit_The_Economy_after_Brexit.pdf. Accessed on April 20, 2018.

Minsky, H. P. (1986). *Stabilizing an unstable economy.* New Haven, CT: Yale University.

Minsky, H. P. (1992). The financial instability hypothesis. Working Paper No. 74. The Jerome Levy Economics Institute, NY. Retrieved from ssrn.com/abstract=16ttp://dx.doi.org/10.2139/ssrn.161024

Moens, G., & Trone, J. (2015). The principle of subsidiarity in EU judicial and legislative practice: Panacea or Placebo? *Journal of Legislation, 41*(1), 65–101, Article 2. Retrieved from http://scholarship.law.nd.edu/jleg/vol41/iss1/2

Mohapi, T. (2017). M-Pesas Origins, iAfrican 2 Dec 2017. Retrieved from https://www.iafrikan.com/2017/12/04/m-pesas-origins/

Monks, K. (2017). M-Pesa: Kenya's mobile money success story turns 10, CNN: Atlanta. Retrieved from https://edition.cnn.com/2017/02/21/africa/mpesa-10th-anniversary/index.html

Moore, E. (1980). Church courts and the people during the English Reformation 1520–1570. By Ralph Houlbrooke. (Oxford Historical Monographs). [Oxford: Oxford University Press. 1979. xii, 272, (Appendices and Bibliography)]. *Book Review: The Cambridge Law Journal, 39*(1), 199–200.

Moore, T. (2011). Detribalizing the later prehistoric past: Concepts of tribes in Iron Age and Roman studies. *Journal of Social Archaeology, 11*(3), 334–360.

Mounsey, C. (1998). More manuscript material by William Stukeley, the arch-druid. *Notes and Queries, 45*(4), 466–468.

Muellbauer, J., & Murphy, A. (1997). Booms and busts in the UK housing market. *The Economic Journal, 107*(445), 1701–1727.

Mussa, M. (1982). Government policy and the adjustment process. In Jagdish N. Bhagwati (Ed.), *Import competition and response* (pp. 73–122). Chicago, IL: University of Chicago Press.

National Museum of American History. (2013). Laffer Curve napkin. National Museum of American History: Washington DC, Catalogue No 2013.0041.01. Retrieved from nhistory.si.edu/collections/search/object/nmah_1439217 (accessed 20 April 2018).

National Research Council. (2009). 21st century innovation systems for Japan and the United States: Lessons from a Decade of Change. Retrieved from https://www.nap.edu/read/12194/chapter/15

Nef, J. (1933). Richard Carmarden's "A Caveat for the Quene" (1570). *Journal of Political Economy, 41*(1), 33–41.

Nef, J. (1937). Prices and industrial capitalism in France and England, 1540-1640. *The Economic History Review, 7*(2), 155–185.

Nickell, S., & Saleheen, J. (2015). The impact of immigration on occupational wages: Evidence from Britain, Bank of England: London, Staff Working Paper No 574. Retrieved from https://www.bankofengland.co.uk/-/media/boe/files/working-paper/2015/the-impact-of-immigration-on-

occupational-wages-evidence-from-britain.pdf?la=en&hash=16F94BC8B55
F06967E1F36249E90ECE9B597BA9C

Nietzsche, F. (1887). *The genealogy of morals a Polemic*, Carol Diethe
(trans.), Student Edition 1994. Cambridge: Cambridge
University Press.

O'Brien, P. K., & Pigman, G. A. (1992). Free trade, British hegemony and
the international economic order in the nineteenth century. *Review of
International Studies, 18*(2), 89–113.

Obstfeld, M. (2012). Does the current account still matter. *The American
Economic Review: Papers and Proceedings, 102*(3), 1–23.

O'Connor, S. (2017). *Left behind: Can anyone save the towns the economy
forgot? Financial Times*. Retrieved from https://www.ft.com/blackpool.
Accessed on November 16, 2017.

O'Connor, S. (2018). *Dark factories: Labour exploitation in Britain's
garment industry. Financial Times*. Retrieved from https://www.ft.com/
content/e427327e-5892-11e8-b8b2-d6ceb45fa9d0. Accessed on May 17,
2018.

O'Malley, J. W. (2013). Is reform possible? Historical and theological
perspectives on the Roman Curia. New York, NY: America. Retrieved from:
https://www.americamagazine.org/issue/reform-possible

Obstfeld, M. (2012). Does the current account still matter? *The American
Economic Review, 102*(3), 1–23.

OECD. (2015). Lifting investment for higher sustainable growth, OECD
economic outlook volume 2015/1. Retrieved from https://www.oecd.org/
investment/Economic-Outlook-97-Lifting-investment-for-higher-sustainable-
growth.pdf

OECD. (2018). *Import content of exports*. Paris: OECD. Retrieved from
https://data.oecd.org/trade/import-content-of-exports.htm

Ojala, A., Evers, N., & Rialp, A. (2018). Extending the international new
venture phenomenon to digital platform providers: A longitudinal case
study. *Journal of World Business, 53*(5), 725–739.

Ollivaud, P., & Turner, D. (2015). The effect of the global financial crisis on OECD potential output. *OECD Journal Economic Studies* (Vol. 2014). Paris: OECD. Retrieved: from https://www.oecd.org/eco/growth/The-effect-of-the-global-financial-crisis-on-OECD-potential-output-OECD-Journal-Economic-Studies-2014.pdf

ONS. (2016). *How is the welfare budget spent?* Wales: ONS. Retrieved from https://www.ons.gov.uk/economy/governmentpublicsectorandtaxes/publicsectorfinance/articles/howisthewelfarebudgetspent/2016-03-16

ONS. (2017a). Overview of the UK population July 2017. Wales: ONS. Retrieved from: https://www.ons.gov.uk/peoplepopulationandcommunity/populationandmigration/populationestimates/articles/overviewoftheukpopulation/july2017

ONS. (2017b). *UK National Accounts, The Blue Book time series dataset.* Wales: ONS. Retrieved from https://www.ons.gov.uk/economy/grossdomesticproductgdp/datasets/bluebook

ONS. (2018a). *Dataset EMP13: Employment by industry.* Wales: ONS. Retrieved from https://www.ons.gov.uk/employmentandlabourmarket/peopleinwork/employmentandemployeetypes/datasets/employmentbyindustryemp13

ONS. (2018b). Contracts that do not guarantee a minimum number of hours: April 2018. Wales: ONS. Retrieved from www.ons.gov.uk/employmentandlabourmarket/peopleinwork/earningsandworkinghours/articles/contractsthatdonotguaranteeaminimumnumberofhours/april2018

ONS. (2018c). EMP07: Temporary employees. Wales: ONS. 15 May 2018. Retrieved from https://www.ons.gov.uk/employmentandlabourmarket/peopleinwork/employmentandemployeetypes/datasets/temporaryemployeesemp07

ONS. (2018d). Balance of payments, UK: Quarter 4 (October to December) 2017. Wales: ONS. Retrieved from https://www.ons.gov.uk/economy/nationalaccounts/balanceofpayments/bulletins/balanceofpayments/quarter4octtodec2017

ONS. (2018e). *Labour productivity by industry division.* Wales: ONS. Dataset, Retrieved: from https://www.ons.gov.uk/economy/

economicoutputandproductivity/productivitymeasures/datasets/
labourproductivitybyindustrydivision

ONS. (2018f). NOMIS query for number jobs created 2015 to 2016 by SIC 2digit code from business register and employment survey: open access dataset, ONS: Wales. Retrieved from https://www.nomisweb.co.uk/query/construct/submit.asp?menuOpt=201&fmt=xls&lr=industry&lc=date&fn=

ONS. (2018g). Pensioners' incomes series, ONS: Wales & DWP: London, data series and document. Retrieved from https://www.gov.uk/government/statistics/pensioners-incomes-series-financial-year-201617

ONS. (2018h). Housing affordability ratio for Newly-Built and existing dwellings, ONS: Wales dataset. Retrieved from https://www.ons.gov.uk/peoplepopulationandcommunity/housing/bulletins/housingaffordability inenglandandwales/2017Chart5

ONS. (2018i). English housing survey 2016–2017 section 1 household tables, ONS: Wales & CLG: London, 25 Jan 2018. Retrieved from https://www.gov.uk/government/statistics/english-housing-survey-2016-to-2017-headline-report

ONS. (2018j). ASHE 1997 to 2017 selected estimates. ONS: Wales. Retrieved from: https://www.ons.gov.uk/employmentandlabourmarket/peopleinwork/earningsandworkinghours/datasets/ashe1997to2015 selectedestimates

Parliament. (2017). Queen's speech. Retrieved from https://www.gov.uk/government/speeches/queens-speech-2017

Parry, G. (2001). Berosus and the Protestants: Reconstructing Protestant myth. *Huntington Library Quarterly*, 64(1/2), 1–21.

Peers, S. (2013). Towards a new form of EU law?: The use of EU institutions outside the EU legal framework. *European Constitutional Law Review*, 9(1), 37–72.

Pessoa, J., & Van Reenen, J. (2013). Decoupling of wage growth and productivity growth? Myth and reality. London: LSE. CEP Discussion paper No 1246. Retrieved from http://cep.lse.ac.uk/pubs/download/dp1246.pdf

Phillips, D., Curtice, J., Phillips, M., & Perry, J. (2018). *British social attitudes: The 35th report*. London: The National Centre for Social

Research. Retrieved from http://bsa.natcen.ac.uk/media/39284/bsa35_full-report.pdf

Pilling, D. (2018). America must allow Rwanda to make its own choices. *Financial Times*. Retrieved from https://www.ft.com/content/44b5cb2e-73a9-11e8-b6ad-3823e4384287

Plato. (c375BC) Phaedo Tr. Jowett B. E doc prepared by Asscher S. 2011. Retrieved from http://www.fulltextarchive.com/page/Phaedo/

Popper, N. (2011). An ocean of lies: The problem of historical evidence in the sixteenth century. *Huntington Library Quarterly*, 74(3), 375–400.

Powell, J. (2018). Trade-war fall out charted, Financial Times Alphaville: London, 3 July 2018. Retrieved from https://ftalphaville.ft.com/2018/07/03/1530614949000/Trade-war-fall-out–charted/

Prescott, S. (1998). *William Stukeley: Archaeologist and archdruid*. Peterborough: Carus Publishing Company, d/b/a ePals Media.

Ramsey, G. (1979). *The politics of a Tudor merchant adventurer*. Manchester: Manchester University Press.

Ramsey, J. (1913). *Genesis of Lancaster*. Oxford: Clarendon Press.

Rees-Mogg, J. (2018a). A vassal state. *The Somerset Guardian*: UK, 20th June 2018 Retrieved from https://www.jacobreesmogg.com/vassal-state

Rees-Mogg, J. (2018b). Mrs May has made many promises on Brexit, now she must keep them, *Daily Telegraph*, 2nd July 2018, page 16.

Reillier, B., & Reillier, L. C. (2017). *Platform strategy: How to unlock the power of communities and networks to grow your business*. London: Routledge Ltd.

Reisen, H. (1998). Sustainable and excessive current account deficits. *Empirica*, 25(2), 111–131.

Richardson, G. (2014). *The field of cloth of gold*. London: Yale University Press.

Richardson, R. (2004). William Camden and the re-discovery of England. *Transactions of the Leicestershire Archaeological and Historical Society*, 78, 108–123. Retrieved from https://www.le.ac.uk/lahs/downloads/05Vol78-Richardson.pdf

Riley, R., & Bondibene, C. R. (2016). Sources of labour productivity growth at sector level in Britain, after 2007: A firm level analysis. Working Paper. National Endowment for Science, Technology and the Arts.

Robertson, A. S., Hobbs, R., & Buttrey, T. V. (Eds.). (2000). *An inventory of Romano-British coin hoards, Royal Numismatic Society Special Publication 20.* London: Royal Numismatic Society.

Rogers, A. (2010). Late Roman towns as meaningful places: re-conceptualising decline in the towns of late Roman Britain, ed. Speed, G; Sami, D, 'Debating urbanism: Within and beyond the walls', Leicester University Press: Leicester, 2010, pp. 57–81.

Roper, S., & Hart, M. (2018). *The state of small business Britain part A.* Warwick: Enterprise Research Centre. Retrieved from https://www. enterpriseresearch.ac.uk/publications/state-small-business-britain-report-2018/

Roper, S., Hart, M., Bourke, J., & Hathaway, K. (2018). *The state of small business Britain part B.* Warwick: Enterprise Research Centre. Retrieved from https://www.enterpriseresearch.ac.uk/publications/state-small-business-britain-report-2018/

Rotherham, L. (2018). It's time to preserve the story of the decades-long campaign for British independence from Brussels, Brexit Central Blog 11 April 2018, blog by Acting Chairman "Museum of Sovereignty" find raising campaign. Retrieved from https://brexitcentral.com/time-preserve-story-decades-long-campaign-british-independence-brussels/

Russell, H. D. (1906). *Lest we forget.* St Joseph, MT: D D Darrow.

Scherer, F. M. (1965). Invention and innovation in the Watt-Boulton steam-engine venture. *Technology and Culture, 6*(2), 165–187.

Schumpeter, J. A. (1934). *The theory of economic development: An inquiry into profits, capital, credit, interest, and the business cycle.* Cambridge, MA: Harvard University Press.

Schumpeter, J. A. (1942). *Capitalism, socialism and democracy.* London; ed Routledge: London 2013. Allen and Unwin.

Scotcourt "Opinion and Referral". (2018, September 21). First Division, Inner House, Court of Session, Edinburgh, Scotland. Retrieved from https://

www.scotcourts.gov.uk/docs/default-source/cos-general-docs/pdf-docs-for-opinions/2018csih62.pdf?sfvrsn=0

Seguino, S. (1999). The investment function revisited: Disciplining capital in South Korea. *Journal of Post Keynesian Economics*, 22(2), 313–338.

Shaw, G. B. (1928). The intelligent woman's guide to socialism and capitalism, Piscataway, NJ: 1984 Reprint Edition Transaction Publishers.

Shelter. (2015). *How much help is help to buy?* London. Retrieved from https://england.shelter.org.uk/__data/assets/pdf_file/0010/1188073/2015_09_how_much_help_is_Help_to_Buy.pdf

Shelter. (2016). *The need for stable renting in England*. London. Retrieved from https://england.shelter.org.uk/__data/assets/pdf_file/0010/1236484/The_need_for_stability2.pdf

Short, M. B., McCalla, S. G., & D'Orsogna, M. R. (2017). Modelling radicalization: How small violent fringe sects develop into large indoctrinated societies. *Royal Society Open Science*, 4(8), 170678.

Skousen, L. (2008). Redefining benefit of clergy during the English Reformation: Royal prerogative, mercy, and the state, masters thesis: University of Wisconsin. Retrieved from https://core.ac.uk/download/pdf/10597893.pdf

Slavin, A. J. (1986). Upstairs, downstairs: Or the roots of reformation. *Huntington Library Quarterly*, 49(3), 243–260.

Smith, A. (1776). An inquiry into the nature and causes of the wealth of nations. Retrieved from http://www.econlib.org/library/Smith/smWN13.html

SMMT. (2018). *SMMT motor industry facts 2018*. London: SMMT. Retrieved from https://www.smmt.co.uk/wp-content/uploads/sites/2/SMMT-Motor-Industry-Facts-2018-online.pdf

Sobolewska, M., & Ford, R. (2018). Brexit and identity politics, in Brexit and public opinion, compendium report with various authors, the UK in a changing Europe: London. Retrieved from http://ukandeu.ac.uk/research-papers/page/3/

Sobolewska, M., Galandini, S., & Lessard-Phillips, L. (2017). The public view of immigrant integration: Multidimensional and consensual. Evidence from survey experiments in the UK and the Netherlands. *Journal of Ethnic and Migration Studies, 43*(1), 58−79.

Spielman, A. (2018). *Amanda Spielman's speech at the Wellington Festival of Education*. London: OFSTED. Retrieved from https://www.gov.uk/government/speeches/amanda-spielmans-speech-at-the-wellington-festival-of-education. Accessed on June 22, 2018.

Spufford, P. (2006). From Antwerp and Amsterdam to London: The decline of financial centres in Europe. *De Economist, 154*(2), 143−175.

Spufford, P. (2010). 4th Ortelius lecture from Antwerp to London, the decline of financial centres in Europe, Netherlands Institute for Advanced Study in the Humanities and Social Sciences and University of Antwerp. Retrieved from www.nias.knaw.nl/Publications/Ortelius_Lecture/Ortelius_04_Spufford/at_download/file

Starkey, D. (1988). Tudor government: The facts? *Historical Journal, 31*(4), 921−931.

Stephens, W. (2004). When Pope Noah ruled the Etruscans: Annius of Viterbo and his forged antiquities. *Mln, 119*(1), S201−S223. doi:10.1353/mln.2004.0038

Stiglitz, J. E. (1999). The World Bank at the millennium. *The Economic Journal, 109*(459), 577−597.

Stone, L. (1947). State control in sixteenth-century England. *The Economic History Review, 17*(2), 103−120.

Stone, L. (1949). Elizabethan overseas trade. *The Economic History Review*, New Series, 2(1), 30−58.

Stone, L. (1965). *The crisis of the Aristocracy (1558−1641)*. Oxford: Clarendon Press.

Stubbs, W. (1875). *The constitutional history of England, in its origin and development*. (2nd Ed.). Oxford: Clarendon Press.

Sufi, A., & Mian, A. (2014). *House of Debt*. Chicago, IL: University of Chicago Press.

Summers, L. (1995). Ten lessons to learn. *The Economist*, 23 December, 46−48.

Surtees. (1882). "The family memoirs of the Rev. William Stukeley, M.D., and the antiquarian and other correspondence of William Stukeley, Roger & Samuel Gale, etc", Surtees Society: London. Retrieved from https://archive.org/details/familymemoirsofr03stuk

Swales, K. (2016). *Understanding the Leave vote*. London: NatCen Social Research. 8 December 2016. Retrieved from http://natcen.ac.uk/media/1319222/natcen_brexplanations-report-final-web2.pdf

Swales, K., & Tipping, S. (2018). *Fragmented communities? The role of cohesion, community involvement and social mixing.* London: NatCen Social Research. Retrieved from http://www.natcen.ac.uk/media/1571059/Fragmented-Communities.pdf

Taleb, N. N. (2007). *The black swan: The impact of the highly improbable* (Vol. 2). New York, NY: Random House.

Temin, P. (2006). The economy of the early Roman Empire. *The Journal of Economic Perspectives*, 20(1), 133−151.

Thomas, A., Lendel, I., & Kanter, A. (2017). Analysis of supply chain opportunities for fuel cell buses using industrial classifications (2017). Urban Publications: Cleveland State University. Retrieved from https://engagedscholarship.csuohio.edu/urban_facpub/1465

Thomas, C. (2016). Fuel cell and battery electric vehicles compared, occasional paper. Retrieved from https://www.energy.gov/sites/prod/files/2014/03/f9/thomas_fcev_vs_battery_evs.pdf

Thomson, J. (2018). Post Brexit customs declaration cost estimate, letter from CEO HMRC to Treasury Select Committee 4 June 2018, House of Commons : London, Retrieved from www.parliament.uk/documents/commons-committees/treasury/Correspondence/2017-19/hmrc-customs-costs-040618.pdf

Thornton, T. (2009). Henry VIII's progress through Yorkshire in 1541 and its implications for northern identities. *Northern History*, 46(2), 231−244.

Times, The. (2018). Johnson accused of four-letter response to industry concerns. The Times: London, 23rd June 2018, reporter Callum Jones.

Retrieved from https://www.thetimes.co.uk/article/johnson-accused-of-four-letter-response-to-industry-concerns-zjrfg8bs9

Tinbergen, J. (1969). The use of models: Experience and prospects, Nobel Prize Lecture December 1969, Sweden: Nobel Foundation. Retrieved from https://www.nobelprize.org/nobel_prizes/economic-sciences/laureates/1969/tinbergen-lecture.html

Tooze, A., & Vallée, S. (2018). Germany's great European heist, 25 May 2018. *Social* Europe. Retrieved from https://www.socialeurope.eu/germanys-great-european-heist

Torotrack. (2018). Torotrak plc Annual Report 2017. Retrieved from http://www.torotrak.com/wp-content/uploads/2017/07/246054-Torotrak-AR-Web_2017.pdf

Tyndale, W. (1528). *The obedience of a Christian man, in the works of the English Reformers vol. I* (1831). Ed. Thomas Russell, Ebenezer Palmer: London.

UN. (2018). UN rights expert hails UK for anti-racism action but raises serious concerns over immigration policy, Prevent programme and Brexit, UN: Geneva. Retrieved from http://www.ohchr.org/EN/NewsEvents/Pages/DisplayNews.aspx?NewsID=23074&LangID=E

UNCTAD. (2018). World Investment Report UK. Geneva: UNCTAD. Retrieved from http://unctad.org/sections/dite_dir/docs/wir2018/wir18_fs_gb_en.pdf

Usher, A. P. (1954). *A history of mechanical inventions*. (rev. ed). Cambridge, MA.

Van de Rijt, A., Kang, S. M., Restivo, M., & Patil, A. (2014). Field experiments of success-breeds-success dynamics. *Proceedings of the National Academy of Sciences, 111*(19), 6934–6939.

Verdoorn, P. J. (1980). Verdoorn's Law in retrospect: A comment. *The Economic Journal, 90*(358), 382–385.

Vienna. (1969). 'Vienna Convention on the Law of Treaties (with annex)'. Concluded at Vienna on 23 May 1969, UN: New York, Registered 27th January 1980. Retrieved from https://treaties.un.org/doc/publication/unts/volume%201155/volume-1155-i-18232-english.pdf

Vise, D. A. (2005). *The Google story*. London: Pan Books.

Von Der Burchard, H. (2018). EU trade partners demand concessions for Brexit transition rollover, Politico Blog: Brussels 2 February 2018. Retrieved from https://www.politico.eu/article/eu-trade-partners-object-to-brexit-transition-roll-over/

Wadsworth, J. (2010). The UK labour market and immigration. *National Institute Economic Review*, 213(213), R35–R42. doi:10.1177/0027950110380324

Wagner, U., & Beer, M. (2009). Life cycle analysis of battery and fuel cell vehicles, occasional paper: Riso energy conference: Denmark. Retrieved from : https://www.ffe.de/download/Veroeffentlichungen/2009_Riso_Energy_Conference.pdf

Walton, P., & Moorhead, S. (2016). Coinage and collapse? The contribution of numismatic data to understanding the end of Roman Britain. *Journal of Internet Archaeology*, 41, University of York: York. Retrieved from http://intarch.ac.uk/journal/issue41/8/toc.html

Waugh, W. T. (1922). The great statute of praemunire. *The English Historical Review*, 37(146), 173–205.

Weaver, J. C. B. (2011). Adolf Hitler's account of the 'Nation' and 'Nationalism', E-International Relations Blog: Bristol. Retrieved from : http://www.e-ir.info/2011/05/16/adolf-hitlers-account-of-the-%E2%80%98nation%E2%80%99-and-%E2%80%98nationalism%E2%80%99/

Wicksell, K. (1898). Interest and prices (tr. RF Kahn, London, Macmillan, 1936).

Wiesen Cook, B. (1981). *The declassified Eisenhower: A divided legacy of peace and political warfare*. New York, NY: Doubleday.

Wilshaw, M. (2018). *Michael Wilshaw's interview at the Wellington Festival of Education*. Retrieved from https://schoolsweek.co.uk/not-all-teachers-do-their-best-and-7-other-things-sir-michael-wilshaw-said-at-the-festival-of-education. Accessed on October 31, 2018.

Winiecki, J. (2002). An inquiry into the early drastic fall of output in post-communist transition: An unsolved puzzle. *Post-Communist Economies*, 14(1), 5–30.

Wood, A. (2016). Tales from the 'Yarmouth Hutch': Civic identities and hidden histories in an urban archive. *Past & Present, 230*(Issue suppl_11), 1 November 2016, 213–230.

Wordie, J. R. (1983). The chronology of english enclosure, 1500–1914. *The Economic History Review, 36*(4), 483–505.

World Bank, The. (2017). GDP per capita in 2010 constant US$ data. Retrieved from http://data.worldbank.org/indicator/NY.GDP.PCAP.KD? locations=KR

World Bank. (2018). GDP (constant 2010 US$), World Bank Washington. Retrieved from https://data.worldbank.org/indicator/NY.GDP.MKTP.KD

Wright, R. (2018). *New project aims to improve teenagers' life chances.* London: Financial Times. June 26 2018. Retrieved from https://www.ft.com/ content/2f49024e-700f-11e8-92d3-6c13e5c92914

Wynne, M. A., & Zhang, R. (2018). Measuring the world natural rate of interest. *Economic Inquiry, 56*(1), 530–544.

Yerxa, D. (2006). An interview with Bryan Ward-Perkins on the fall of Rome, historically speaking March/April 2006 p 31. Retreived from http:// www.bu.edu/historic/hs/perkins.pdf

YouGov. (2017a). The Arab world: A perspective from Britain, YouGov and Arab News. *YouGov.* Retrieved from https://mena.yougov.com/en/news/ 2017/09/25/arab-world-perspective-britain/

YouGov. (2017b). The challenge. YouGov Survey, 26–28 November 2017. *YouGov.* Retrieved from https://d25d2506sfb94s.cloudfront.net/cumulus_ uploads/document/j689my8z0m/TheChallenge_Nov17_Results_w.pdf

YouGov. (2018). Two years after the referendum. YouGov Survey, 19–20 June 2018. *YouGov.* Retrieved from https://d25d2506sfb94s.cloudfront.net/ cumulus_uploads/document/3flpkaywfj/InternalResults_180620_Brexit_w.pdf

YouGov. (2018). YouGov/The Times Poll. *YouGov.* Retrieved from http:// d25d2506sfb94s.cloudfront.net/cumulus_uploads/document/s696bae4gb/ TimesResults_180924_Brexit_.pdf Accessed on September 21/22, 2018.

INDEX